Advance Praise for
Reasons for Success

This work will become not only influential but also a solid basis on which to build programs that respond to the most enduring problems of development.

—*John D. Montgomery*
FORD FOUNDATION PROFESSOR OF INTERNATIONAL STUDIES, EMERITUS
HARVARD UNIVERSITY

I found the draft manuscript for *Reasons for Success* so useful that I am keeping a copy for myself as an instructional manual and reference book and to give copies to my colleagues. I hope other practitioners will also benefit in the same way from this excellent summing up.

—*Akhter Hameed Khan*
ORANGI PILOT PROJECT
PAKISTAN

Deserves to become a classic in its field. This book is one of the few books written recently whose authors have been both willing and eminently able to tackle the entire field of rural development.

—*Roland Bunch*
DIRECTOR
COSECHA, HONDURAS

During my years in the development field there are only a handful of books and articles that have strongly influenced my thinking about development. *Reasons for Success* is now added to that list. It is an exceptional book which I hope gets a very wide reading by those who work with development.

—*Thomas R. Carter*
ADVISOR
NATIONAL DAIRY DEVELOPMENT BOARD OF INDIA

A volume filled with facts and unorthodox ideas. It richly answers decision-makers' and developers' most anxious and frequent questions. The book's well-known authors have crafted an outstanding tool to facilitate the replication of success.

—*Michael Cernea*
ESSOR, THE WORLD BANK

D1017853

An important affirmation that it is possible to promote rural development activities that are both effective and sustainable. While the focus is on the local community, the study examines the important partnership role that external parties can play, including governments, NGOs, and the private sector.

—*Louise G. White*
PROFESSOR
GOVERNMENT AND POLITICS
GEORGE MASON UNIVERSITY

A powerful commentary about the continuing need to keep rural issues at the front and center of the development paradigm. The authors have marshaled compelling evidence to prove that rural development matters . . . can be done successfully, by appropriate policies, ideas, leadership, and nurturing local institutions.

—*Ismail Serageldin*
VICE PRESIDENT
ENVIRONMENTALLY AND SOCIALLY SUSTAINABLE DEVELOPMENT
THE WORLD BANK

This book makes a vital and unique contribution to agricultural and rural development. It shows that there are ways to improve peoples' livelihoods whilst sustaining the environment. It adds to the literature of hope. It is a must for all professionals.

—*Jules Pretty*
DIRECTOR
CENTRE FOR ENVIRONMENT AND SOCIETY
UNIVERSITY OF ESSEX

The authors have dedicated their long careers to promoting and understanding the conditions for successful participatory rural development. Here they summarize the wisdom they have accumulated and do so in a wonderfully readable manner, well illustrated with case examples.

—*David K. Leonard*
PROFESSOR
UNIVERSITY OF CALIFORNIA, BERKELEY

REASONS FOR SUCCESS

The SEWA Tree
A Women's Support Network

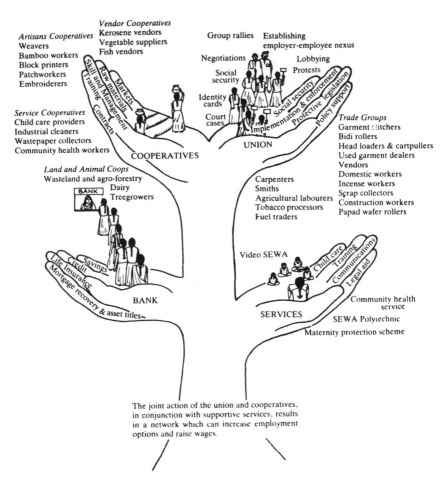

Vendor Cooperatives
Kerosene vendors
Vegetable suppliers
Fish vendors

Artisans Cooperatives
Weavers
Bamboo workers
Block printers
Patchworkers
Embroiderers

Group rallies   Establishing
employer-employee nexus

Negotiations   Lobbying

Social   Protests
security

Service Cooperatives
Child care providers
Industrial cleaners
Wastepaper collectors
Community health workers

Identity
cards

Court
cases

Social security

Implementation & enforcement

Protective legislation

Policy support

Markets

Raw materials

Skill and Management

Training   Contracts

COOPERATIVES

UNION

Land and Animal Coops
Wasteland and agro-forestry
Dairy
Treegrowers

BANK

Carpenters
Smiths
Agricultural labourers
Tobacco processors
Fuel traders

Trade Groups
Garment stitchers
Bidi rollers
Head loaders & cartpullers
Used garment dealers
Vendors
Domestic workers
Incense workers
Scrap collectors
Construction workers
Papad wafer rollers

Video SEWA

Child care

Training

Communications

Legal aid

Savings
Credit
Life Insurance
Mortgage recovery & asset titles

BANK

SERVICES

Community health
service

SEWA Polytechnic

Maternity protection scheme

The joint action of the union and cooperatives,
in conjunction with supportive services, results
in a network which can increase employment
options and raise wages.

REASONS FOR SUCCESS

LEARNING FROM INSTRUCTIVE EXPERIENCES IN RURAL DEVELOPMENT

NORMAN UPHOFF
MILTON J. ESMAN
ANIRUDH KRISHNA

Kumarian Press

Dedicated to
John M. Cohen
February 14, 1939 — December 24, 1997

An active intellectual, versed in many disciplines, John
worked and traveled widely and participated fully in
the communities and cultures of the countries he visited.
A valued colleague, he contributed much to the art as
well as the emerging science of rural development.

Reasons for Success: Learning from Instructive Experiences in Rural Development.

Published 1998 in the United States of America by Kumarian Press, Inc.,
14 Oakwood Avenue, West Hartford, Connecticut 06119-2127 USA.

Production supervised by Jenna Dixon
Copyedited by Linda Lotz   *Typeset by CompuDesign*
Text design by Jenna Dixon   *Proofread by Beth Richards*
The text of this book is set in 10.8/13 Monotype Sabon.
The display type is Rockwell Condensed.

Printed in Canada on acid-free paper by Transcontinental Printing and Graphics.
Text printed with vegetable oil-based ink.

♾ The paper used in this publication meets the minimum requirements of the American
National Standard for Information Sciences—Permanence of Paper for Printed Library
Materials, ANSI Z39.48-1984.

Library of Congress Cataloging-in-Publication Data
Uphoff, Norman Thomas.
    Reasons for success : learning from instructive experiences in rural development /
Norman Uphoff, Milton J. Esman, Anirudh Krishna.
      p.   cm. — (Kumarian Press books on international development)
    Includes bibliographical references and index.
    ISBN 1-56549-077-0 (cloth : alk. paper). — ISBN 1-56549-076-2 (paper : alk. paper)
    1. Rural development—Developing countries. 2. Agricultural development projects—
Developing countries. 3. Human services—Developing countries. 4. Natural resources—
Developing countries—Management. I. Esman, Milton J. (Milton Jacob), 1918–   . II.
Krishna, Anirudh, 1958–   . III. Title. IV. Series.
HN981.C6U66   1998
307.1'412'091724—dc21   97-38550

07 06 05 04 03   10 9 8 7 6 5 4 3   1st Printing 1998

Contents

Illustrations

Preface

This book was written as a companion volume to *Reasons for Hope: Instructive Experiences in Rural Development,* a collection of case studies of programs that have succeeded in improving the lives and prospects of large numbers of rural households, often in very inhospitable settings. We felt that those cases, reported by initiators and managers of the programs, spoke for themselves. As editors, our role was to facilitate the expression of hopes, plans, strategies, and hindsight from which others could learn. To use a term employed by anthropologists, that was an *emic* volume, reflecting views of purposeful rural change from inside the projects, programs, organizations, or movements that mobilized resources, both internal and external, to alter undesirable conditions.

In this volume, we draw lessons from those cases and others that can assist both planners and protagonists of rural improvement. In anthropological terms, this is an *etic* view, offering a more comparative and analytical perspective. We do not profess to be neutral about rural development, having been planners and protagonists ourselves in several contexts. But we have tried to distill in an objective way the state of the art of people-centered rural development.

As explained in the concluding chapter, in the past we tried to steer clear of the word *success.* It is a judgment that is susceptible to contradiction and invites disappointment, if only because all human enterprises fall short of perfection and are destined for downward as well as upward movement. It is an outcome sought assiduously by development agencies and their public- and private-sector supporters, but it is achieved with no certainty of sustainability. Having been distrustful of claims of success, we concluded, however, that such a view taken to extremes is injurious to development hopes and accomplishments.

Albert Hirschman in *Journeys toward Progress* (1963) warned against the mentality that "nothing works." He pointed out how pessimism and skepticism contribute, in a self-fulfilling way, to paralysis and failure. Therefore, without swinging the pendulum to either extreme, we decided to address the question of "what works?" We know from personal experience and observation, as well as from the now extensive literature, that it is possible to help poor and disadvantaged households make progress, even if the odds against doing so are still long. It is good to know that success, although requiring funding, depends more on ideas, leadership, and appropriate strategies than on money.

The majority of failures in rural development projects and programs stem not, we are convinced, from any intrinsic incapacity among rural people but rather from the ways that governments, donor and international agencies, and some nongovernmental organizations usually proceed. It is now popular to scorn top-down, bureaucratic methods, for good reason. They have contributed to an overall record marked by failure. But simply reversing these faults is not enough. We find from a wide range of successful experience that outside initiatives can be fruitful and that local initiatives can be made more effective and widespread through amicable and respectful collaboration between external and community actors. Understanding how such initiatives can become not just successful but also generalizable was the task we set ourselves.

The cases reported in *Reasons for Hope* are not without faults and shortcomings, but they demonstrate the kinds of strategies and activities that can inaugurate processes of beneficial change elsewhere. What institutional arrangements, technologies, modes of communication, structures of decentralization, and, most of all, ideas, attitudes, and values can alter possibilities for production and well-being in desired directions?

Success and sustainability could not be absolute criteria for our selection of cases, since these qualities cannot be fully proved in the present. Rather, we were interested in experiences that provided promising lessons for undertaking rural development initiatives in other settings. The selection of cases was thus purposive rather than random. We were naturally constrained by the availability of data and the lack of funding to survey, select, and study cases. Some of the cases included in this volume were ones we had hoped to include in the first one, such as the Self-Employed Women's Association in India and the Organization of Rural Associations for Progress in Zimbabwe, but at the time, the persons best able to write about them were preoccupied with other tasks.

We wanted to consider a variety of programs, across sectors and across regions. We think that we have chosen a good and instructive set, reflecting a wide range of experience. There is a predominance of South Asian cases (thirteen), but that proportion reflects South Asia's share of population in the Third World if China is not counted. There are five cases from Southeast Asia, six from Africa, and six from Latin America (see page ix).

We have probably overlooked some worthy projects and programs. We would be glad to hear from readers about any experiences that compare

Distribution of Cases by Type

Rural Development
    Aga Khan Rural Support Program (AKRSP), Pakistan
  * Bangladesh Rural Advancement Committee (BRAC)
  * Center for Economic and Social Development (DESEC), Bolivia
    Khorat Integrated Rural Development Program (IRDP), Thailand
    Moneragala Integrated Rural Development Project (MONDEP), Sri Lanka
    Organization of Rural Associations for Progress (ORAP), Zimbabwe
    Program for Integrated Rural Development (PIDER), Mexico
  * Six-S, Burkina Faso and other West African Sahelian countries
    Small Farmer Development Program (SFDP), Nepal

Agriculture
  * Anand-Model Dairy Cooperatives, India
  * Gal Oya Water Management Project, Sri Lanka
  * Integrated Pest Management (IPM) Program, Indonesia
    Kenya Tea Development Authority (KTDA)
  * National Irrigation Administration (NIA), Philippines
    North Potosi Program (World Neighbors), Bolivia
  * Plan Puebla, Mexico
  * San Martin Jilotepeque Program (World Neighbors), Guatemala

Health/Family Planning/Women's Programs
  * Iringa Child Survival and Nutrition Program, Tanzania
  * Population and Development Association (PDA), Thailand
    Posyandus (Health Posts) and PKK (Women's Associations), Indonesia
    Self-Employed Women's Association (SEWA), India

Natural Resources
  * Agroforestry Outreach Project, Haiti
  * CAMPFIRE Association, Zimbabwe
    Nepal-Australia Forestry Project (NAFP), Nepal
  * Rajasthan Watershed Conservation and Development Program, India

Infrastructure
    Baglung Bridge Program, Nepal
  * Orangi Pilot Project (OPP), Pakistan
  * Self-Help Rural Water Program, Malawi

Credit and Savings
  * Grameen Bank, Bangladesh
  * SANASA Savings and Credit Cooperatives, Sri Lanka

---

*Cases also presented in *Reasons for Hope.*

favorably with those we have reviewed and, even more important, any lessons that may have been omitted from our analysis. We hope to prepare a future edition that keeps abreast of the evolving state of the art.

We owe debts to the many people from whom we have learned through personal acquaintance and visits to their programs and, of course, to the many more who have contributed to the rich literature on rural development experience. The contributors to *Reasons for Hope* gave us many insights, both from their chapters and from other reading. A number of them offered suggestions and criticisms for strengthening our analysis. We thank especially Thomas Carter, an adviser to the National Dairy Development Board of India, and Laura Meitzner, a graduate student at Cornell with considerable experience abroad, for their careful reading of the manuscript, and Virginia Montopoli of the Cornell International Institute for Food, Agriculture, and Development (CIIFAD) for her excellent and unstinting assistance in this project from start to finish.

CIIFAD provided logistical and some financial support for this undertaking, in connection with its concern for strengthening local management capabilities as part of overall strategies for sustainable agricultural and rural development. This institute operates on an interdisciplinary, problem-focused and collaborative basis and represents an unusual undertaking by a U.S. university to be actively engaged with colleagues in Africa, Asia, and Latin America. CIIFAD seeks to advance the state of knowledge and to improve human and institutional capacities for achieving lasting improvements in productivity and well-being that are compatible with equitable and sustainable development.

1 Why Rural Development Remains Important

In some circles, rural development appears to be an outmoded issue. This is not because the incidence or severity of rural poverty in Third World countries has declined in recent years—quite the contrary in large parts of the world—but because the priorities of governments and the paradigms of many donor agencies have been shifting during the past ten to fifteen years. By its conservative definition, the World Bank estimates that more than a billion persons in Third World countries still live in poverty, with all the misery and insecurity this entails; in many countries, especially in sub-Saharan Africa and South Asia, the rural poor constitute half the population.

During the 1970s, the prevailing paradigm among development assistance agencies focused on the alleviation of poverty, recognizing that the benefits of macroeconomic growth had largely bypassed the majority of households, especially in rural areas. Enhancing the capacities and well-being of the poor could make them greater net contributors to their economies and societies. Accordingly, government and donor-supported programs were expected to address the basic needs and raise the productivity of the neglected majority.

This antipoverty emphasis was eclipsed in the 1980s by a neoclassical formula that prescribed marketization, privatization, deregulation, and minimal government to cure the ills of Third World economies. These measures were proposed to rescue Third World countries from the debt in which many found themselves as a result of excessive short-term borrowing. Some were responding to declines in the prices of their export products, which benefited the richer countries; others were compensating for budget imbalances that stemmed variously from the dissipation of resources on military establishments, prestige projects, official corruption, overstaffed bureaucracies, and lax collection of tax revenues.

Stringent actions, collectively referred to as structural adjustment, were advocated and often imposed. These aimed to reduce domestic consumption so that public debts could be serviced, external payment accounts would be returned to equilibrium, fiscal balance would be restored, and

1

the groundwork would be laid for future export-oriented growth led by domestic and multinational private enterprises. Although this doctrine is still dominant, there is some evolving thinking that poverty alleviation needs to be resurrected as a prime concern, with concern for sustainable development now legitimating the incorporation of environmental considerations into policy and planning.[1] This does not signal the end of trickle-down economic theories, but it may mean that the predominance of "ooze-out" approaches for reducing poverty and raising the productivity of the world's underclass is being reconsidered, at least in some circles.

The ascendancy of neoclassical economic logic, after decades of dormancy, owed much to the electoral successes of Ronald Reagan and Margaret Thatcher in the 1980s. These were fueled by growing public protest against chronic inflation, high taxes, and abuses of welfare programs in the industrialized countries. Rehabilitated in the wake of this protest was an orthodox strategy in which capital accumulation and investment guided by profit-seeking private entrepreneurs were expected to produce self-sustaining economic growth. This would draw underutilized "surplus" labor from rural areas into higher-productivity industrial jobs, which would lead in the long run to full employment and increasing incomes. This would induce the modernization and mechanization of agricultural production to cope with labor shortages in the rural sector.

Such a process, which appeared to explain the success of high-income countries such as the United States, Japan, and most of Western Europe, overlooked the huge subsidies paid to agricultural producers, contradicting free-market principles. What is most relevant here is that such a strategy stipulates no role for rural development as a priority for government or donor resources, since rural poverty is seen as a residual phenomenon, destined to be eliminated eventually by vigorous and continued industrial growth.

There are, however, a number of conditions associated with this conventional model of development. These include a high, sustained rate of domestic savings; substantial investment of those savings in industries, whether domestic or foreign owned, that utilize labor-absorbing rather than labor-saving technologies; and a relatively slow rate of population growth. In most of today's less developed countries, few of these conditions prevail. Savings rates tend to be low, and savings are invested in land, urban real estate, or trading rather than in manufacturing. Considerable domestic capital flows overseas to safe havens in the industrialized countries. Contemporary industrial technologies absorb relatively little labor, and population continues to increase at relatively high (but diminishing) rates.

The unrelenting growth of population in rural areas has created a young labor force far exceeding the numbers that can be productively

employed in the rural economy, given the technologies in use and the prevailing systems of land tenure and organization of production. The consequences of these trends can be observed in the burgeoning slums,
shantytowns, and squatter settlements in urban areas throughout the
Third World. There, redundant workers from rural areas search desper-
ately for any kind of work, mostly in the informal sector, thereby depressing
wage rates even among the lucky few who find more or less regular work
in offices, shops, and factories. Some of them swell the ranks of menial
employees in overstaffed government agencies.[2]

Some of the more venturesome emigrants from rural areas take advantage of opportunities to migrate, legally or illegally, to industrialized
countries and find work, which enables them to remit part of their earn-
ings to their families back home. This movement might in the long run
equilibrate the marginal productivity of labor across countries. But however desirable this might be for overall economic efficiency and equity, it is
politically unacceptable in the receiving nations. Closing this "safety
valve" aggravates the problem of urban unemployment in less developed
countries, which have a continuing influx of fresh arrivals into cities and
towns from labor-surplus rural areas. Given these demographic realities,
especially in South Asia, most of Africa, and many areas of Central and
South America, how can the neoclassical model of development resolve
the massive problems of rural and urban poverty in the foreseeable future?

What has been emerging in both urban and rural areas is a dualistic
society. A "modern" sector provides relatively secure and comfortable living
standards for owners, managers, and employees in the "formal" sector—
financial institutions, commercial companies, manufacturing firms, and
government offices, including parastatal organizations and the military.
Associated with them are independent professionals and shopkeepers who
serve the modern enterprises and members of the urban middle class, plus
persons in the informal sector who have established niches that yield them
and their families assured incomes.

Persons in these favored circumstances can aspire to occupy decent
housing, equip their families with modern appliances (often including
motor vehicles—motorcycles, if not cars), and send their children to technical colleges and maybe even to universities. Their numbers gradually
grow as the modern economy expands and incorporates additional
recruits into its ranks. These opportunities do not increase fast enough,
however, to benefit most of the residents of the shantytowns, whose numbers continue to expand with new arrivals from rural areas.

In rural areas, the modern sector is composed of landed farmers with
sufficient resources and initiative to gain reliable access to institutional
credit, mechanized equipment, modern production inputs, and marketing

channels. Because productive land is limited in most countries, however, their numbers do not increase and indeed may decline if rules and practices of inheritance limit the division of holdings into uneconomic parcels, and landownership becomes consolidated in fewer families. Associated with such "middle" farmers are rural merchants, moneylenders, contractors, and government employees. As in the urban areas, they do not constitute a single "class." What they have in common are reasonably secure living standards that maintain them safely above the subsistence level.

Outside the modern sector are small landholders who often work the poorer soils, have access to few if any modern production inputs, find themselves often in debt, and must seek wage employment to supplement farming incomes. Many are tenants or sharecroppers with insecure tenure. Even more precarious are the landless who have no assets except their labor. They live on the margins of subsistence, and their only security may come through dependence on well-endowed patrons. The most vulnerable are women, especially those who have been abandoned or widowed, who, though having few assets and fewer rights, are responsible for supporting themselves and their children.

This diverse category of individuals and families is designated as the rural poor. Illiterate, often malnourished, afflicted with serious health problems, sometimes stigmatized by ethnic prejudices, living often in remote, isolated areas, and having limited access to productive resources, the rural poor nevertheless manage by dint of necessity to devise coping or survival strategies that can be quite innovative (Chambers 1997, 162–87). Often there is sharing among kinfolk as the rural poor create their own "safety nets." The labor of all family members, including women and children, is allocated between urban and rural locations to produce income for the family's daily survival.

Third World governments are seldom in a position and often are not disposed to assist the rural poor, who are mostly unorganized, "out of sight and out of mind," having little political clout. For the most part, the poor must cope on their own. Governments, donors, and intellectuals who espouse the current orthodox, neoliberal model of development are not unconcerned with poverty, including rural poverty. They know that the buildup of a massive underclass could topple the political-economic edifice their policies have constructed, no matter how encouraging the aggregate per capita gross national product statistics may be. But there is a lingering hope, not supported by evidence, that economic growth will gradually eliminate poverty and put the national economy on a firmer foundation for long-term and equitable productivity.

Policy prescriptions continue to insist that government be kept small and that taxes be kept low to provide a favorable climate for private enterprise, domestic and foreign. Assistance to the poor is likely to be confined to the diffusion of recommended agricultural practices, modest health service provision, access to primary education (whose quality is generally declining), and, when necessary, famine relief. Few governments see making greater direct investments in raising the productivity and increasing the well-being of the poor as the leading edge of development strategy.

It is not impossible that a combination of favorable circumstances might enable a few Third World countries to achieve and maintain high rates of growth over extended periods, sufficient to allow the neoclassical model to succeed. An example is Malaysia, where natural resource endowments (petroleum, minerals, fertile soil, and rainfall), competent management by a stable government, and a long tradition of external trade, combined with a strategic geographic location and a conducive environment for foreign investment, have quadrupled the size of the economy in twenty years. The incidence of rural poverty has been reduced from 55 to 9 percent, and Malaysia has even begun to attract migrant workers from neighboring countries. But there have been few such successes. More typical are situations in which a few urban growth poles—Manila, Nairobi, Shanghai, Mumbai, São Paulo—industrialize rapidly while large populations in the hinterlands are barely touched by modernization and continue to harbor growing populations that stagnate in poverty and insecurity and conditions for the majority of urban residents become less and less livable. Not all countries can become net exporters.

TAKING DIRECT ACTION

Given this pervasive reality, the most promising strategy is to address the problems of rural underdevelopment directly, not waiting for the benefits of industrialization to trickle down to rural people. This requires measures that will improve the productivity and quality of life for the hundreds of millions of smallholders and landless men and women who, with their children, will continue to live and earn their livelihoods in rural societies for decades to come, often on a natural resource base that is itself fragile and in need of special protection.

Measures are needed to increase the productivity of both land and labor in agricultural and nonagricultural occupations, for rural women as well as rural men. Land use needs to be intensified and diversified in ways consistent with preserving soil fertility, while remunerative forms of nonagricultural employment are created to supplement income from cropping and livestock activities. Rural communities need improved nutrition and health services, including environmental sanitation and access to family planning; elementary education aimed at universal literacy; basic shelter; and the essentials for a dignified existence.

One of the tragedies of rural poverty is the destructive pressures it can exert on natural resources—land, forests, and water—on which the livelihoods of future generations depend. Land is being overused and its natural fertility depleted, forests are being ravaged, rangelands overgrazed, water supplies exhausted, and wildlife eliminated. Sometimes these pressures are exploited and exacerbated by wealthy interests that use the rural poor as advance parties to open up forests or rangelands that can then be taken over for large-scale operations. Some of the environmental degradation attributed to the rural poor is a matter of blaming the victims rather than the instigators. But in any case, farming and grazing practices in the future must optimize productivity, with sustainability an urgent concern.[3]

Critics may castigate any substantial support for rural development by saying that it restricts the mass of people to rural areas for the indefinite future while other, more fortunate persons enjoy the opportunities, status, and amenities of urban life. We are not proposing that the process of national transition toward more urbanized societies and economies be halted. Nor are we glamorizing rural alternatives. Rather, we want people to have freer choices about where they will make their homes. Urban growth that is driven by rural "push" more than urban "pull" cannot produce cities and towns that are desirable and sustainable. We are also mindful of the legitimate desire of rural parents to offer their children attractive life opportunities in the places where they are growing up. We are distressed by the plaintive worries of mothers and fathers who see their children drawn into drugs, crime, and destructive lifestyles if they enter into the reality of today's cities. So we are talking about a development strategy that aims to give people good choices rather than forces them to choose between undesirable lives in either rural or urban areas.

What is required to implement the broad-based strategy suggested by this concept of rural development? Although self-help strategies are important for many reasons, at least some resources and services external to rural society need to be provided, normally by governments. These contributions to rural development include public works such as roads, irrigation facilities, and electricity; assistance to agriculture through research and extension; elementary schooling; public health measures and health clinics; and encouragement of rural industrial production, small or larger scale.

Such services, when provided by government agencies, commonly fail to reach the rural poor. They may be preempted by rural elites, but more often they are simply irrelevant or inaccessible to poor households, which are scattered across large areas, many in remote locations. Increasingly the services are insufficient to cover the large numbers of persons needing them. Often they are regarded as "welfare" measures and thus of low priority (unless the area in question happens to be the constituency of an influential political leader). However, we see a need for new commitments to provide the poor majority with access to credit, appropriate technologies, relevant education, natural resource conservation measures, and the like.

Such improvements need not be expensive, although their total cost can add up because so many people are involved. An exemplary rural development program initiated by World Neighbors with poor villagers in Guatemala in the 1970s increased yields of maize and beans fourfold within seven years at a cost of about US$50 per family. This must be considered a highly profitable investment by any standard, particularly because the people doubled their yields once more after external assistance was withdrawn (Krishna and Bunch 1997).

Nongovernmental organizations (NGOs) have emerged over the last two decades as important contributors to rural advancement, but not all are as effective as the above example (Tendler 1997, 157–63). Those that are effective can provide useful information, services, and resources through dedicated staff to a few communities and programs. But most NGOs operate on a fairly small scale, with a few exceptions, such as the Bangladesh Rural Advancement Committee (BRAC). Moreover, despite the enthusiasm expressed by many policy makers for reliance on the private sector, for-profit companies are not likely to find it very attractive to operate among the rural poor. They may market rural produce and supply some production inputs, but usually they serve the larger-scale, more prosperous farmers better. When there is no competition among private providers of goods and services, the poor may indeed be taken advantage of by monopolistic enterprises.

That governmental, nongovernmental, and private (for-profit) institutions all have limitations for promoting rural development does not make them irrelevant. Rather, it means that none can be relied on as an exclusive channel for bettering rural livelihoods and quality of life. The main resources for broad-based rural development must come from the energy, ideas, and determination of rural people themselves, from collective self-help and what we call *assisted self-reliance* (Esman and Uphoff 1984, 258–61). In most successful cases we know of, the efforts, resourcefulness, self-discipline, and latent management skills of the rural poor have initially been mobilized and organized by outsiders, overcoming the lack of experience and self-confidence among people who have known only deprivation, hardship, social and economic oppression, and a sense of powerlessness.

3 actors.
Govt, NGOs, private sector

The rural poor are not inherently more unselfish or committed to group solidarity than are persons raised under more favorable circumstances, although the former may have become accustomed to cooperating and communicating among themselves out of necessity for survival. Romanticizing the poor is a naive error among some who sympathize with their plight and would like to help them. This error should be avoided, as should its converse, underestimating what the poor can contribute to their own development. Although they are vulnerable to the same human frailties as the rest of us, they are by the same token innately no less intelligent and no less desirous of improving their lot. They have considerable capability for "getting ahead collectively" (Hirschman 1984). This does not substitute for individual initiative and responsibility, but especially for the poor, it is an essential element in any large-scale strategy for rural development.

In devising survival strategies under constrained conditions with very few resources, poor rural households demonstrate high levels of resourcefulness. In most Third World countries, the rural poor increasingly know that they cannot depend on benevolent governments, on the trickle-down effects of industrialization, on the generosity of powerful patrons, or on migration to the cities to transform their prospects to ameliorate their poverty and insecurity. If their lot is to be improved during their lifetimes, they must take their futures into their own hands, in those rural settings that they have called home all their lives. This is why rural development is not an obsolete concern. It is as urgently needed as it was decades ago and deserves as much priority as it enjoyed then. But is it possible?

LEARNING FROM EXPERIENCE

Contrary to conventional wisdom, there are some encouraging prospects. Experience over the past quarter century demonstrates that broad-based rural development has been attempted, achieved, and sustained on every continent among the poorest and most deprived classes, including rural women. Many initiatives have indeed failed. But some have succeeded, even under what seemed unpromising circumstances.

Successful experiences have often been inspired, initiated, and guided in their early stages by unusually able and motivated persons from outside rural communities. But from their beginnings, these efforts have involved rural people and a dedicated cadre of staff, managers, and technicians, sometimes from the communities and sometimes from outside, in the development of new organizational arrangements and the use of new techniques. Responsibility for decision making and implementation has become increasingly exercised by local bodies so that capacities for management are institutionalized at village as well as at higher levels.

These development entrepreneurs brought to rural communities certain appropriate technologies, simple but effective management methods, social organization compatible with local experience and preferences, and, most important, a willingness to continue experimenting and learning as successive sets of problems emerged. They have been able to persuade rural publics that they can gain more by collective self-help and by cooperating with their neighbors than would be possible through separate individual efforts.

These social innovators have come from government departments, from NGOs, from the private sector, from donor agencies, from universities. Like the authors of this volume, what they have in common is a commitment to broad-based, participatory development, inspired by a deep conviction that people who happen to be poor and uneducated can, with some outside encouragement, assistance, and support, take control of their lives, work together for their respective and collective self-improvement, institutionalize viable patterns of cooperation, and continue to innovate on their own.

These protagonists of broad-based, participatory rural development reject as mistaken and patronizing the notions of inherent fatalism among peasants and of amoral familism determining behavior in poor countries. For them, participation implies not only that the rural poor will share in the benefits of development and that they will contribute labor and funds but also that they or agents accountable to them will take responsibility for planning, managing, and evaluating the activities undertaken by their organizations and having ownership of these organizations and their products.

Not succumbing to the pathologies of "localitis," these innovators were willing to take advantage of external assistance from governments, donors, and NGOs, gaining access to services, technical information, and funds that could help launch and nourish their programs, as long as these resources did not create dependency on outsiders or impair the ability of rural people to manage their own affairs.

We were persuaded that the reports of some of these successful experiences with broad-based rural development would be instructive for persons wishing to initiate or support similar ventures. As explained in the introduction to *Reasons for Hope*, the companion volume to this one, we arranged for case studies to be written on eighteen impressive initiatives for development with and by, not just for, the rural poor. That volume presented retrospectively, in the words of protagonists who established and/or supported these ventures, what was attempted, what was accomplished, and, most important, what were the strategies and methods employed—how they learned from hands-on experience and adjusted their strategies accordingly, and how rural people took greater responsibility for their organizations and programs.

This volume draws on the experiences and insights presented in the first one. It offers comparative analyses and identifies practical implications from those case studies and from others with which we are acquainted through the literature or from personal observation and involvement. The main features of the cases presented in that first volume are summarized in Table 1.1, and another dozen cases offering significant lessons about successful rural development are described briefly in Table 1.2.[4] These additional cases expand on the range of experience considered and maintain a geographic spread across Asia, Africa, and Latin America, although there is still a preponderance of cases from South Asia. This region not only has more rural population than other parts of the Third World; it also has launched more large-scale efforts to improve rural people's productivity and well-being. We undertake in this volume to distill from these and other experiences some general principles and operational guidelines that should be useful to practitioners of the art, to planners, implementers, and evaluators contributing to the emergent science of broad-based and purposefully promoted rural development.

NOTES

1. The elements of "the emergent development policy consensus," according to a senior fellow in the Institute for International Economics, are fiscal discipline, shift in public expenditure priorities, tax reform, financial liberalization, exchange rate unification, trade liberalization, encouragement of foreign direct investment, privatization, deregulation, and protection of property rights (Williamson 1994, 2–3). When the World Bank's chief economist had suggested in 1990 that poverty reduction also be emphasized, Williamson felt that this "was unjustified at the time. However, [t]his prediction that the issue would become increasingly salient proved to be correct" (1994, 3). The World Bank, the U.S. Agency for International Development (USAID), and other donors are now devoting more resources to "socially oriented projects" and giving more attention to environmental problems, but within neoclassical presumptions.

2. Complicating and accelerating this growth is an increasing sense that there is no future in rural areas, so that even if there were economic opportunities there, people might pass them up to gamble on finding acceptable income streams in urban areas, where they could enjoy the public services, entertainment, and psychological excitement found in towns and cities. Perhaps more important, such a move might be seen as giving one's children better life opportunities. Urban "pull" may

not contribute to greater economic efficiency, however, and it can have long-term effects that depress both rural and urban areas.

3. Chambers (1997, 23–9) challenges the conventional wisdom that the poor invari-ably undermine their natural resource base. He cites examples from Kenya, Guinea, and Nepal in which either poor rural households enhanced their land, forest, and water resources or the deterioration resulted from having too few peo-ple rather than too many. Chambers's discussion of erroneous opinions held by diverse experts and authorities should be read by all students and practitioners of development.

4. We wanted to include seven of these cases in *Reasons for Hope*: the Self-Employed Women's Association (SEWA) in India, the Aga Khan Rural Support Program (AKRSP) in Pakistan, the Small Farmer Development Program (SFDP) in Nepal, the Posyandus and Mothers' Clubs (PKK) in Indonesia, the Kenya Tea Development Authority (KTDA), the Organization of Rural Associations for Progress (ORAP) in Zimbabwe, and Mexico's Program for Integrated Rural Development (PIDER). For various reasons, the persons most deeply involved in establishing these initiatives were unable to contribute to that volume. Others cases listed in Table 1.2 and included in this volume are less well known but very instructive.

Table 1.1 Rural Development Cases Documented in *Reasons for Hope*

Program	Start of Idea	Start of Program	Organizational Structure	Program Objectives	Achievements	Donor Support
Grameen Bank BANGLADESH	1976 Personal loans	1983 Bank created	Innovative bank plus borrower groups	Loans for the rural poor, especially women	2 million borrowers, 94% women, in 34,000 villages; daily loan volume of $1.5 million; 98% repayment; 16,000 rural schools started	Ford Foundation initial support, then IFAD and other donors provided funds
Bangladesh Rural Advancement Committee (BRAC) BANGLADESH	1972 Relief work	1977 Target group approach	NGO plus village organizations	Multisectoral development for the rural poor through village organizations	Programs in 35,000 villages with 1.2 million households; 1.1 million pupils in rural schools; $86 million budget, with 40% from own funds	NOVIB, ODA, CIDA, World Bank, SIDA, KFW, NORAID, DANIDA, UNICEF, Swiss aid, AKF, Ford Foundation
Center for Social and Economic Development (DESEC) BOLIVIA	1963 Group meetings	1963 NGO formed	NGO working with community organizations	Create income opportunities for rural communities	Programs in villages with 50,000 households; achieved 4-fold increase in potato production; artisan cooperative; reforestation	Misereor, Deutsche Welthungerhilfe, and many other European NGOS; FAO, Swiss, Belgian, and Spanish aid

(cont.)

AKF   Aga Khan Foundation
ANU   Australian National University
ATI   Appropriate Technology International, U.S.
BCCI   Bank of Credit and Commerce International
CAA   Community Aid Abroad (Australian nongovernmental organization)
CIDA   Canadian International Development Agency
CIMMYT International Center for Maize and Wheat Improvement
CLUSA   Cooperative League of U.S.A.
DANIDA Danish International Development Agency
EC   European Community
FAO   Food and Agricultural Organization of the United Nations
GTZ   German Society for Technical Cooperation
HIVOS   Dutch nongovernmental organization
IDB   Inter-American Development Bank

IFAD   International Fund for Agricultural Development
IRRI   International Rice Research Institute
JICA   Japanese International Cooperation Agency
KFW   Credit Fund for Reconstruction, Germany
NORAD   Norwegian International Development Agency
NOVIB   Dutch nongovernmental organization
ODA   Overseas Development Administration, U.K.
SCF   Save the Children Fund
SIDA   Swedish International Development Agency
UNDP   United Nations Development Programme
UNICEF United Nations Children's Fund
USAID   United States Agency for International Development
WCCU   World Council of Credit Unions
WHO   World Health Organization

Table 1.1 Rural Development Cases Documented in *Reasons for Hope* (cont.)

Program	Start of Idea	Start of Program	Organizational Structure	Program Objectives	Achievements	Donor Support
Six-S BURKINA FASO/ SAHEL	1975 Conference	1977 First funding	Loose federation of rural organizations supported by NGO	Use dry season in Sahel to create better livelihood opportunities in agriculture	Mobilizing/assisting 1 million villagers in 1,500 communities in Burkina Faso, Niger, Togo, Gambia, and Guinea-Bissau	Swiss aid, Misereor, and other European NGOS
San Martin Jilotepeque GUATEMALA	1962–68 Health program	1972 Project started	NGO giving technical assistance to farmers and their cooperative	With farmers, devise technologies to raise agricultural production and reduce soil erosion	5,000 households able to more than triple yields within 7 years, for less than $50 per household; farmers doubled yields again after project ended	World Neighbors, Oxfam; USAID project rejected by villagers as likely to undermine self-reliance
Agroforestry Outreach HAITI	1979 Anthropological study	1981 Project started	Project working with local NGOS and farmer groups	Get farmers to plant trees to reverse deforestation and to augment their incomes	200,000 households (20% of rural total) involved in planting 60 million fast-growing trees over 10-year period	USAID assistance positive for first 10 years, then USAID policy shift undermined project
Anand-Model Dairy Cooperatives INDIA	1946-47 District co-op started	1970 Operation Flood with World Bank funding	Cooperative with primary societies at base, district and state unions, and national board	Increase milk production and farmer incomes	10 million members, mostly poor, who get 70% of consumer price; incomes increased by 30% or more	Initial UNICEF aid; World Food Program and FAO next; then EC, World Bank, USAID, Danish and Swiss aid; also Ford, CIDA, CLUSA
Rajasthan Watershed Program INDIA	1990 Funds offered by donor and GOI	1991 Program started	Government program working with user committees	Conserve watersheds and raise local production and incomes	Devised and extended new technologies to raise production and halt erosion; covered 442,000 ha. within 5 years involving 15,000 user committees	World Bank

(cont.)

Table 1.1 Rural Development Cases Documented in *Reasons for Hope* (cont.)

Program	Start of Idea	Start of Program	Organizational Structure	Program Objectives	Achievements	Donor Support
Integrated Pest Management (IPM) Program INDONESIA	1979 IPM endorsed	1986 Presidential decree	Government program with farmer field schools and farmer groups	Reduce use of chemical pesticides without lowering yields by educating farmers	650,000 farmers trained by 1996, starting to train other farmers; saving $150 million/year in foreign exchange without yield declines, indeed with production growth	FAO, USAID, World Bank, JICA, IRRI
Self-Help Water Supply Program MALAWI	1968 Pilot project	1969 Scaling up	Government department working with village committees	Provide potable water to villages through gravity flow systems	Water provided for over 1 million rural people, 30% of rural population, at less than $10 per capita with reliable maintenance	USAID, DANIDA, CIDA, Oxfam, UNICEF, Dutch aid, Christian churches of Malawi
Plan Puebla MEXICO	1966 Proposal	1967 Funding	Project with farmer groups plus university and government and private institutions	Develop appropriate technology for farmers growing rain-fed maize	Increased yields and incomes for almost 50,000 farmers, plus institutional changes; model for other rain-fed agricultural programs	Rockefeller Foundation, CIMMYT support, ATI support
Orangi Pilot Project (OPP) PAKISTAN	1980 Explorations	1981 Construction started	Project with lane committees and other local organizations	Provide low-cost, self-help sewer facilities, then other services	Sanitation provided for $33/household; mobilized 17 times more local resources than donor funding; health, education, housing, employment	BCCI, UNICEF, World Bank, AKF, USAID, UNDP, Swiss aid, Rockefeller Foundation
National Irrigation Administration PHILIPPINES	1976 Pilot project	1980 Scaling up	Government agency plus water user associations	Improve water distribution and fee collections to finance operations and maintenance	Over 500,000 ha. with participatory irrigation management; most of operation and maintenance funded by farmers	Ford Foundation, USAID, IFAD

(cont.)

Table 1.1 Rural Development Cases Documented in *Reasons for Hope* (cont.)

Program	Start of Idea	Start of Program	Organizational Structure	Program Objectives	Achievements	Donor Support
Gal Oya Irrigation Project SRI LANKA	1980 Reconnaissance	1981 Organizers trained/fielded	Government agency plus farmer organizations	Improve water distribution and solve agricultural and other problems	Water use efficiency doubled; rice produced per unit of water up 4-fold; led to national program involving 250,000 farmers	USAID
SANASA Savings and Credit Cooperatives SRI LANKA	1978 Village observations	1979 Expansion after Walgama seminar	Savings and loan cooperative societies	Mobilize rural savings for benefit of members, including rural poor	750,000 members have built up $40 million in savings with little outside aid; $32 million in loans, 100% repayment	NGOs and co-ops: CAA, WCCU, CCA, HIVOS; USAID and World Bank funding was detrimental
Iringa Child Survival and Nutrition TANZANIA	1983 Pilot project	1986 Expansion after evaluation	Government program plus local committees	Reduce malnutrition and improve health of children	Reduced severe child malnutrition by two-thirds within a few years; scaled up to national coverage by 1996	UNICEF, WHO, Italian aid, GTZ, World Bank, IFAD, NORAD, SIDA
Population and Development Association THAILAND	1974 NGO started	1975 Reorganized in new NGO structure	NGO working with local organizations	Reduce rate of population growth and promote economic development	Helped to lower population growth rate to 1.2%; developed own funding base for development services	AgroAction (German NGO), many donors, also now many private corporations
CAMPFIRE Association ZIMBABWE	1986 District conference	1989 Devolution of authority to districts	National association with local committees	Protect wildlife by giving communities stake in preserving it	Cooperation of villagers in conservation efforts in all major wildlife areas in country	SCF, World Wide Fund for Nature, Zimbabwe Trust (national NGO)

Table 1.2 Additional Rural Development Experiences Considered in *Reasons for Success*

Program	Start of Idea	Start of Program	Organizational Structure	Program Objectives	Achievements	Donor Support
North Potosi Program BOLIVIA/ANDES	1973 Two field visits	1974 Pilot project with communities	Network of volunteer promoters assisted by World Neighbors staff	Improve food security for rural communities using low-cost technologies developed with farmer participation	120 rural communities with 2,500 households gained skills for identifying and diffusing appropriate technologies, doubling barley, wheat, and potato production; health and education improvements also made	World Neighbors; some support now from World Bank, UNICEF projects
Self-Employed Women's Association (SEWA) INDIA	1971 Poor women asked TLA union for assistance	1972 SEWA registered as trade union	Membership organization with features of trade union and cooperative	Organize and assist poor women: small-scale sellers, home-based producers, and laborers	One million poor women now involved through network of 16 autonomous SEWAs in Indian cities, though not all are as successful as Ahmedabad SEWA	Some Ford Foundation support; no major external assistance
Posyandus and Mothers' Clubs (PKK) INDONESIA	1960s Mothers' clubs started spontaneously	1979–84 80,000 health posts consolidated in 41,000 villages	Local health posts (posyandus) operating with support of mothers' clubs (PKKs)	Improve health, nutrition, family planning, and immunization services at village level through self-help activities	By 1995, 264,000 village posyandus reaching 23 million children, with 1.4 million volunteers; critical factor in lower birthrate; cut infant mortality by one-third; 94% of children immunized	Mostly national and local resources; many donors working with posyandus
Kenya Tea Development Authority (KTDA) KENYA	1950s Special Crops Development Authority	1964 New parastatal agency created	Central government agency with outgrower groups attached	Promote tea cultivation by smallholder farmers; processing and marketing tea on commercial basis	Smallholder tea output went from 1,000 tons in 1960s to 30,000 tons in 1980s, with improved prices and top quality; from 6,000 to 130,000 farmers (110,000 acres)	Commonwealth Development Corporation, World Bank

See Table 1.1 for list of acronyms

(cont.)

Table 1.2 Additional Rural Development Experiences Considered in *Reasons for Success* (cont.)

Program	Start of Idea	Start of Program	Organizational Structure	Program Objectives	Achievements	Donor Support
Integrated Rural Development Program (PIDER) MEXICO	1973 Multidisciplinary research group formed	1975 New participatory methodology field-tested	Municipalities work with multidepartmental committees at state, regional, national levels	Multisectoral development through involving local communities in planning government-funded development activities	Infrastructure, soil conservation, and other sectors accelerated; methodology used again in "safety net" and social development programs in 1990s	World Bank main donor ($2 billion); also IDB and IFAD
Baglung Bridge Program NEPAL	1971 Local member of Parliament had idea for program	1974 Government agreed to assist program	Construction committees within village *panchayat* system	Build improved bridges throughout Baglung district	Built 62 bridges in 5 years, twice as fast and at one-fourth the cash cost of government, using local resources, management, and technology	Small government grant plus UNICEF provision of cables
Nepal-Australia Forestry Project (NAFP) NEPAL	1966 Australian technical assistance for forestry began	1978 Pilot project for people-centered forestry	Government department with village user groups plus ANU advisers	Community management of forests; conservation with sustainable yield for local harvesting	Established over 15,000 ha. of new community-managed forests, overseen by 150 *panchayats*; got new national policy for community management	Australian government (about $12 million)
Small Farmer Development Program (SFDP) NEPAL	1973 Field workshops organized by FAO	1975 Pilot projects in Dhanusha and Nuwakot	Farmer groups organized and assisted by Agricultural Development Bank of Nepal	Improve household incomes and security through individual and group action supported by loans and technical assistance	Program expanded to include 40,000 households in rural, often remote areas; greater economic and political security	FAO provided $30,000 to initiate program; IFAD, GTZ, and others

(cont.)

Table 1.2 Additional Rural Development Experiences Considered in *Reasons for Success* (cont.)

Program	Start of Idea	Start of Program	Organizational Structure	Program Objectives	Achievements	Donor Support
Aga Khan Rural Support Program (AKRSP) PAKISTAN	1980 Initial planning	1982 Program established	Project supporting activities through village organizations	Support multi-sectoral development through local self-help	Over 2,600 men's and women's village organizations benefiting almost one million persons; income doubled, compared with 26% increase in rest of country; cost of $26 per capita	Aga Khan Foundation major donor; also funding from others
Moneragala Integrated Rural Development Program SRI LANKA	1979 Prior IRDP started in Hambantota district	1984 Moneragala IRDP started	Project unit in district administration plus local organizations	Participatory diagnosis and project activities to promote all-round rural development at district level and below	Broad-based improvements through school renovation, revolving funds, primary health care, etc.; some group incomes increased 6–10 times through dairy co-ops, sericulture, etc.	NORAD, with 20-year commitment
Khorat Integrated Rural Development Program THAILAND	1981 Discussions among officials started	1983 Basic minimum needs (BMN) program established	Provincial office coordinating ministry staff working with village groups	BMN status monitored at level of household cluster; promote self-help and government action	BMN program became national program after 1986; 95% of rural villages using these indicators to assess their programs	UNDP helped institutionalize national program after 1985
Organization of Rural Associations for Progress (ORAP) ZIMBABWE	1980 NGO Rural Development Coordinating Council	1981 National independence	Federation of village groups	Food security, drought relief, income-generating projects, literacy meeting basic needs	Serves almost a million persons; technical and managerial skills being upgraded to match high levels of group solidarity	20 agencies, but member contributions greater than donor aid

2 Learning Process and Assisted Self-Reliance

The impetus for broad-based and sustainable rural development may come from government, from nongovernmental organizations (NGOs), from individuals, from the private sector, or from communities themselves. Whatever the source of initiative, it is important that rural development programs be undertaken in a *learning process* (LP) mode and with *assisted self-reliance* (ASR) as both end and means. LP and ASR are both methodologies as well as objectives, representing philosophies of development at the same time that they are practical strategies.

Given the complexity of socioeconomic processes of change and of their interactions with technological alternatives, it is hard to imagine how anyone could anticipate all or even most of the salient factors in any serious rural development initiative. Although frameworks for action can and should be formulated, it is not possible or useful to prepare a detailed blueprint in advance specifying all actions, sequences, investments, staffing, and criteria. Not enough is known about the many elements involved or about their varied causal relationships.

For *sustainable* development, the capacities and orientations that are created must remain flexible, open to new information, ideas, and instructions. Economic, social, ecological, political, and other aspects of the world are always evolving and changing, sometimes favorably, but often adversely. For innovations to remain relevant and effective, they must be continually checked against new realities and revised accordingly. This makes "learning" a goal with long-term implications as well as a means for accomplishing short-term objectives.

The value of an LP approach is vividly demonstrated by a conversation that a colleague of ours had with the manager of a World Bank–funded project in an East African country some years ago as the five-year project was coming to an end. After discussing the many problems that the project had encountered, not atypical ones, the manager volunteered that basically most of what they had initially thought they knew about the project's task and its task environment had turned out to be wrong. It had taken three years to ascertain this, however. Then another year was needed to reassess the situation and redesign the program. This meant that just one year was left to begin doing useful things. The project's manager and the participants would have gotten more results for their expenditure if they had started out assuming that they knew little or nothing about the task and the task environment. That way, they could have had four years, instead of one, to attempt more reasonable developmental changes.

This is probably an extreme case. But such self-critical candor from managers of donor-funded projects is rare, so we will never know how common this circumstance is. Such shortcomings plague too many development efforts around the world. Laborious efforts are made to design a project; large commitments of resources are made; intricate implementation procedures are prescribed; and the results are seldom commensurate with the efforts made, even if a post hoc evaluation indicates an acceptable economic rate of return. That an LP approach is advantageous for rural development has been increasingly accepted in principle. But bureaucratic processes and requirements continue to distort and truncate efforts to work in this more inductive mode.[1] To be sure, this approach requires some prior assumptions and commitments. Learning itself cannot proceed with a "blank slate"—all perceptions and conceptions require some preconceptions. The challenge for development initiators is to provide for optimal degrees of flexibility and specification that will structure and support a learning process. This is discussed later.

Assisted self-reliance, also considered in this chapter, seems a paradoxical idea. It links assistance with independence to arrive at outcomes of self-determination, self-financing, and self-sustainability (Esman and Uphoff 1984, 258–61; Uphoff 1988). Unfortunately, assistance too often creates dependence, the antithesis of self-reliance. ASR requires providing assistance in certain ways and on specified terms that have the effect of building up capacities, incentives, and confidence for self-management rather than undermining them. That this developmental alchemy is possible can be seen from the cases presented in *Reasons for Hope*. Here, we analyze and synthesize the reasons for their success and that of other instructive cases.

LEARNING PROCESS

To accept learning process as the mode of operation in rural development is to recognize the nature of reality, which is highly contingent and interactive, locally variable, and continually changing (Chambers 1997, 162–74). Any a priori plans are bound to be inadequate, although this does not mean that planning is unnecessary. What is needed is planning for contingencies rather than for certainties. As is increasingly appreciated within the planning profession, the *process* of planning is generally more important than its *product*. Plans themselves will surely need to be revised and superseded; the shared understandings and the consensus built up during the process of producing them should make subsequent efforts more coherent and more usefully focused on both obstacles and objectives, with funding from more diverse sources.

Learning process was "discovered" by David Korten (1980) from his review of five rural development programs in Asia that had distinguished themselves by the late 1970s. That three of them have continued since then to expand and diversify their activities supports the validity of his analysis; the two other programs that did not prosper so impressively were not as imbued with the LP philosophy. It is not entirely coincidental that the program with the longest investment in learning how to mesh organizational structures and incentives with technological innovations and investments has had the greatest impact, now benefiting about fifty million persons in India, most of them the rural poor. Dr. Verghese Kurien devoted over twenty years to devising and refining the Anand system of dairy cooperatives before he agreed to launch "Operation Flood" on a massive scale with Government of India and World Bank funding in the 1970s. This program, which has spread across most of the states of India, many of them with larger populations than most of the world's countries, took great perseverance on the part of Dr. Kurien and his associates, but it also took an experimental frame of mind, which is seen from his case study in *Reasons for Hope*, where he advocates the use of "living laboratories" in the field for any development program.

The Bangladesh Rural Advancement Committee (BRAC), which was also featured in Korten's analysis, has grown and strengthened its capacities to the point where it is probably the largest development NGO in the world, with 17,000 staff and over 47,000 volunteers. The leadership of BRAC makes a point that should be clear with any application of learning process: the process should never stop, as the staff must continue to experiment (Abed and Chowdhury 1997, 45). This conclusion is also supported by experience from the Gal Oya irrigation management project in Sri Lanka (Uphoff 1992a), where Korten's prescriptive framework was applied from the beginning of the program design (he was a member of the initial design team). When C. M. Wijayaratna visited the farmer organizations in Gal Oya ten years after external assistance was withdrawn, leaders proudly demonstrated the diverse activities their groups had undertaken since project support had ended. Their orientation toward problem identification and problem solving had prepared them to cope with the new problems, opportunities, and challenges that continually arise.

Learning process must be ongoing, and it should be carried forward not just by program planners and implementers but even more so by rural people themselves. They need to see themselves as capable of and responsible for continual innovation, as must the government or NGO personnel working with them. A key actor on the team that introduced integrated pest management (IPM) on a national scale in Indonesia says, "The entire system must keep learning," developing, testing, and improving methods, and pioneering new approaches. "Only if the system keeps evolving and learning does it stay committed and clear on its goals" (Oka 1997, 194).

Some of the more recent rural development initiatives are working more explicitly in this LP manner. The CAMPFIRE program in Zimbabwe promotes the protection and management of wildlife for the benefit of rural people as well as for posterity. Its success has attracted favorable attention worldwide. Writing about this experience, Simon Metcalfe says, "Apart from following some basic principles, CAMPFIRE's implementation was never seen as following a blueprint" (1997, 277). The most recent case included in *Reasons for Hope*, documenting the introduction of watershed conservation and development measures in the Indian state of Rajasthan, is impressive because it shows that a government agency working in an LP mode can proceed both quickly and effectively. Within two years, 100,000 hectares were being protected and improved by villagers who had previously been contributing to the watersheds' degradation. Anirudh Krishna, who directed this effort, describes it as an "iterative search for approximate solutions"; the plans prepared with local participation for each microwatershed were "not cast in concrete" (1997, 264–6). They could be revised, with villagers' suggestions and consent, whenever it was felt that new knowledge could improve them. This gives a new meaning to the concept of planning.

Guiding Ideas

One key to success was not as evident in Korten's analysis as it is to us now, after considering a wider range of successful cases over a longer period of time. Clearly, having an effective leader or a core group of persons playing leadership roles is essential (see the next chapter). But in successful cases, we find novel and significant approaches being put forward to deal with particular problems impeding development progress. Some basic concept provided the gyroscopic guidance for maintaining and directing the learning process that taught program implementers and participants how to achieve higher levels of productivity and well-being.

The Agroforestry Outreach Project in Haiti was able to get twenty million tree seedlings planted mostly by impoverished smallholders in its first four years, vastly exceeding the project's target of four million seedlings in five years. In ten years' time it proceeded to involve 200,000 households in planting sixty million seedlings, with 60 percent or higher survival rates, countering the deforestation that has turned that unhappy country into an environmental disaster. The core idea was that trees should be treated as a cash crop, contrary to previous governmental policy and environmental protection logic. If farmers could cut and profit from trees, they would be more willing to plant them on their tiny parcels of land, at the same time accepting new practices that contributed to soil conservation and increased agricultural production. This idea was similar to the one that launched the CAMPFIRE program in Zimbabwe. There, conservationists proposed that villagers should benefit financially from maintaining a large population of wild game animals in their locality. This required many institutional, procedural, and incentive innovations, which is where the learning process came in, but the important element was the concept of local ownership of and benefit from wildlife, which reversed previous governmental policy and law.

Some persons have rejected an LP approach because it seemed too indeterminate, too likely to waste scarce resources in ambiguous searching. Surely some efforts undertaken in the name of learning process have been poorly conceived, with inadequate understanding of the problem and of promising solutions. With a process of open-ended planning and implementation, however, persons who aim to accelerate development are informed about the situations in which they work, the major problems that exist, and a range of possible solutions. The most productive part of the learning process begins once a good appreciation of the problem, the context, and some tenable solution has been achieved. These need to be expressed in general, strategic terms rather than in specific, tactical details, with the latter being decided along the way toward realizing the overall goal. Provided the initial concepts are sound, they will be expanded, enriched, and modified through experience.

In Thailand, Mechai Viravaidya identified rapid population growth as a major obstacle to improving the lives of the rural villagers he encountered during his trips up-country from Bangkok in the early 1960s. His bold insight was that the practice and means of family planning should be demystified, making the subject one that everyone could talk about and act upon, free from the taboo of silence that had impeded previous family planning programs. His approach was audacious, initially gaining recognition when he blew up condoms like balloons in public, even on television. Many broader socioeconomic forces have contributed to lowering the population growth rate in Thailand from 2.4 percent in the late 1970s to half that now, but surely the efforts of the Population and Development Association were instrumental in this. Mechai's linking of family planning and community development was a related "big idea" that proved to be important and effective. Exactly how to do this had to be worked out through LP practice.

Innovations can be technical or organizational, but preferably they are some productive blend of both. The Self-Employed Women's Association (SEWA) in Ahmedabad, India, has improved the income and security of thousands of the poorest women in that large city, and SEWA has spread to fifteen other cities. Ela Bhatt, who initiated and led this effort, recognized that poor women suffered from lack of capital but also from harassment by the police and municipal authorities and from poverty-induced family problems. Attacking only one of these sources of oppression would not suffice, so she got the idea of an organization that combined two types of joint action: a trade union (militant, activist, willing to use the force of numbers to protect and advance members' rights) and a cooperative (pooling resources, making investments, sharing benefits). To make the latter effective, technical training, appropriate technologies, and reliable sources of raw materials were needed, but the key to success was a new and better concept (Sebstad 1982; Rose 1992).

This basic idea behind SEWA, a hybrid form of organization, was elaborated and amplified over time as many different services and opportunities were generated (see frontispiece). Such core innovations are important for successful development because they can be modified for use elsewhere. We summarize in Table 2.1 what we understand to be the conceptual advances that guided and propelled the cases included in *Reasons for Hope* and several other important cases.

These ideas should not be considered the basis for a blueprint to be used in some other setting. The process of giving such ideas social and institutional life in a new setting always requires considerable experimentation and modification, if only to give the persons involved a sense of ownership and responsibility. But this is a different aspect and will be discussed later. Here, we state a caveat: the learning process does not end in some finished model that can be replicated. The word *replicated*, widely used among development specialists and policy makers, is inappropriate and self-deceiving, implying that successful rural development efforts can be multiplied like documents from a photocopier.

Initiating the Process

The learning process can start in a variety of ways. Some are very dramatic and direct, based on *personal immersion* in the situation, getting close to the circumstances and the thinking of rural people.

- Dr. Kurien, fresh from higher education in the United States, settled into a rural community in the Indian state of Gujarat to help manage a local creamery, from which base he acquired knowledge of the needs and possibilities for larger-scale and participatory dairy production.

- Akhtar Hameed Khan, having already spent a lifetime in public service, moved into the squatter settlement of Orangi outside Karachi, Pakistan, and started walking around the streets, making acquaintances, asking questions, gaining an understanding of that society while he established himself in the community.

- Dr. Muhammad Yunus, a young lecturer at the University of Chittagong in Bangladesh who had recently returned from the United States, began visiting villages around his campus, getting to know the people living there, and then bringing along his students to get acquainted.

- P. A. Kiriwandeniya, after working with a large NGO that was not as close to the grassroots as he had hoped, went back to his home village in Sri Lanka and became involved with the local savings society. Within a year, its members had gained an understanding of how to expand and upgrade its operations so that it would be more than a savings club and could operate as a financial institution. Using Korten's terminology, Kiriwandeniya says that he sought first to learn how savings societies could become more effective, then more efficient, and then how they could grow (1997, 59).

A variant of this strategy is to build on the *knowledge and experience of someone else* who has been immersed in rural conditions. The World Neighbors program in Guatemala benefited from more than a decade of work by a medical missionary in the same district (Bunch 1982; see also Gow et al. 1979, 2:153–70). Dr. Carroll Behrhorst had learned that rural people's health problems could not be solved by medical means alone, or even primarily. Agricultural development, he concluded, was necessary to improve human nutrition; otherwise, the rural people would continue to be vulnerable to more ailments than doctors could cure. This provided the basis for an integrated rural development program that started by improving maize and bean yields while also conserving the soil. Fortunately, a simple technology could be identified—grass-strip live barriers—which farmers evaluated favorably and readily adopted, thereby serving both objectives.[2] The learning of Dr. Behrhorst was important for the quick progress that could be made after some admittedly ill-chosen initial efforts. Learning does not have to be direct; it can come through and from others.

The most common way to initiate a learning process is through some

Table 2.1   Core Ideas for Rural Development Success

Agroforestry Outreach Project / HAITI   Even small and poor farmers will plant trees if they are assured that they can benefit from the full-grown trees. If the government is too weak or corrupt to implement the project, NGOs and local groups can take this responsibility.

Anand Dairy Cooperatives / INDIA   A village-based structure of cooperatives, investing in and supported by state-of-the-art facilities for milk transport and processing and for veterinary services and feed, can raise the incomes of large numbers of poor rural households.

Baglung Bridges / NEPAL   Bridges in a mountainous terrain can be constructed more quickly and at a much lower cost through local self-help measures using indigenous technologies and management, if supplemented by outside aid providing essential inputs that must be purchased.

BRAC / BANGLADESH   The poor will benefit more from homogeneous membership groups. A variety of productive activities can be undertaken on this basis. (This had to be learned from failures when BRAC worked with and through more heterogeneous groups.)

CAMPFIRE / ZIMBABWE   Giving rural villagers the right to manage and derive economic benefits from wild game animals will give them a stake in the conservation of wildlife and contribute to local economic development.

DESEC / BOLIVIA   An NGO operating as a service organization can facilitate rural communities' efforts to raise production in a variety of sectoral activities, through whatever form of organization already exists or is thought appropriate.

Gal Oya Project / SRI LANKA   Same basic idea as for the National Irrigation Administration in the Philippines (see below), with the additional concept that these would be the farmers' own organizations, and their scope of work would expand to other areas of improvement as confidence and competence grew.

Grameen Bank / BANGLADESH   Poor people, especially women, can benefit greatly from even small loans and will repay these. Group-based lending can replace lending based on physical collateral. Later, groups can be aggregated for greater efficiency and empowerment.*

Integrated Pest Management / INDONESIA   IPM is more than a technical activity. Success requires the development of farmers' human resources so that they become more knowledgeable and committed managers of their own agroecosystems, that is, their farms.

Iringa Nutrition Program / TANZANIA   Children's nutrition can be improved through a network of organization from the household cluster up to the village, ward, district, and provincial levels. This can mobilize and mesh parental and governmental efforts, taking a holistic approach. The triple-A cycle of assessment, analysis, and action enlists community initiative and makes it effective.

National Irrigation Administration / PHILIPPINES   If farmers become organized through the efforts of organizers who live among them in rural areas, they will assume greater responsibility for the management and financing of irrigation systems.

Orangi Pilot Project / PAKISTAN   Poor households can afford to pay for sewerage and water in urban slums through self-help means and appropriate technologies, if organized into committees. These groups can provide the organizational basis for a variety of other self-help undertakings.

---

*Two recent books trace how the ideas that animated the Grameen Bank were evolved and elaborated in practice. See Bornstein (1996) and Counts (1996).

Population and Development Association / THAILAND   Reducing population growth is essential for the development of the country, and gaining acceptance of family planning depends on demystifying the means of contraception. Family planning can be linked to community development.

Plan Puebla / MEXICO   A university and international research center, working closely with small farmers under rain-fed conditions, can devise and deliver more appropriate technologies, especially if the farmers become organized.

Rajasthan Watershed Program / INDIA   Dividing large watersheds into microwatersheds and devolving responsibility for planning and implementation to village user committees working with interdisciplinary government teams can result in large-scale programs being carried out quickly.

San Martin Jilotepeque / GUATEMALA   Farmers who are encouraged to experiment and carry out their own extension activities can develop appropriate technologies that both raise yields and conserve soil. Continued improvements can be made without outside aid.

SANASA Savings and Loan Societies / SRI LANKA   Traditional savings clubs can be transformed into financial institutions to help whole communities, and particularly their poorer members, through the mobilization of savings and the making of loans under more "modern" conditions.

Savings Development Movement / ZIMBABWE   Illiterate, poor people can mobilize large amounts of savings for their own benefit through a decentralized structure of organization using simple means for crediting savings and by providing ready cash on demand.*

Self-Employed Women's Association / INDIA   Poor women can be benefited by combining the functions of a trade union and a cooperative organization to achieve both protection through advocacy and solidarity and economic improvement through self-help initiatives.

Self-Help Water Program / MALAWI   A simple technology for water supply can be implemented at very low cost through community participation, provided appropriate technical support and a well-articulated system of local organization are available.

Six-S / WEST AFRICA   The underutilized labor in Sahelian communities during the long dry season can be tapped through traditional work groups to construct facilities and make investments that will raise living standards and help communities better withstand the drought.

---

*This program, discussed in the text, was not included in our set of thirty cases because the government took it over in the late 1980s, displacing its central leadership and breaking its momentum of growth. Local chapters continue to function autonomously, however.

kind of a pilot project or program. The National Dairy Development Board in India considers these "living laboratories," whereas BRAC and the National Irrigation Administration (NIA) in the Philippines call them "learning laboratories." The purpose is the same: to try out ideas, to test, evaluate, and refine them. Extensive baseline information can be gathered in a systematic way, as was done for the Gal Oya project in Sri Lanka and Plan Puebla in Mexico. Whatever is learned in these "laboratories" should be carefully and systematically evaluated to assess the generalizability and robustness of findings, with local people participating in the collection, analysis, and evaluation of information.

Although it is not common—partly because development agencies are usually in a hurry and may not have much respect for scholarly studies—the learning process can begin with *academic research*. For the Agroforestry Outreach Project in Haiti, an anthropologist with extensive knowledge about rural Haitian society, Gerald Murray, was contracted by the U.S. Agency for International Development (USAID) to contribute ideas based on his own and others' research about how to launch a successful reforestation effort. The remarkable results of this innovative program surely justified the investment of time as well as money by the donor.

But there are also situations in which the learning process starts with *no preparation*. BRAC grew out of efforts by educated Bangladeshis to rehabilitate rural areas of their war-torn country after independence. They found themselves in the middle of a chaotic and difficult situation. Knowing little about the realities of rural Bangladesh, they quickly accepted the need for intellectual modesty and never assumed that they knew enough to design effective initiatives without testing (Lovell 1992).

In the more recent Rajasthan case referred to earlier, Krishna tells us that the government department charged with watershed management had to "plunge right in, get hands dirty, and refine our methods as we went along." The instructions given to field staff were: "Start with what you know, what resources you have or can find, and what people want; do small-scale experiments of whatever you think might work" (Krishna 1997, 259). This is appropriate advice as long as a program operates in a supportive administrative climate, accepting that some mistakes will be made and believing that these are the price of rapid and eventually widespread progress.

For long-term success, learning process needs to be accompanied by a number of components that are examined in subsequent chapters: creative leadership (Chapter 3); effective local organizations and people's participation (Chapter 4); an adaptive system for the management of program activities (Chapter 5); appropriate technologies and training that shares needed knowledge among people at many levels of the operation (Chapter 6); systems that use information as a management tool—process documentation as well as monitoring and evaluation (Chapter 7); linkages with key local, regional, national, and international actors (Chapter 8); and political support, deftly mobilized and managed (Chapter 9). These should not be seen as prerequisites, since they can be put in place and improved as implementation proceeds. They are, rather, elements that make it possible to translate the original inspiration of a core idea into coherent and cumulative actions by large numbers of people. Although such elements should be provided for in initial planning, they cannot be designed in any detail in advance.

In this sense, plunging in is not inconsistent with learning process, provided there are realistic expectations about how quickly results will accrue. The USAID project manager who oversaw the Gal Oya program in Sri Lanka was correct to press project implementers (including Norman Uphoff) to get into the field as quickly as possible, without spending many months preparing for this exposure to operational realities. It is said in military doctrine that no battle plan survives its first encounter with the enemy. Although the field is not the enemy, it does present many uncertainties and unknowns, even unseen obstacles and traps. Recognizing that a lot of room needs to be left for tactical maneuvers, what is most important for success in rural development is strategic thinking, which flows from the core idea, the basic doctrine that lays out the desired ends and basic means around which program efforts and resources will revolve.

Flexibility and Self-Criticism

Although there are common characteristics of successful rural development programs, one must avoid the "one-size-fits-all" mentality that most government programs exhibit, seeking to simplify administrative operations by across-the-board regulations and standard plans and procedures.

- BRAC emphasizes in all its training and publications the importance of maintaining flexibility by avoiding "fix-all" approaches. It operates on a very large scale, assisting villages with a combined population of 1.7 million, but its staff expect that adjustments and adaptations will be the rule rather than the exception.

- The Six-S association, which supports nearly a million residents of the West African Sahel in self-help activities across half a dozen countries, has developed a highly decentralized system of flexible funding. It avoids the conventional project approach, which has many fixed requirements, by delegating allocation decisions to local assemblies. These can judge the feasibility and desirability of community proposals better than could a more centralized decision-making process.

- The Agroforestry Outreach Project in Haiti started out with a standard package for farmers who were willing to plant trees on their small farms. But it soon made adjustments, varying the number of trees and the mix of species in the packages made available, and relying more on indigenous species and less on exotics, as experience was gained. This helped the project achieve an implementation rate more than six times greater than planned.

Readers should note that Bangladesh, the Sahel, and Haiti are commonly regarded as some of the most difficult places to work in the less-developed world.

Keeping an open mind about the technical aspects of a rural development program is not enough. Organizational structures should also be introduced on a tentative and experimental basis. The Orangi Pilot Project in Pakistan had the idea of forming "lane committees" to initiate sewerage development, as this technology needs to be installed lane by lane, but it offered no prescribed structure for these committees. Irrigation improvement likewise faces certain technical constraints regarding how people will relate to one another. But the system of farmer organization in Gal Oya, which became a national system for all major irrigation schemes in Sri Lanka, began with no proposed structure or roles, leaving these decisions to the farming communities. The resulting organizations were more clearly "owned" by rural people. The Center for Economic and Social Development (DESEC) in Bolivia similarly started with no fixed criteria for community organization, working with whatever structures existed, such as village committees, trade unions, or mothers' clubs.

When rural people are given choices to make based on their own priorities, capabilities, and evaluations, it must be recognized that mistakes will be made. Errors should be "embraced," to use Korten's provocative phrasing, so that they can be instructive. Obviously, one does not want to maximize mistakes, but these should be expected and accepted as part of the process. This was something that Akhtar Hameed Khan stressed when he helped create the network of small farmer cooperatives at Comilla in Bangladesh (at the time, East Pakistan), which inspired a whole generation of participatory development efforts in South Asia (Milliken and Hapgood 1967, 108–12; Raper 1970). The leadership in Six-S makes a point of reviewing mistakes as well as successes, as this is considered necessary to free member groups from the need for tutelage (Lecomte and Krishna 1997, 89).

In the establishment of BRAC, it is not surprising that a number of mistakes were made. What is unusual is that that organization's leadership openly encourages risk taking, explicitly accepting that errors are bound to happen (Abed and Chowdhury 1997, 42–3).[3] The founder and the general manager of DESEC in Bolivia acknowledge that they now better understand the processes of local self-management after making a number of mistakes, such as handing over responsibility for a major agricultural program before the membership was strong and confident enough to discipline their leaders (Demeure and Guardia 1997, 92–3). Roland Bunch's assessment of the earlier World Neighbors program in Guatemala is that the initial plan spread efforts too thinly and over too large an area, and "errors were made." According to an internal evaluation, the agricultural project as it was first conceived was almost totally ineffective (Krishna and Bunch 1997, 140). Such candor is not just refreshing but also badly needed; it is one of the ingredients for success.

There seems to be a correlation between top-level acceptance and institutionalization of self-criticism and a program's movement toward long-term success. Otherwise, it moves toward increased rigidity and becomes resistant to criticism. A learning organization is a self-critical organization; one that does not accept and embrace errors, seeking to learn from them, is a self-deceiving organization, likely to perpetuate mistakes and even accelerate their occurrence (Korten 1980). The Rajasthan watershed program explicitly followed Korten's advice, agreeing that no penalties would be imposed for failures from experimentation that was carried out with honest intention and care. The CAMPFIRE case in Zimbabwe shows how a learning process can occur even when a false start is made, provided that values and goals, with appropriate modifications, are not abandoned (Metcalfe 1997, 280). Embracing error is a disturbing notion, but it has proved to be a productive one.

Systematized Learning

Not all successful experiences in rural development have formalized processes for learning, but they make some provision for accumulating and assessing knowledge as they proceed. Bernard Lecomte describes this process for Six-S as one of "reflection, information, and correction" (Lecomte and Krishna 1997, 89); Akhtar Hameed Khan talks of the Orangi Pilot Project's action research as leading to solutions devised and grounded in community-based organizations (1997, 26).

Two-thirds of the successful experiences reported in *Reasons for Hope* either had an initial connection to a knowledge-generating institution or established such a linkage once they got more deeply enmeshed in processes of socioeconomic change. The Grameen Bank, Plan Puebla, NIA, Gal Oya, Iringa, the Agroforestry Outreach Project, and CAMPFIRE were started by or involved persons from universities or research institutes from their beginning.[4] The Orangi Pilot Project, the Indonesian IPM program, and the Rajasthan watershed project involved faculty or students from nearby universities once work was under way.

The Anand dairy cooperative movement had early interaction with the Indian Institute of Management at Ahmedabad and later established its own teaching and research institution, the Institute for Rural Management at Anand (IRMA), to strengthen human and knowledge resources for cooperative and rural development throughout the country, not just for its own organization. SANASA now has an informal link for research and evaluation with the University of Manchester in the United Kingdom. BRAC has various connections with university faculty and students in its own country and some from overseas, but its knowledge needs are met mostly through its own active Research and Evaluation Wing, established to give BRAC in-house capacity for improving technology and organization.

This is not to suggest that involvement of university or research institutions is a requirement for rural development success. A majority of academics and researchers are probably not inclined to get involved in the kind of work required, and perhaps not many are temperamentally or theoretically well-prepared for these tasks. But doing analysis and acquiring, utilizing, and disseminating knowledge are important aspects of development work. There needs to be someone involved in successful programs, if not their executives, who will engage in formulating, assessing, communicating, and revising the essential ideas that undergird a new initiative. Although successful programs may emphasize practice and empiricism, the ones we studied show respect for the role of knowledge in preparing and implementing programs for substantive change.

The Fit between Technology and Organization

One of the key insights in Korten's analysis of rural development experience is the importance of concurrently devising and acquiring appropriate kinds of technology and establishing appropriate forms of organization, usually through some trial and error. Fashioning a good fit between the two is an even greater challenge. One of the criteria of appropriateness for either technology or organization is whether it is compatible and fruitful with the other. To be effective and diffusible, technology must lend itself to application within available organizational capabilities, and a good organization for rural development is one that can help raise levels of productivity through the application of better techniques.

The Malawi self-help water program is one of the best examples of how a learning process over half a dozen years worked out compatible and mutually productive technical and organizational solutions to villagers' need for potable water. Determining the correct location and dimensions of settling ponds to reduce silt, ensure water quality, and control the flow was as important as devising a sensible operational division of local responsibilities that ensured ongoing maintenance and repair. Villagers were selected and trained to serve as paratechnicians so that there would be technical knowledge in the communities after the construction was completed and so that the construction itself would be done in a more collegial manner.

The child nutrition program in the Iringa district of Tanzania expected that lasting and effective solutions would have to be sociotechnical. The system of local organization that was developed enjoins parents and village committees to find the means whereby the food intake of malnourished children can be increased with local resources on a sustainable basis.

Technical advice is available, but no particular solutions are pushed. Rather, a problem-solving approach is advised. Each seriously undernourished child is seen as a challenge to all the adults—parents, officials, and community representatives—who learn about the child's disadvantaged status during the regular public weighing days. A similar animation occurs with the Posyandu primary health system in Indonesia (Rohde 1993).

The Agroforestry Outreach Project in Haiti appears to have been successful primarily because of its organizational structure and the incentives it introduced, but its decentralized system of nursery production was crucial for getting millions of tree seedlings into farmers' hands. This was made possible by acquiring and using inexpensive plastic root trainers. This simple technology greatly increased the transportability and survivability of young trees. With all the deserved attention given to organizational aspects of rural development, it is easy to underestimate the role played by appropriate, low-cost technology. (This is considered more in Chapter 6.)

Exactly what technical or organizational factors will produce sticking points or breakthroughs cannot be known in advance. These factors are interactive, and making them mesh requires testing and adjustments, usually through an iterative process exemplified by the Anand model for cooperatives. Advances were made sequentially on the technical and organizational fronts, recognizing that it is their mutual reinforcement that ultimately leads to success.

Starting Slowly and Accelerating

The objection most often heard to an LP approach is that it is too slow. In fact, this perception comes mostly from a linear way of thinking about schedules, expecting to accomplish equal amounts of work during each time period, rather than having a logistic (S-shaped) curve in mind. With LP, one is willing to begin slowly, gain knowledge and experience, and build up a cadre of capable and dedicated personnel, with the expectation that at some point a critical mass will be achieved and work can be accelerated productively.[5]

It took ten years for the Anand dairy cooperatives in India to get organized and to operate effectively in the first and second districts where they were started in Gujarat state. A third district took four years, and the fourth, fifth, and sixth districts took two years each. Between 1949 and 1970, although progress was slow, the pace was accelerating. Having devised appropriate means for meshing technology and organization through experience, Operation Flood over the next twenty years covered most of the major "milksheds" of India with cooperative marketing and technical support opportunities.[6]

Akhtar Hameed Khan found that organizing the first lane committee in Orangi took three months. But then lane groups began forming themselves and coming to the project for assistance to put in their own water and sewerage lines. The program spread quickly once appropriate low-cost technologies for installing sewers had been devised and a suitable scheme for managing and financing their installation was agreed upon (see Chapter 8). In Gal Oya, the first organizers were able to work with only seventy-five to a hundred farmers each. But once effective techniques for communicating with farmers had been learned, and once farmers began to see positive results from their cooperation, organizers could achieve similar results each working with 200 to 300 farmers at a time. Probably the most dramatic evidence that an LP approach does not need to be slow is the Agroforestry Outreach Project in Haiti. Its spread accelerated remarkably once the organizational and technological components were mastered by local participants, both NGOs and farmer groups.

Many rural development projects try to "run" before they have learned to "walk." An LP approach validates the natural sequence of starting slowly, crawling for a while if necessary, before measurable steps are taken. The skills of walking need to be mastered before trying to speed up the pace. The limitation of this metaphor is that it implies certain inborn limitations, holding progress down to some rate of biological maturation. Since in rural development efforts we are dealing with adults, such limitations do not apply in this way. There may be constraints of confidence and trust to overcome, and learning complex skills, whether technical or organizational, can take time. But there can also be rapid learning and the quick dissemination of new behaviors and values. This is what we see at some point in the progress of successful rural development programs.

ASSISTED SELF-RELIANCE

Taking a learning approach to the *process* of planning and implementing new initiatives to improve the lives of thousands and eventually millions of people is not enough. The *philosophy* that animates these efforts is similarly important, as it gives substance and value-oriented direction to such programs. After considering the life histories of many programs, we have found a common element that can be characterized as assisted self-reliance.

BRAC considers self-reliance among the poor to be the "only abiding answer" (Abed and Chowdhury 1997, 42). But BRAC's experience shows that self-help activities need not be limited to what the poor can accomplish only with their own resources, for example, their savings. BRAC provides credit to member groups to support the process of uplift once they have demonstrated both self-discipline and group cohesion, undergoing systematic training and starting their own savings accounts. When entering into a financial and organizational relationship with villagers, BRAC is self-conscious that it should never become their "patron," which means that they become acquiescing "clients." Rather, it sees its mission as one of bringing to life "the entrepreneurial spirit latent among all people" (Abed and Chowdhury 1997, 56). Such confidence in the innate abilities of the rural majority is common among successful programs.

The SANASA savings and loan cooperatives in Sri Lanka have been able to operate essentially with the resources mobilized by its more than 700,000 members, achieving and maintaining a high degree of financial independence (Hulme, Montgomery, and Bhattacharya 1996). Its primary societies are self-supporting, while the higher levels of the SANASA federation have benefited from modest assistance from NGOs and cooperative movements in Australia, Canada, and Europe. Higher levels of the federation provide education to members on cooperative principles and operation; they also handle interlending among branches and assist in the trading of commodities produced by members in different districts to capture and retain the value otherwise extracted by middlemen. This strategic blend of internal and external resources is similar to that of Six-S, which utilizes NGO funding from Europe to evoke and support local initiatives from villages across the West African Sahel. When Six-S cofounder Lecomte says that members' resources are combined with outside resources, he adds that Six-S takes care not to become the "patron" of its members (Lecomte and Krishna 1997, 81). This represents the same philosophy of assisted self-reliance as expressed by BRAC's director.

The Anand dairy cooperative movement aims to assist the rural poor by setting up institutions that can harness the best of modern science and technology to improve their production base and bring them sophisticated marketing skills. The private sector cannot do this for the poor, and the state sector has not shown that it has much to contribute in this regard (Kurien 1997, 105–6). People need institutions of their own to take advantage of science and technology, but they cannot do this in a vacuum. Dealings with the state and with private-sector organizations should be on terms that protect rural producers from exploitation or neglect, and their own organizations give them power to bargain.

When Oxfam decided to assist the World Neighbors project in Guatemala, its guiding principle was that development must be carried out by local people themselves. Experts could provide new ideas and help establish new institutional mechanisms, but the goal was to hand over program leadership to local people within two years. This was quite a radical idea for the mid-1970s, but the result was that when external assistance had to be withdrawn in 1979 because of the government's undeclared war against native communities, the testing and adoption of improved agricultural practices that had quadrupled yields in just seven years continued with entirely local leadership and resources, further increasing yields on their own and maintaining their lead over communities that had not joined the program.

Conditionality

There is a lot of discussion in development circles about the acceptability of "strings" attached to aid, known as conditionality. Debate on this will continue at the national level, but at local levels, the question is not whether there should be conditions attached to the provision of outside resources but rather what is the purpose of any such strings. If it is to build up local resources and empowerment, such an end can justify the means.

Giving aid with no strings attached can be criticized as a dole or a handout. But more important is whether the provision of outside resources contributes to the creation and maintenance of capacities for local management or whether it has a discouraging or deterrent effect. If local capacities are strengthened, many other productive improvements can be made in the future, which makes such assistance "the gift that keeps on giving."

It is not unreasonable for gifts and contributions to be accompanied by certain conditions and requirements, provided these are intended not to benefit the giver but rather to encourage and even enforce among recipients a level of discipline and an assumption of responsibility that puts them in a better position to be self-managing and self-sustaining. The Grameen Bank and BRAC in Bangladesh, the Orangi Pilot Project in Pakistan, Six-S in the Sahel, SANASA in Sri Lanka, and DESEC in Bolivia all require the poor to start building up their own savings, to attend group meetings regularly, and to participate in training to acquire knowledge and skills as a prerequisite for assistance. The SANASA savings societies in Sri Lanka—without any capital infusion from outside, only technical assistance—have built up over US$40 million in savings deposits by their more than 700,000 members, who are on average poorer than the rural population as a whole. Similarly impressive is the Savings Development Movement in Zimbabwe, which, before government interference in the late 1980s, had built up over $2 million in deposits from its 250,000 members, over 90 percent of whom were women and most of whom were illiterate and poor. As in the case of SANASA, the outside aid was more technical than financial, coming from a priest, a businessman, and an adult educator in the capital city who saw a need and established a simple organizational mechanism to mobilize resources for self-help.[7]

In some situations, the legacy of government handouts is so strong that rural people are reluctant to put up any of their own resources, hoping or expecting that if they decline self-help they can get something for free.

Benjamin Bagadion (1997), who provided leadership for participatory irrigation management in the Philippines, notes that it was difficult for the NIA to reverse the prevailing psychology of pork-barrel gifts, which politicians had been doling out for years to gain and maintain political support. The NIA found that the most it could require was a 10 percent contribution of local resources for rehabilitation of irrigation schemes. This was accepted by farmers once they learned that the quality of the work done could thereby be improved. This contribution gave them a voice in how the resources would be used, and they could play a watchdog role to ensure that construction met agreed-on standards.

In the Rajasthan watershed program, there was a similar legacy of government handouts, which made getting any local contributions difficult at first. The program required that at least 10 percent of the cost of local projects come from the affected community, contributing resources in kind if not in cash. Some politicians tried to make their own political capital from this, insinuating that officials were benefiting from this payment. But once benefits started to accrue, the logic of making local contributions became accepted, and the program has been trying to change the cost-sharing formula to get more grassroots resource mobilization.

Such requirements have the budgetary advantage of permitting larger areas and more people to be served by a given amount of government or donor funding. But more important, local resource mobilization can have the effect of empowering local communities, possibly in unexpected ways. In Gal Oya, Sri Lanka, USAID project designers decided without consulting farmers that field-level channels would have to be rehabilitated through voluntary labor, describing this as "farmer participation." Wijayaratna and Uphoff protested that this was unfair, pointing out that private firms rehabilitating main and branch canals were going to be paid for their work. But since no money had been budgeted to pay for field channel improvements, and since farmers would be the most direct beneficiaries of this activity, their cooperation was enlisted. This had the effect of creating power for the farmers, because the Irrigation Department now depended on them to do this work; otherwise, little benefit would result from improved flows of water at higher levels of the irrigation system. Engineers for the first time became solicitous of farmers' needs and suggestions, and a working partnership was established between officials and farmers, benefiting the latter, who had previously been ignored or bossed around.

Local contributions of labor can give villagers some leverage vis-à-vis officials and authorities, just as the accumulation of large capital reserves can give the poor a louder voice. Money talks, even if the accumulation comes from many small contributions. People's labor can become more valuable when it is required to implement development programs. Accordingly, we do not object to requiring resources from members to carry out programs, provided these programs will indeed benefit them. Such expectations should not be determined unilaterally but rather in consultation with representatives of those groups whose participation and advancement are sought. In our experience, once the concepts of partnership and assisted self-reliance are understood, rural people are quite willing to set strict standards for contributing labor or money, for attending meetings, and for taking responsibility.[8]

Local Capabilities as a Priority

Assisted self-reliance can be applied to a variety of programs—for agricultural improvement, better health care, water supply, forest protection, or soil or wildlife conservation. Local capacity is most effectively built in connection with meeting some particular need that communities identify as pressing. But success is not to be measured just by how well certain material or social needs are met. Rather, the aim is to create local capabilities for mobilizing and managing resources so that needs can be met on a sustainable and expanding basis. Such capacities are commonly extended or extrapolated to solve still other problems that local people experience (explored in Chapter 10).

BRAC emphasizes group solidarity as a means for further development, and we agree. Six-S in the Sahel aims to strengthen local capabilities by "filling in gaps," a good ASR concept. Groups affiliated with Six-S are helped to gain expertise and confidence, so that they become more viable, independent agencies for local development. Many of the programs we reviewed are prepared to invest in the formation of groups, which will then be assisted. But Six-S requires groups of interested individuals to incur their own organizational start-up costs; it is then willing to help existing groups meet and cooperate, which Six-S considers to be more important than the money it makes available. The CAMPFIRE program in Zimbabwe has a fairly narrow objective—protecting wildlife through community action—yet it stresses that local people must be involved and debate the issues themselves, so as to develop "their own capabilities to tackle these problems" (Metcalfe 1997, 288). Once these capabilities are in place, they can be used by local people to tackle still other problems. The aim of protecting wildlife is served, but more is accomplished by strengthening local management capacities.

The World Bank recently completed a detailed and quantified evaluation of 121 rural water projects worldwide (Narayan 1995). It aimed to identify those factors that best explain the effectiveness and efficiency of rural water systems once they have been established. Not surprising to us, one of the strongest correlates of a successful rural water project is the extent to which planners and implementers emphasized building local capabilities at the community level. This proved to be statistically more significant than the technical solutions employed or the amount of capital expended on the project. Capacity building thus has technical and material consequences, as discussed in more detail in Chapter 4.

Recycling and Expanding Resources

A key concept in assisted self-reliance is that communities be encouraged and enabled to manage and multiply both the funds they receive and the funds they raise from their own efforts. Revolving funds have been introduced around the world, but most of the time they do not revolve—or, better said, they revolve only once. This lack of success stems largely from the terms on which the outside resources are provided. Cases in *Reasons for Hope* show that such funds can be made to succeed, within a framework that sets clear and rigorous standards and expectations and when it is clear that those who will lose the most if the funds fail to revolve will be local friends and neighbors. Programs such as the Grameen Bank, the Orangi Pilot Project, SANASA, BRAC, Six-S, and DESEC can point to repayment rates from the rural poor that would make most banks that lend to the rich quite envious—95 percent and higher. Why? Because a sense of social responsibility coexists with individual self-interest, at the same time that the interests of members are being served.

An ingenious, extrapolatable practice in this regard is the idea of "son and daughter" grain-grinding mills disseminated by Six-S groups in the Sahel. This scheme was developed by rural villagers themselves, not thought up in Ouagadougou or Geneva. When a village group receives funds to put up its own grain mill, it agrees that part of the fee that each member pays to have his or her grain milled will go into a "son mill" fund and part will go into a "daughter mill" fund. Local tradition requires daughters to marry out of the village, while sons remain. The money in the first fund is eventually used to replace the original mill when it wears out beyond the possibility of repair; the money in the second fund is given to some other village to set up its own "daughter" mill. This beneficiary village, in turn, makes the same allocation of funds so that valuable capital facilities are maintained and extended in rural areas without additional outside funding. Similar conditionality was established by the Population and Development Association in Thailand in its program to extend facilities for potable water collection and storage in villages otherwise suffering from water shortages in the dry season (Mechai 1997, 208–9).

One question always comes up: whether provision of outside resources should not be considered a "subsidy" and thus of dubious legitimacy. Lecomte, one of the founders of Six-S, initially emphasized the importance of giving only loans, but he now says that, on reflection, he would favor some judicious mixing of grants and loans to help groups get started faster. With more of an initial grant element, he thinks that groups in the Sahel could become self-reliant in six years. Now the average is more like twelve years, which he considers too long, because long tutelage can become "like a cancer." Developed countries are often quite willing to provide subsidies; dairy producers in the European Community enjoy a 69 percent subsidy from their governments (Kurien 1997, 119). Commenting critically on a 1991 USAID decision that tree seedlings would no longer be given free of charge to Haitian farmers, Murray (1997, 249) notes that the U.S. government has found that it cannot get reforestation, a social good, accomplished in its own country without providing free seedlings. USAID wanted to require payment from farmers who had to feed their families from tiny plots of poor land when it had accepted that such a policy would not work in its own country with much richer households.

We would focus not so much on whether cash or materials are provided free in the first instance but on what happens in subsequent periods. Is there sufficient increase in productive capacity or in other social values to justify the initial contribution of outside resources? Does the expenditure of outside resources (from a donor, government, or NGO) elicit matching and increasing management and contribution of resources? When we see how programs following an LP approach with an ASR strategy assisted self-reliance have managed to launch thousands and even millions of households on upward paths more quickly than before—particularly by establishing mechanisms that recycle financial resources as well as mobilize them on a self-help basis—we think that there are many circumstances in which subsidies from richer countries can be justified.

The relevant test is whether the insertion of outside resources leads to a positive-sum outcome, that is, a win-win situation in which all or most stakeholders gain, or to a zero-sum outcome in which a fixed amount of benefits is being redistributed or contested. To be sure, outcomes can be negative-sum, subtracting from the total available resources, in which case outside contributions are harmful and should be avoided or terminated. Assisted self-reliance obviously aims to establish and sustain a positive-sum dynamic.

Division of Responsibilities

One way to make ASR last is to work out a sharing of functions that is equitable and manageable. This also reduces management requirements, as discussed in Chapter 5, but here we are interested in how it serves to engage local resources and responsibility. The Orangi Pilot Project, for example, identified four components of an urban sewerage network: those facilities in the home, those in the lane, those in the locality, and those at the metropolitan level. The project negotiated with the Karachi Municipal Council to assume responsibility for the main drains and treatment plants at this fourth level if communities would provide the other facilities through their lane committees. Once properly organized, households could handle these tasks, but constructing main drains and treatment plants was not feasible. The city, which had made only minimal plans to provide sewerage to the Orangi area, was persuaded that expenditure for system-level facilities would be a good investment, mobilizing much greater investment in sewerage than the municipal government could make on its own.

In the Philippines, the NIA, no longer assured of adequate government funding, had to strike a deal with farmers who got water from its systems. Farmers agreed to provide 10 percent counterpart funding for capital improvements and to cover all operating and maintenance costs at middle and lower levels of their systems. As a "sweetener," the government made it clear that farmers would not be expected to pay for the reconstruction of systems after typhoon damage, as special funds could be made available for this. The principle that farmers should cover normal costs of system operation and maintenance has been accepted in the Philippines, which now has the highest level of farmer financing of irrigation in Asia—except for Taiwan, where irrigation associations carry out practically all operations with local resources (Repetto 1986; Small, Adriano, and Martin 1986).[9]

Such sharing is easiest to see and negotiate with infrastructure programs. The Malawi self-help water program informs communities that it will provide materials, technical advice, and training if they contribute the necessary labor to construct new water systems—and if they will make organizational and financial provisions to maintain the systems in good working order afterward. The Malawi self-help water scheme provides materials and technical advice only to communities that contribute the necessary labor and local management. A similar sharing of responsibility was devised in the Baglung bridge-building program (see Chapter 5).

Exactly which division of responsibilities will prove to be most productive and sustainable is something that needs to be assessed through experimentation and learning in particular settings, but the arrangements that have been worked out in successful programs offer a starting point for thinking through these issues. The basic principle is that of comparative advantage: expecting to get from the different parties what they are in the best position to contribute without opportunity costs acting as a deterrent. The agroforestry project in Haiti hit upon a simple formula that is easy to understand and explain and that appears to be quite fair: if farmers provide the land and labor for planting trees, the project, on behalf of the donor agency and government, will provide the capital—in this case, the biological capital of seedlings.

The Iringa child nutrition program articulated the principle that, starting at the lowest level, each party should do as much as it could to counteract malnutrition. The problem-solving process started with the family. Each cluster of households was expected to act on problems that individual families could not manage. Higher levels—the community, the ward, and on up to the district, region, and nation—were called upon to take actions that lower levels could not. Most malnutrition problems for individuals could be solved at local levels at low cost, so higher levels were left to find more generalized solutions, following the principle of comparative advantage. This principle has also been followed in the national nutrition improvement program in Thailand, as discussed in Chapter 7 (Piyaratn 1993).

Assisted self-reliance can have large payoffs. The Orangi Pilot Project estimates that for every rupee it received from outside, this was multiplied seventeen times by the resource contributions of the people of Orangi (Khan 1997, 33). Installing sewers in squatter settlements is one of the more challenging kinds of development. This project shows us that where there is a felt need and a carefully constructed program to enlist the ideas and management skills of local people, as well as their money and labor, a resource-multiplying process can be created. The social relationships and value commitments that started with providing sewerage have since been extended to women's education, health clinics, literacy, low-cost housing, family enterprises, social forestry, and still other benefits where outside resources are less than those mobilized internally.

The rural Guatemalan communities that World Neighbors assisted showed that despite civil warfare and ethnic oppression, once people have bought into self-reliance as a strategy, they can achieve further gains without outside assistance and despite adverse government actions. Evidence of local people's commitment to self-help was seen in 1978, when they petitioned USAID and the government to exclude their area from a regional project that paid farmers to introduce soil conservation measures on their fields. They feared that this would undermine the solidarity and independent capacities they had built up (Krishna and Bunch 1997, 148). This kind of commitment was what enabled them to continue agricultural progress without outside aid.

This same spirit prompted the farmer-representatives in the Gal Oya irrigation scheme in Sri Lanka to tell one of the advisers who had helped them establish their organizations: "Come see what we have accomplished since you left." They had built up over $100,000 in savings and assets and were now effectively comanaging the largest irrigation scheme in the country (Wijayaratna and Uphoff 1997, 179). Previously skeptical engineers and officials had become supportive of farmers' assumption of responsibility. Such skepticism is, unfortunately, fairly common. Most development projects operate without a belief in or a commitment to self-reliant outcomes. They assume that *their* resources are the critical ones, and they often seek to take credit for all or most of the accomplishments. Although most projects welcome local people's contribution of money or labor, their managers do not understand how and why to invest in the self-management capacities of ordinary people. This is what much of the rest of this book addresses.

NOTES

1. We have experience in Nepal, where USAID wanted to build on the successful experience of the Gal Oya irrigation management project in Sri Lanka (presented in Chapter 11 of *Reasons for Hope*). Despite explicit language in the design documents for the Nepal Irrigation Management Project providing for a "learning process" approach, the project agreement signed by the governments of the United States and Nepal had the effect of freezing all ideas in place. As a result, the experimentation and adaptation envisioned and promised in the project documentation were difficult to achieve. With donor resources becoming scarcer in recent years, one often sees less rather than more willingness to proceed with flexibility, incorporating the lessons learned from experience into revised budgets and schedules as implementation proceeds.

2. This was similar to some of the technologies used in the Rajasthan watershed conservation case (Krishna 1997).

3. In this spirit, the young organizers who catalyzed the farmer organizations in Gal Oya, Sri Lanka, were told that mistakes will be made but that most need not be repeated if they are discussed openly and learned from collectively. In the training program, organizers were told: "Nobody will be punished for mistakes made from lack of foresight or lack of skill. As trainers and supervisors, we must share responsibility for any shortcomings in performance. But we will be very unhappy if problems are neglected or concealed. Everybody makes mistakes, and that includes foreign consultants. Anybody can be wrong [including the trainers]. We do not expect perfection. But we do expect sharing of positive and negative learning" (Uphoff 1992a, 69).

4. Respectively, Chittagong University, the Postgraduate College for Agricultural Sciences at Chapingo-Montecillo, the Ateneo de Manila's Institute of Philippine Culture and the Asian Institute of Management, Cornell University, the Tanzanian Food and Nutrition Center, the University of Florida, and the University of Zimbabwe. Although the Agrarian Research and Training Institute in Sri Lanka, which was the lead institution for establishing farmer organizations in Gal Oya, was under the Ministry of Agriculture, it functioned like a quasi-academic institution and had a number of former university lecturers on its staff. Part of the success of the Nepal-Australian Forestry Project can be attributed to the innovative and continuing role of the Australian National University in its implementation.

5. An excellent case study showing the advantages of thinking in terms of this kind of logistic curve when choosing among alternative technologies is provided by

John Thomas (1975), who evaluated the merits of different technologies for installing tubewells in Bangladesh. The more mechanized approach could meet targets fairly predictably by drilling a set number of wells each year, whereas the more labor-intensive method would have to start slowly but could meet the five-year target with accelerating levels of activity after several slower start-up years. A big difference between the alternatives was that there would still be capacity at the village level to install and maintain water supplies once the project providing labor-intensive wells was completed. Villagers could continue digging wells after the capital-intensive drilling rigs were worn out and their capacity to expand water supplies was lost.

6. This process is described in Kurien (1997; see also Doornbos and Nair 1990). During this massive expansion stage, the program became more target-oriented and less adaptive, tending toward "one-size" approaches; the National Dairy Development Board has been trying to modify this orientation in recent years. Some routinization was necessary and even desirable, but a more self-conscious appreciation of the dangers inherent in this process could have mitigated at least some of this effect of scaling up.

7. In this case, a very simple technology was employed. Because most members were illiterate, there was considerable distrust of the formal banking system. The Savings Development Movement introduced a passbook system in which members were given different-colored savings stamps, representing certain amounts deposited, to be pasted into their respective passbooks. This gave members a tangible sense of receiving something in return for having handed over their savings. Stamps could be converted into cash on a week's notice, which enabled members to get fertilizer for their garden crops, put tin roofs on their houses, and do other things that improved their quality of life entirely from their own resources (Chimedza 1985).

8. Members of farmer organizations in the Weeragoda area of Gal Oya decided after one year that they would collect 100 rupees per acre per season from themselves to build up a savings fund from which personal loans could be taken. Farmers decided to charge themselves 16 percent interest *per month* on short-term loans. When asked why they would extract such exorbitant interest, they said that since local moneylenders were getting as much as 25 percent interest per month on their loans, charging themselves two-thirds that much would help them build up their own capital more quickly, thereby reducing their dependence on richer persons.

9. In recent years, the degree of self-sufficiency of these systems has fallen as more and more farmers, having more attractive income options in nonagricultural employment, invest less time and money in their irrigated production of rice and other crops. This underscores that institutional as well as technical solutions need to evolve and change with new conditions.

3   Initiation and Leadership

Successful large-scale and sustainable programs for rural development are, unfortunately, much more the exception than the rule. How do they get started? We have considered this question by looking at rural development programs that have had important impacts in their countries, and some with impacts well beyond their national borders. Often this question points to the vital but elusive factor of leadership, which begs for elaboration and illumination. Being acquainted with a number of persons who have played such roles, and having found ourselves in such roles,[1] our thoughts on this subject are more than "academic." It is a subject that has not been dealt with very well in the social science literature, perhaps because there are few characteristics of leadership that have any predictive power.

We find a fairly consistent theme running through the accounts by persons who have established and sustained large-scale development undertakings: success depends on the quality, creativity, and commitment of the personnel who staff an organization from bottom to top. The concept of *cadre* is usually associated in the literature with political movements, and with leftist ones at that. But this factor we find particularly prominent in successful rural development programs. Of particular interest is a special kind of cadre characterized as *catalysts*.

This perspective makes more comprehensible and operational the concept of leadership for rural development. It enlarges on the preoccupation in some accounts with the individual vision and capability of some successful programs' progenitors and chief protagonists. It would be as much a mistake to overestimate this consideration as to underestimate it. Anyone who has managed a large operation knows that massive credit must go to the staff who accept a programmatic vision and transform it into reality through hundreds, thousands, even millions of explanations and actions.

Thus the concept of leadership should be expanded from one fixated on the most visible individual to a more collective vision of leadership, which we elaborate in this chapter. In doing so, we do not depreciate the role of visionary initiators such as Muhammad Yunus or Akhtar Hameed Khan. When their successes are understood analytically, similar advances can be achieved by others. Nobody should be deterred by the aura of personal greatness that attaches to the top leadership of ventures once they are successful. A wide variety of personalities have played formative and decisive roles in large-scale rural development efforts. This indicates that there are many leadership styles and many routes for successful programs. Indeed, some of the most successful leaders possess great, even excessive, personal modesty.[2]

Leadership for rural development has multiple focuses. The most fundamental focus is rural people themselves, whose efforts, ideas, and commitment are being mobilized. Effective program leaders, rather than performing decision-making and spokesperson roles in rural communities themselves, aim to bring forth or strengthen *local* leadership, as discussed in Chapter 4. Strong program leaders who subordinate or displace local leadership defeat their own purpose of establishing sustainable improvements in productivity and well-being. At the same time, leadership on behalf of rural development must relate to various agencies and actors at national and international levels, establishing linkages to sources of financial and technical support (Chapter 8) and dealing with political interests and actors (Chapter 9). But this role is expected to be transitional, fashioning institutional relationships that enable local communities and their representatives to attain some direction and control.

The major role of national leaders is to initiate and help shape productive roles for others, not to play these roles personally beyond a formative period. This transition is not an easy or a natural one, however. In several of the cases reported in *Reasons for Hope*, there is presently some concern whether the program's initiator has provided sufficient opportunity for the next generation of leaders to emerge and eventually take full responsibility. Unless a leader makes explicit efforts to broaden the skills and increase the visibility of supporting leadership cadres, a program is likely to become fixated on an individual and lose its long-term capacity to grow and evolve.

The main focus of rural development leadership should be the personnel of whatever organizations are working to engage and empower rural communities. A number of different kinds of persons can play such intermediary roles. They can be from the communities themselves or from cities or other regions; they can be part of a government bureaucracy that is adopting a new approach and new tasks, or the staff of a nongovernmental organization (NGO), cooperative, bank, university, or research institute. Although the progenitors of successful rural development efforts play important leadership roles vis-à-vis rural communities and external actors, the abiding and most critical leadership role belongs to the cadre of rural development workers, no matter what their backgrounds or titles, who take the grand new idea for self-improvement literally, through several tiers of organization, to the grassroots. This realization, we think, puts the factor of leadership in its proper perspective, while making it no less essential and no less unusual and commendable.

INITIATIVE

Some programs have depended heavily on the vision, energy, steadfastness, and skills of one individual. This is true for about a third of the cases considered in *Reasons for Hope*, where one finds remarkable accounts by Muhammad Yunus and F. H. Abed in Bangladesh, Akhtar Hameed Khan in Pakistan, V. Kurien in India, P. A. Kiriwandeniya in Sri Lanka, Mechai Viravaidya in Thailand, and Lédéa Ouedraogo and Bernard Lecomte in the Sahel. They recount diverse initiatives to open up multiple opportunities for their less advantaged compatriots.

But in as many cases, one sees some form of collective leadership accomplishing similar kinds of national program development and spread. These include Plan Puebla in Mexico, the Center for Economic and Social Development (DESEC) in Bolivia, the participatory irrigation management program in Sri Lanka, the national integrated pest management program in Indonesia, the Iringa child nutrition program in Tanzania, and the CAMPFIRE program in Zimbabwe. Although certain key personalities gave impetus and direction to each of these efforts, these contrast with situations in which a particular individual was the principal source of ideas and leadership.

Along a continuum between the Anand cooperatives in India and Plan Puebla are a variety of programs in which certain personalities were primarily associated with the design and implementation of the initiative but there was a broader base of leadership and inputs to the initiatives than in the first group of programs listed above. This middle range includes the World Neighbors program in Guatemala, the National Irrigation Administration (NIA) in the Philippines, the self-help water program in Malawi, the Agroforestry Outreach Project in Haiti, and the Rajasthan watershed conservation program. Interestingly, in three of these cases (Guatemala, Haiti, and Rajasthan), the persons who played key roles in launching these efforts (Bunch, Murray, and Krishna) handed over leadership responsibility after the first two years; it was up to others to carry forward the initial vision, adapting and innovating as learning indicated and circumstances dictated.[3]

There are some remarkable, indeed legendary, beginnings of several successful rural development efforts. In 1949, Verghese Kurien began his work as a government employee with an experimental creamery in a rural subdistrict in India; the next year, he began to work with a district union of dairy cooperatives. From this base, he improvised and experimented, learning how to devise appropriate organization as well as technology. He can now say proudly that for almost fifty years he has "worked for farmers," being responsible to elected boards of directors all this time.[4]

A few years before Kurien began his work in Gujarat, Akhtar Hameed Khan resigned from the Indian Civil Service to protest the British colonial government's lack of response to the 1943 Bengal famine, giving up a promising administrative career. He went to live in a village for two years as a laborer and locksmith, seeking to get to know rural life firsthand, before starting a new career as a teacher. When the Pakistani government, with support from the U.S. government and Michigan State University, established the Academy for Rural Development at Comilla in the eastern wing of that country, he was drawn into this enterprise. His ideas and personality elicited such impressive performance from smallholder cooperatives that agricultural development in Comilla soon distinguished it from neighboring districts (Raper 1970).

After retiring at age sixty-five, Khan wanted to see how much improvement could be achieved through self-help in a poor periurban setting. He once again spent a year (1980) living among what development agencies (but not he) would call the "target population." While walking about the streets of Orangi to get acquainted with people and their problems, he began identifying potential local leaders to draw into his endeavor. Once accepted by and better informed about the people, he began eliciting local efforts to transform Orangi.

Many have heard how Muhammad Yunus began visiting villages near the University of Chittagong where he taught in the mid-1970s, seeking to understand what kept the people there submerged in poverty. Using his own resources, he began experimenting to see whether even quite small loans could help reduce the burdens oppressing the poor. He learned that loans much too small for conventional banks to bother with could make a world of difference to the disadvantaged, particularly poor women. This direct experience propelled his efforts to create accessible institutional alternatives to usurious village moneylenders and remote, indifferent banks.

Less well known is how P. A. Kiriwandeniya, dissatisfied with the operating style of a prominent NGO in his country, returned to his village and lived there for a year, working with the community savings society. This local institution was well accepted but rather small and staid. Through discussions and experiments, he started a process that transformed village savings clubs in rural Sri Lanka into financial institutions. (Given the smaller size of this country, 700,000 members in Sri Lanka is equivalent to about 5 million in Bangladesh.) SANASA's current $40 million in deposits was built up entirely by its members, not by any infusion of outside funds. Although the members are not as poor as most of the borrowers from the Grameen Bank, a higher percentage of SANASA members are below the poverty line than in the rural sector generally, and the resulting system of savings and loans has made the capital deposited by richer members available for poorer ones to borrow.

At the other end of the continuum for initiation is Plan Puebla in Mexico. This grew out of the discussions of a group of faculty members and researchers at the National Agricultural University at Chapingo. By 1970, Plan Puebla was considered a model for small farmer development utilizing modern agricultural research. The founding group was able to enlist the support of the International Center for Improvement of Maize and Wheat (CIMMYT), one of the new international agricultural research centers established to make a "green revolution." The group sought and received foundation and then government support. Their sense of group responsibility was such that none of the four persons involved in initiating and overseeing Plan Puebla would write the case study for *Reasons for Hope* by himself. What is presented in that volume is, appropriately, a collective product.

The Gal Oya program in Sri Lanka was initiated as a result of the U.S. Agency for International Development (USAID) deciding to include a farmer organization component in an irrigation rehabilitation project. It asked the Agrarian Research and Training Institute (ARTI) and Cornell University's Rural Development Committee to take responsibility for designing and implementing this part of the project. Four Cornell faculty members worked with a similar number of Sri Lankan colleagues to conceptualize the effort, advised by Ben Bagadion, Carlos Isles, and David Korten from the Philippines during several short-term consultancies.

With less expenditure and institutional support than in the Philippines, a national program of participatory irrigation management was launched over a five-year period; however, this progress and speed were certainly facilitated by the precedents and learning available from the Philippines as well as Nepal.[5] Three persons played the most central roles in the Sri Lankan effort, but half a dozen other individuals made crucial contributions, such as field supervisor S. Munasinghe and district engineer S. Sentinathan, without whose leadership the program could well have languished in the field (Uphoff 1992a).

These contrasts show how a range of leadership structures and styles can contribute to institutionalized change in rural areas. Indeed, what may be considered "charisma" once a program has become successful may not have been so evident to villagers or government staff when first confronted with a persistent, unfamiliar, and maybe even deviant rural reformer. So while it is true that so-called charisma can be an important factor in some situations, it is likely to be a post facto explanation, and even a post facto phenomenon.[6]

Since we know most of the persons who contributed to *Reasons for Hope*, we can say that a major source of their effectiveness has been their conviction and consistency regarding the potentials of rural people. To make a program succeed and to expand it certainly requires unusual talents for organization and communication, supplemented by a good sense of human psychology and how to use incentives. But the characteristics often associated in the public mind with charisma—a dominating personality, a spell-binding speaking style, a demeanor of utmost confidence—are not evident prerequisites for leadership of rural development endeavors.

Along with similar philosophical perspectives in such leaders, another factor in common was their persistence and perseverance in the face of early opposition and disappointments, plus a willingness to incur some personal costs to promote a larger social benefit. This was sometimes seen as zealousness, but for the most part, it was fueled not so much by inner compulsion as by the continuous reinforcement from rural people, who confirmed the feasibility and fruitfulness of the new approach through their words and actions. To see the stirring of human potentials otherwise lying invisible and neglected gives persuasive reason for continuing to try to "break the mold." This we can say from personal experience in Sri Lanka and India, but we know from others that it has been a powerful motivating factor elsewhere.

Being able to connect with rural people is crucial for success, but so is the ability to mobilize, inspire, and lead the staff of a learning organization, whether this is a government agency, an NGO, a cooperative, or a university program. We would thus focus the discussion of leadership for successful rural development on the contributions made by personnel who are called on to exercise varied but continuous leadership at headquarters and in the field, by proxy and in their own right. This concept of *diffused leadership* needs to be taken more seriously than journalistic accounts of rural development successes suggest.

In part, our emphasis on collective leadership reflects the democratic impulse that drives these various rural development initiatives, but it also reflects the pragmatic realities we have observed with such programs. It underscores the importance of a participatory style of leadership if the program is to promote the assumption of responsibility for self-management among rural people, since it is difficult to establish a genuinely participatory program using autocratic means. A proposition from organizational theory that can be applied to rural development is that any organization tends to replicate in its environment the same values and social relationships that it maintains internally. A support agency that does not operate according to participatory and egalitarian ideals will find it difficult to establish community organizations that operate according to such principles.

RURAL DEVELOPMENT CADRES

Quite a variety of roles can be employed in introducing and sustaining changes in the productive possibilities of rural people. We group them into three general categories of cadres according to the tasks they perform: staff, technicians/trainers, and catalysts. A program such as the Anand dairy cooperatives can have all three roles.

Staff

These are persons whose tasks are, for the most part, defined administratively, though this does not mean that all their work is routine. They need to be adapting as well as carrying out programs under conditions of uncertainty and flux. This category includes persons with such innovative responsibilities as the "bankers on bikes" who have brought Grameen Bank services to some 35,000 villages in Bangladesh. Less dramatic are the roles of the large number of SANASA staff who manage cluster, divisional, and district union operations as employees of this now-national cooperative federation. Their contribution has been to provide easily accessible and trustworthy services to member-depositors throughout the rural areas of Sri Lanka—a significant accomplishment. The bulk of the staff members of cooperatives based on the Anand model in India have similar roles, unglamorous but crucial for the maintenance of the organization's integrity and functioning.

The staff of government agencies can perform similarly if they are well motivated and well directed. The Iringa nutrition program in Tanzania, the Malawi self-help water program, the Rajasthan watershed conservation program, and the CAMPFIRE wildlife conservation program in Zimbabwe have all utilized public-sector personnel in ways that have impressed villagers and outsiders; these staffers exhibited more seriousness and dedication than is the norm for government employees. In the CAMPFIRE case, this small cadre is supplemented by NGO personnel. The Agroforestry Outreach Project in Haiti relied entirely on NGO staff to reach 200,000 rural households in that country. Our point is that one need not be working with "elite" cadres. Large numbers of staff are able to function effectively if they are given better than usual leadership within government or nongovernmental organizations, as Krishna found in Rajasthan. This is one of the main findings of Tendler (1997) in her analysis of successful programs in Brazil.

Paraprofessionals

During the 1970s, there was considerable interest in the possible contributions to rural development of field staff operating in roles such as paratechnicians or paraveterinarians (Esman 1983). Many designations have been used to refer to non-Chinese equivalents of the "barefoot doctors" who, with elementary technical training and material support, were able to provide needed knowledge and services in rural communities of China that were otherwise poorly served. For the most part, paraprofessionals were persons from villages who were willing to be purveyors of knowledge or services for modest payment or in some programs as unpaid volunteers.

The paratechnicians who were recruited, trained, and utilized under the Malawi self-help water program exemplify this category.[7] They operated under the supervision of a project engineer, but as they gained experience and confidence, they worked increasingly independently. The Anand cooperatives have large numbers of paraprofessionals, who are crucial to those cooperatives' success. The veterinary cadre now administers 4 million artificial inseminations annually and gives farmers advice and assistance on the health and nutrition of their cattle. Six-S in the Sahel takes persons nominated from its federated member groups and trains them in a wide variety of skills for agriculture, health, well construction, mechanical maintenance, handicrafts, and account keeping, which they then put to use for community benefit directly through their own efforts or multiply through training. DESEC's paratechnicians in Bolivia are similar in their background and function.

This category can also include persons who are responsible more for training than for providing technical services. Most of the cadre of the national integrated pest management program in Indonesia operate as trainers or as trainers-of-trainers. The lowest-level cadre in the program are regular agricultural extension agents who have been assigned to it and are given both training on its participatory philosophy and technical knowledge. The staff above them are especially recruited, trained, and highly motivated. Their enthusiasm and teaching skills have been crucial for the program's progress to date.

The farmer-experimenters and farmer-extensionists who were recruited and trained in the San Martin Jilotepeque program in Guatemala represent

another variant of the paraprofessional role. Whereas persons in paraprofessional roles in most government programs are fairly closely supervised
and managed, reflecting limited confidence in their knowledge and skill, in
the World Neighbors' program, such persons, chosen from the communities, were considered the *most* qualified to make judgments about innovations and to plan and carry out dissemination efforts. The strategy of
farmer-to-farmer extension now gaining acceptance around the world was
given impetus by this program's experience and by the impressive accomplishments of these unschooled or little-educated farmer-scientists and
farmer-communicators (Bunch 1982).

The field staff of Plan Puebla in Mexico initially worked in technical
roles, as intermediaries between scientists and farmers, assisting the latter
to participate in agronomic research conducted on their fields and to manage "high production plots" where the new technology could be demonstrated. As they also became involved in helping farmers form groups at
local and regional levels, their role verged on being a catalytic one.

Catalysts

The third role emerged during the 1970s, as documented by Lassen (1980),
and became more widely accepted thereafter. If staff are to administer and
manage, and paraprofessionals are to transfer appropriate knowledge and
technology to users, catalysts are to mobilize and motivate rural people.
Catalysts induce people to organize, or, if there are already organizations,
they help make these stronger and more effective. The concern is not so
much with efficiency or expertise as with empowerment. But the aim is
not just to bolster people's ability to make claims on government or other
outside sources for funds, as is sometimes proposed. Rather, it is to create
self-management capacities that can support self-reliant development.

Catalyst roles did not suddenly appear twenty years ago. Rather, they
evolved out of previous roles that were introduced in the 1950s and 1960s
through programs for community development in Anglophone parts of
the Third World (Holdcroft 1978) and for *animation rurale* in Francophone
regions (Charlick 1984). Persons in these roles were variously called community development officers, *animateurs* (in French), *promotores* (in
Spanish), or sometimes change agents. None of these terms is, however,
apt for the kind of rural development we are proposing.

The term *catalyst* comes from chemistry. Social actors, when introduced into certain community settings, can be seen as analogous to certain substances that, when put into a chemical solution, precipitate or
accelerate a reaction that changes the nature of that solution. Social catalysts can change the nature of a social situation like chemical catalysts

alter a physical one. In both situations there is a potential already existing to be activated. To give an example from chemistry, nitrogen and hydrogen can combine naturally to form ammonia, but when iron is present, this speeds up the chemical reaction that creates this compound. The iron is activating an inherent potential. This is different from causing changes that would not occur otherwise, that are in some sense against the interests or destiny of those affected by the transformation.

Catalysts in chemistry can start a process whereby the chain reaction either ceases when the catalyst is removed from the solution or continues even when the catalyst is no longer present. Both kinds of outcomes are possible in social situations, but obviously our interest is in the latter alternative, where the presence of a catalyst serves to create capacities that can continue functioning without further outside stimulus or reinforcement.

Persons in catalyst roles are supposed to bring out potentials for change that already exist in rural communities rather than assume that their task is to change, indoctrinate, motivate, and manage rural people. Catalysts show explicit respect for what local people already know and can accomplish under conducive conditions. The analogy between chemical and social dynamics can be taken too far, however. In chemistry, a catalyst is something that is unchanged by the reactions it evokes and that occur around it. We find that not only do social catalysts have some personal impact on the people with whom they work and interact, but those people invariably have some reciprocal effect on the persons who serve in their communities. The part of the analogy that is most relevant is that social catalysts are not attempting to *change* people and communities so much as to *facilitate* their emergence as self-managing and empowered agents.

The newer concept implies that the catalyst will be withdrawn at some point, but the process of transformation will go on. In some programs, this is what happens, yet the continuity of effort may be problematic. Maintaining some connection between the program and communities is advisable. Abrupt, complete removal is not necessary and is destructive of relationships that have been built up; however, the locus of initiative should shift. The amount of effort that program personnel commit to capacity building compared with operational activities should be reduced.

When the Gal Oya program was explained to engineers, the farmer organizations being established were described as "social infrastructure." This analogy to physical infrastructure suggests an initial process of design and construction that is followed by a more extensive and less costly ongoing phase of operation and maintenance, which engineers know as O&M. When a dam or a road is built, it is expected that there will need to be some continuing investment in O&M. One does not build a physical structure and then walk away from it, expecting it to retain its strength and productivity without any further supplementary inputs. Similarly, local organizations need some maintenance investments, such as further training of members, orientation of new officers, monitoring and evaluation, conflict resolution, and troubleshooting. As much as possible, these tasks should be handled by the organizations themselves. But for some time, at least, a continuing catalytic role is appropriate to help operate and maintain social infrastructure. Less expense and less effort are needed to the extent that the structures created are reasonably solid.[8]

The question often asked about an organizing effort—how soon can you withdraw?—is therefore not a good indicator of success, as discussed in Chapter 10. Rather than expecting or demanding total withdrawal, more meaningful questions are whether local organizations are assuming greater responsibilities and whether the economic and social benefits resulting from some continuing external investment are sufficient to justify further expenditures.[9] The catalyst role should change over time both quantitatively and qualitatively. Fewer persons should be needed in such roles, and what they do will change as local capacities are strengthened. But withdrawal by itself is not an appropriate measure of success.

It is instructive to see how many of the programs in *Reasons for Hope* were aided and accelerated by the use of catalysts, operating in roles quite different from those of the earlier promoters or *animateurs*. Although the Grameen Bank field staff function much like other bank employees in a number of respects, during the organizing phase of program expansion, these "bankers on bikes" are catalysts. They operate much like the social organizers who spread the work of the Orangi Pilot Project and the Aga Khan Rural Support Program in the northern districts of Pakistan, the program officers for the Bangladesh Rural Advancement Committee (BRAC), the group organizers for the Small Farmer Development Program in Nepal, the community organizers for the National Irrigation Administration in the Philippines, and the institutional organizers for the Gal Oya project in Sri Lanka.

The National Dairy Development Board in India spreads cooperatives through "spearhead teams" that include both veterinarians to address technical problems of animal health and production and persons trained in social science to deal with local organizational issues. DESEC's *promotores*, despite their name, function more as catalysts than as promoters, maintaining what Demeure and Guardia call a "subsidiary" role, supporting locally elected leaders and never substituting for them (1997, 95). Even SANASA, which now operates in a relatively routine way, in its early years had persons, many of them volunteers, who traveled to villages to encourage the savings societies functioning there to join the emerging national movement.

It is hard to classify programs as depending primarily on staff, on para-professionals, or on catalysts, since most have persons in two or even three of these roles, and sometimes roles evolve. Once SANASA became effective in mobilizing and utilizing savings, the catalytic role within that program receded. A general assessment of the experience reported in *Reasons for Hope* suggests that these three roles have roughly equal weight among the cases. If organizational capacity or innovation is most important, catalysts have a larger role to play; if the development and diffusion of technical knowledge are critical, paraprofessionals are more central; when a program is already established and the scale and spread of operations most concern it, the need for capable, committed staff is paramount.

The Importance of Cadres

The persons in the best position to judge how essential cadres and their leadership performance are to program success are the chief protagonists of programs, who usually are given credit for that success. Muhammad Yunus describes the Grameen Bank's "bankers on bikes" as that program's "greatest asset," emphasizing that they are trained and encouraged to think creatively and take independent decisions (Yunus 1997, 17). The program officers who carry BRAC's program into thousands of villages in Bangladesh are recruited competitively and told to think for themselves (Abed and Chowdhury 1997, 55). Program officers are chosen and rewarded for their "firm commitment to the agency's values and objec-tives," echoing a principle for effective management of large-scale organi-zations articulated by Peters and Waterman (1982, 318–25). Such a situation enables the top managers to run a "loose-tight" operation, with much decentralization to field operators because they share a common set of core values.

Such sentiments are expressed by other program leaders. Verghese Kurien writes about the "high standards of professionalism and respon-siveness" that are expected of, and by and large manifested by, employees in the cooperatives following the Anand model (Kurien 1997, 113). The Plan Puebla originators say, "The most critical factor for success or failure in a development program is the ability and dedication of the technical team members" (Diaz Cisneros et al. 1997, 133). An Indian government official visiting the Rajasthan watershed conservation program spoke of "a widespread unleashing of the creative talent of field staff" (Krishna 1997, 259). The engineer in the Ministry of Community Development who launched the self-help rural water supply program in Malawi concluded his assessment of the program by saying, "The success of this project did not, of course, happen overnight, but has taken ten years of patient under-standing and persistent hard work from dedicated field staff" (Robertson 1981, 11).

Although the top leadership of a program is the most visible and in some ways the most crucial because of its level and position, for such lead-ership to be effective, there must be comparable and reinforcing ideals and articulations leading to decisions and actions at multiple levels, all the way down to the grassroots. The directions and purposes identified with top leadership will have little impact unless they are expressed similarly, if not identically, at many lower levels. With a dominating leader, even one com-mitted to building an institution, there will be paralysis if others wait for decisions to be made at the top. What are generally referred to as "subor-dinate" levels in an organization are more appropriately called those lev-els that are closer to the field.[10]

This is what we found in the Gal Oya irrigation program. The ideas and purposes that animated the ARTI and Cornell leadership were expressed in turn by the organizers who carried the program into the field, living in communities and encouraging the formation of farmer organiza-tions. The farmer-representatives chosen by their peers to improve the effi-cient and equitable use of water articulated and promoted the purposes of the program, exercising leadership within the farming communities. The "virus" of leadership eventually "infected" engineers and other officials, and they became additional points for the creation and dissemination of new impetus to achieve program goals. At some point—quite soon, in this particular case—the net flow of energy and ideas was reversed, flowing from bottom to top.

Leadership can and should become a collective phenomenon, despite top-down initiation. This can also occur in programs that depend more heavily on a single individual to start the process than in the Gal Oya case. This is one reason why a participatory style of leadership within organi-zations for rural development is so important—better late than never, but also the sooner the better. This generalization supports the suggestion made at the start of this chapter that it would be as misleading to overes-timate the contributions made by a program's top leadership as to under-estimate them. Practically by definition, leadership will be crucial to the success of any major rural development program that changes patterns of resource use, political and social relationships, and local capabilities. But evaluators—and imitators—should not focus only on the most visible aspects of leadership, those that are nationally and internationally known. Especially for rural development, leadership must be seen as a socially and organizationally embedded phenomenon.

WHERE TO START?

Even if it is agreed that a learning process approach should be adopted and that a pilot effort or "learning laboratory" is necessary, there is no agreement on the best place to start. A logical focus would be to begin in the most typical location—community, locality, district, region—so that any methods or techniques devised would have the most likelihood of wide applicability. This is the approach taken by many programs setting out to operate on a national scale, such as the integrated pest management program in Indonesia, the irrigation program in the Philippines, Six-S in the Sahel, and self-help water supply in Malawi.

It can be argued, however, that it is better to start in somewhat more favorable or better endowed areas, expecting that if rapid progress can be made, greater cooperation and subsequent support will be enlisted more quickly. The child nutrition program supported by UNICEF in Tanzania chose to start in Iringa district because it had a strong administrative infrastructure and a net food surplus, but also because the incidence of malnutrition there was greater than average. World Neighbors' program in Guatemala chose to work in San Martin Jilotepeque because it appeared more promising than average—partly because it had a cadre of local leadership accessible through rural churches, and because people in the area had the reputation of being receptive to change. Still, by other measures such as average size of landholding (small) and percentage of landless households (high), San Martin was not a very favorable area. Actually, the criteria for what constitutes a "more favorable" place to begin are not simple or self-evident. The fact that food-surplus Iringa district in Tanzania had higher-than-average malnutrition could have meant that it was a more difficult place to begin an ambitious program.

The initiators of Plan Puebla in Mexico argue for choosing a location where ecological conditions are somewhat above average but then working with the more disadvantaged households in that area (Diaz Cisneros et al. 1997, 121). The state of Puebla could be considered better off in terms of its accessibility, being near the capital and to research and educational institutions. But in terms of maize yields, size of holdings, use of traditional technology, and low family incomes, the area was not more favorable.[11]

The CAMPFIRE program in Zimbabwe first devised local financial and natural resource management rules in a district (Nyaminyami) that was quite favorable in terms of the amount of wildlife available to protect, meaning that potentially more revenue could be generated. This meant, however, that there were also more local and national vested interests to be dealt with, which reduced the degree of freedom for experimentation and produced a less participatory system of wildlife management. A more satisfactory set of principles and practices was developed when the program was started in a more typical district (Guruve).

A counterargument can be made, based on the Gal Oya case, that beginning in a "disadvantageous" place has some advantages. The Gal Oya scheme, not chosen by ARTI or Cornell but rather by USAID and the government of Sri Lanka as the place to initiate improvements, was considered the most difficult and run-down system in the country. "If we can make progress in Gal Oya, we can make progress anywhere in Sri Lanka" were the encouraging words offered by the Irrigation Department's director for water management when planning began. The farmers there were considered some of the most conflictual and uncooperative. The organizers were told by the top district official as they prepared to enter the field: "If you can bring even ten or fifteen farmers in Gal Oya to work together, that will be a big achievement." Their task was to get somewhere between 10,000 and 15,000 farmers to form water management associations. In fact, within four years, this was accomplished, and the organizations are still functioning well more than a decade after the project ended. The structure of organization that was devised jointly by farmers and organizers has now been extended to all major irrigation schemes in the country.

In this case, it could be argued that the "worst" place was actually the "best" place to begin. At least farmers were likely to be receptive, because after thirty years of neglect, they were prepared to accept the principle of self-reliant development. More important, even small gains could fuel enthusiasm and build up momentum for further advances. Political and administrative as well as technical leadership soon began supporting the initiatives that the farmers were taking.[12]

When USAID invited Cornell to assist with a participatory irrigation management project in Nepal, the irrigation system chosen as the pilot was Sirsia-Dudhaura, located right on the border with India. This scheme was terribly run-down, but more significant, it was right next to the Indian state of Bihar and was beset by the same kinds of caste, poverty, illiteracy, and other problems that have made Bihar one of the most intractable states of India. *Dacoits* (outlaws) operated freely in the area, and officials had abandoned their efforts to control the system between sundown and sunrise. Yet within four months, organizers working in the same catalytic way as in Gal Oya had gotten effective irrigation associations started. The same kind of dynamic was seen with the Orangi Pilot Project in a depressed and conflict-ridden squatter settlement outside of Karachi.

There is some statistical support for the idea that the "worst" can be "best." A quantified analysis and evaluation of 150 cases of local organization in Asia, Africa, and Latin America found that a number of environmental variables such as topography, resource endowment, infrastructure, economic diversification, income distribution, settlement patterns, and literacy had negative or nil correlations, all insignificant, with overall scores of local organization contributions to rural development (Esman and Uphoff 1984, 104–28). A hypothesis that more "favorable" environmental conditions would be correlated with greater success of local organizations was not supported by the data.

This suggests that plausible arguments can be made for beginning almost anyplace, except presumably in areas that are especially violent and conflicted. The physical conditions are probably considerably less important than the capabilities and disposition of the people in an area: are they ready, willing, and able to take responsibility for improving their lives in one or more respects? This often cannot be known in advance. When the watershed program started in Rajasthan, the communities were not very cooperative. There had been a widespread breakdown in traditional forms of social organization, and there was considerable alienation of local people from the government administration; at the same time, the most prevailing "tradition" was that of dependency, expecting that the state would work its will and provide communities with at least some resources to improve their welfare.

The rural areas of Rajasthan are among the most unapproachable, given infrastructure and climatic difficulties, compounded by scattered, even nomadic settlement patterns and low levels of literacy. The interdisciplinary teams deployed to engage these communities in new measures to reduce soil erosion, reforest denuded areas, and increase food and fodder production were able, surprisingly quickly in many places, to establish enough credibility and rapport that a process of experimentation could begin. The rate of program expansion, approaching 100,000 hectares a year across large expanses of the state—ten times more than the area covered previously—was driven by government and donor imperatives. Yet with leadership that stressed initiative and responsibility by both administrative cadres and communities, new starts were made in state-local relationships, repeating the kind of turnaround seen in Gal Oya.

This and other experience indicate that *how* a program is initiated is more important than *where* it is started. This has been appreciated by various programs that have succeeded in introducing large-scale changes in rural areas. Initiative for change has come from adept and persevering leadership, whether from individuals or from small groups of committed professionals. They fashioned systems of organization with a central capability for planning and projecting overall strategy, mobilizing government and donor resources, and engaging in communication and education that connected to a growing number of local associations. Such systems can be effective only if significant numbers of supporting personnel, whether in staff, paraprofessional, or catalytic roles, take up the challenge and opportunity of making major social and economic changes and help give it reality at local levels.

The thrust of such initiatives has not been simply to achieve certain objectives—increased milk production, greater savings and loans, reduced population growth, potable water supplies, reforestation, soil conservation, or wildlife protection. In the cases we have considered, the essential goal was to establish local capabilities that evoke and strengthen long-term leadership as well as active membership within rural communities. The processes of innovation and behavioral change initiated from above are converted into activities that are carried forward and managed by local communities through their own institutions. This gives life and energy to assisted self-reliance.

NOTES

1. Uphoff played an active role in the Gal Oya irrigation project in Sri Lanka, and Krishna was the administrator responsible for establishing the Rajasthan watershed program in India. Esman has served as development administration adviser in the prime minister's office in Malaysia.

2. A difficulty we encountered in assembling case studies for *Reasons for Hope* was that many of the key figures in the successful programs we wanted to document were reluctant to call attention to themselves and their roles, feeling that credit should be widely shared and not claimed by themselves.

3. In the successful primary health care case in Brazil documented by Tendler (1997, 21–45), its architect and visionary leader similarly served less than two years. The additional dozen cases considered for this volume are divided about equally among the three categories described in text.

4. We should note that although his involvement with the Anand cooperative model has been longer, Dr. Kurien considers T. K. Patel, an extraordinary political and social leader in Gujarat, to be the cofounder of this movement. Patel served as chair of the Kaira District Cooperative Milk Producers' Union (AMUL) until the 1980s.

5. Along with NIA, the Small Farmer Development Program (SFDP) established in Nepal with technical advice and modest financial assistance ($30,000) from the United Nations Food and Agriculture Organization (FAO) provided a role model and precedents for the Gal Oya program (Ghai and Rahman 1979). The other

SFDPs that FAO established concurrently during the late 1970s in Bangladesh and the Philippines never achieved half as much success as did the program in Nepal. The leadership of the general manager of the Agricultural Development Bank of Nepal, S. K. Uphadyay, and of the initial field supervisor, Chandra Adhikary, is generally credited in Nepal with devising a workable and effective set of roles and operational procedures through experimentation that was carried out with a self-critical spirit. Eventually 40,000 households were brought into the program.

6. See the discussion of the limited role of charisma in successful rural development programs by Tendler (1997, 17–9).

7. "The technical assistants are carefully selected for their practical experience and their suitability for working with people in the field. They are trained in all the necessary skills, mainly through in-service training. They become very proficient at their work and are respected by the people. They are personally involved in the success of their section of the project and become highly motivated" (Robertson 1981, 11).

8. The cadre used to catalyze the organizational capacities may itself be quite fluid. The institutional organizers in the Gal Oya project were on one-year contracts with no guarantee of any long-term employment. Consequently, when they got offers of permanent jobs elsewhere, most (but not all) accepted them. The Sri Lankan government was periodically recruiting large numbers of teachers to absorb the many unemployed university graduates, so the organizer cadre was depleted every six to twelve months. At the end of four years of organizing effort, out of the 169 organizers recruited, trained, and deployed in the field, only eight were left. The period of service averaged about nine months. But each new batch of recruits was able to learn quickly from the few remaining organizers, absorbing their values and organizational culture, as well as learning techniques and strategies. As a result, the farmer organization program proceeded successfully despite a dismaying and potentially devastating rate of turnover—95 percent.

9. These are often considered "subsidies," but there is no analytical way, except by definition, to differentiate these from other government or NGO "expenditures." This is an important issue for the Grameen Bank and SANASA—whether outside resources that enable them to maintain a program of organization and training that serves social purposes such as education, health, and sanitation are to be considered subsidies or developmental expenditures.

10. One contributor to *Reasons for Hope*, whom we will not identify here, has sometimes been described as autocratic in his management of the program he pioneered. He was asked by Uphoff to comment on the role of cadres at lower levels. Uphoff suggested that one function of staff could be to take the ideas of the central leadership and communicate these ideas in the field, making them a reality on the ground. This program leader responded without hesitation, "And to improve upon them," referring to the ideas coming from above. This supports our proposition about the importance of seeing cadres as leaders, not just implementers.

11. One unstated consideration was that the president of Mexico at the time came from this state, so working there gave more promise of high-level political support.

12. The Mennonite Central Committee's agricultural program in Bangladesh was started in an area with some of the worst land in terms of soil, overcrowding, and flooding. But because the situation was so desperate, farmers had already started to innovate, experimenting with alternative crops and cropping cycles. This made it easier to promote farmer experiments and changes in the cropping system (Laura Meitzner, personal communication).

4 Local Organization and Participation

How can the participation of rural people in planning, managing, financing, adapting, and extending programs that are expected to benefit them in important ways be assured and sustained? To maintain effective popular engagement in rural development programs, systems of local organization are needed that are appropriate to the task and to the capacities of rural people. Such organizations must be ones that they can and will take possession of as their own, even if the organizations were instigated by others.

Creating and maintaining such social infrastructure is not an easy or simple task. It requires considerable investment of effort, ideas, and material resources from rural people and also from supporting agencies, whether sponsors, partners, or providers of services. In a computer age, people increasingly appreciate the importance of "software." Government investments in the "hardware"—the physical facilities—of rural development will not produce the desired results without some reliable means for command and control, not in the hands of planners so much as in the hands of users and intended beneficiaries.[1] The latter need to have the means of sequencing and reconciling instructions, communicating, building up memory and routines, merging efforts, checking inconsistencies, and making decisions. Without carrying this analogy too far, we consider in this chapter the means and strategies for developing such organizational capacities, which are more crucial to effective and sustainable rural development than is any other element.[2]

We begin by considering the structures of local organization that are most likely to support the "weight" of widespread participation. This leads to a consideration of how organizations can operate most effectively, and then to a review of participation issues and opportunities. Quite a wide variety of organizational arrangements can help empower rural people and make them more effective at meeting their development needs. What we are looking for are principles and examples rather than recipes or rules. To the extent that self-managed and self-correcting organizations are established, we can expect the improvements they implement to be of lasting value. The kinds of management needed to extend and support such systems of development participation are considered in Chapter 5.

ORGANIZATIONAL STRUCTURE

The grassroots organizations fostered by programs reviewed in *Reasons for Hope* ranged from the strictly prescribed arrangements for Grameen Bank borrower groups—always five members, with the groups linked upward through centers and branches—to the "open arms" approach of Six-S and the Center for Economic and Social Development (DESEC), which work with any group that can meet certain performance tests. Even though the Grameen Bank now has a clearly specified structure for organization, this was arrived at through considerable experimentation in the program's early days. DESEC has no fixed formula for community organization partners, assisting existing peasant associations or even local trade unions if they come forward. It works either with whole villages or with subsets of villagers, depending on the activity being undertaken. Forestry, irrigation, and animal health tend to be whole-village undertakings, whereas other efforts, DESEC finds, can be better carried out with smaller groups.

The Orangi and Gal Oya projects and the Rajasthan watershed program started with no prescribed structure, encouraging prospective members to design their own organization. As experience was gained, organizations began to learn from one another, and the forms of their structures tended to converge, instructively, on simple rather than more complex forms of organization. The approach in Gal Oya was to start with informal committees and to encourage members to formalize their organizations later, when they felt the need for this next step. The intention was to create *demand-led* organizations rather than adopt a *supply-side* approach, presenting rural people with a predesigned model.

A program can build on existing local organizations, often "traditional" ones such as the *naam* groups that were reconstituted and drawn into the Six-S movement in the Sahel or the *groupmans* (Creole for *groupements*) that planted 60 million trees in Haiti under the Agroforestry Outreach Project.[3] The Orangi Pilot Project worked with existing political, social, and commercial networks but channeled local efforts into and through lane committees, because initial project activities had to proceed according to contiguous spatial units. By working with potential groups on their own terms and encouraging the formation of more explicit and empowered groups as needed, successful programs have avoided the "cookie-cutter" approach, also known as the "Xerox" approach.

The concept and goal of *replication* has become pervasive in the thinking of donor agencies, but it is a mechanistic and misconstrued idea. *Propagation*, a term with biological roots, is more appropriate for the spread of local organizations. It implies the planting of seeds (ideas) and then the nurturing of organisms, not all of which may survive. The analogy suggests that the variety should not be a hothouse plant that requires extensive and expensive husbandry but rather one that is self-seeding or can propagate from cuttings or from roots that spread and push up new plants in an expanding plant community. Such new organisms should be able to nourish and protect themselves, not be dependent on the "gardener," once they have become established in the particular environment. They should be able to adapt successfully over time to variations in their surroundings.

Size of Base Groups

A variety of structures have emerged around the world for organizing local efforts to develop rural communities, but there are some recurrent patterns that offer guidance. Large, amorphous mass movements have not been successful anywhere without some structure. The most effective programs have had systems of "nested" organizations that start from a base-level group or association that can maintain solidarity and discipline. Smaller organizations have lower transaction costs, that is, easier communication, and members are able to observe and discourage "free riding" (Olson 1965). At the same time, smallness by itself contributes to weakness, so it is important for groups to be linked with one another, as discussed in the next section.

The size of base groups can vary. The Grameen Bank decided, after some experimentation, that its basic unit would be a five-member group, and this is being replicated in programs in other countries using the Grameen Bank model. This represents, we think, a minimum size. Also, it is desirable for members themselves to have some say in the size of their organization, to make it more truly "theirs." The more common size of base-level organizations is between ten and twenty members. In such a group, everyone can know one another well, communication and transaction costs are not very great, and any free riding or shirking will be fairly evident. The range of twelve to fifteen members seems to be optimal, at least for irrigation groups (Coward 1979; Uphoff 1986a, 67–75). In the Gal Oya irrigation system in Sri Lanka, if more than twenty farmers drew water from a field channel, they usually formed themselves into two groups of about ten each; if there were more than forty farmers, they were likely to form three groups.

When economies of scale figure prominently, larger organizations may be preferable and sustainable. This is suggested by the experience of SANASA savings and loan cooperatives in Sri Lanka, where primary societies range from 30 to 300 members, though 50 to 150 is more usual, with about 100 members being the norm. When local organizations get to be large, experience shows that they function better if they are composed of smaller suborganizations that can facilitate collective action, like the village organizations assisted by the Bangladesh Rural Advancement Committee (BRAC). Or membership may include all residents in a village, but the operating organization may be a smaller representative body, such as the Rajasthan watershed program's user committees of five to ten members acting on behalf of the whole community.

Successful local organizations are likely to grow in size, with the option of subdividing into smaller operating groups if the diseconomies of scale outweigh the economies. The cooperative established in San Martin Jilotepeque with encouragement from World Neighbors grew from 32 to 732 members in seven years' time, with assets expanding from $177 to $38,000; $23,000 in savings was accumulated from very poor members, with a default rate of only 8.5 percent on its loans (even after an earthquake had damaged or destroyed most of their homes). Membership continued to grow, to almost 1,000 members, after World Neighbors withdrew from the area as civil war raged. But sadly, size and success of a localized organization could not protect the cooperative from the effects of violence, which eliminated many of its leaders and led to its dissolution.

A quantitative analysis of local organization performance carried out on 150 cases from Africa, Asia, and Latin America found a small but not significant positive correlation (.09) between the size of an organization at its base and its contributions to rural development (Esman and Uphoff 1984, 149). Since, as noted already, successful organizations are likely to attract more members, a higher coefficient was expected. However, the observed low correlation between size and performance resulted from the fact that small base-level organizations, if active and especially if federated upward, contribute to effective operation.

Federated Organizations

Small organizations by themselves may be beautiful, but their impact will be limited if they are not joined in some larger enterprise. Any program that aims to produce widespread benefits must address the question of how to organize a hierarchical structure that is animated from below even more than from above.[4] There is an ever-present danger when small groups are federated that they will be dominated by higher levels of the organization. This hazard should be forthrightly acknowledged, and steps should be taken to resist it, as discussed later.

Certain rural development tasks obviously require some form of multi-level organization. With irrigation, for example, water from a reservoir or river gets divided into smaller and smaller supplies until it reaches the field channel level where users have access to it (Uphoff 1986a, 59–78). The National Irrigation Administration (NIA) in the Philippines encouraged a two-tier structure, with turnout service associations at the base level and irrigation associations encompassing them at the project level. The Gal Oya project in Sri Lanka, whose organizational structure became the model for all major irrigation systems in that country, involved a very large area. It started with informal groups at the field channel level. Their representatives formed a management committee at the next higher level, for the distributary canal, and an area assembly at the branch canal level, with an overall project committee at the level of the main canal. In smaller systems, three-tier rather than four-tier organizational structures suffice. Interestingly, in Sri Lanka, farmers around Polonnaruwa have taken the initiative to form a district-level association, and there is continuing aspiration for a national federation.[5]

Putting in rural water supplies or installing sewers requires a hierarchical organizational structure, corresponding to the physical pattern of water distribution or waste aggregation. The Orangi Pilot Project outside Karachi, Pakistan, started with lane committees, which could install sewers for their own streets and make home hookups, but it also had to form neighborhood associations in order to construct secondary sewers, which fed into the primary sewer lines that were built and maintained by the city government. In Malawi, the self-help water supply program worked through four levels of organization, from tap committees up to main line committees.

A function like savings and credit does not have the same kind of physical connections and interdependence, but similar organizational structures are appropriate. There can be productive financial connections and interdependence, such as when funds built up by groups with surplus savings are made available to groups with greater demand for loans. The Grameen Bank starts with the small groups discussed earlier, which are joined into centers, and these centers are associated with branches. Conferences of borrower-representatives are held annually in each zone, covering two or three districts. There is no national organization of Grameen Bank members, but borrower-representatives serve on the Grameen Bank's board of directors to complete the circuit of organization from the villages to the capital.

SANASA savings and loan cooperatives in Sri Lanka started with village-level primary societies at the base, joined in district associations and finally in a national federation. As the program has grown to over 700,000 members, two more levels have been introduced: the cluster organization of five to ten primary societies, and a divisional (subdistrict) organization. This does not add a costly or impeding layer of bureaucracy, because the cluster and division organizations are operated mostly by volunteer or elected personnel, who expedite and aggregate transactions. There is interlending among district associations. SANASA's structure is almost an ideal type of "nested" organization in which each level is an extension upward of lower levels.

Even more complex and heterogeneous structures are possible and can be beneficial, depending on the task and scale of organization.[6] The Iringa nutrition program has one of the most complete structures in terms of number of levels, being a hybrid organization combining local membership committees with political and administrative bodies at higher levels. Throughout rural areas in Tanzania, in order to facilitate communication and small-group action, groupings of ten households have been clustered into cells, at the initiative of the government party. Above the cells, there are village health committees (VHCs) made up of elected members given party and administrative support. These committees work under the guidance and monitoring of their respective ward development committees (WDCs) operating at the locality (multivillage) level. WDCs are overseen by their respective divisional development committees and district development committees. All these bodies have both elected and appointed membership. Above them are regional and national coordinating committees made up of representatives of the relevant government departments. No special structure was created just for child survival and nutrition, as only the VHCs and the coordinating committees are devoted primarily to this program. Multipurpose organizations operating at different levels were co-opted and expanded to give support to this campaign, which showed quick and dramatic results because each level was called upon to do what it was best able to contribute. This structure as a whole has had substantial impact, changing behavior to ensure better child health (Jonsson, Ljungqvist, and Yambi 1993).

We cannot say that any particular structure for federation will be the best everywhere. Simpler structures are preferable, other things being equal, but more levels can give more varied capabilities. Factors such as population density (or sparsity), transportation and communication facilities, topography, cultural homogeneity (or heterogeneity), and existing political jurisdictions need to be considered. The Six-S federation operating across the Sahelian region of West Africa is built on work groups operating at the village level. Thirty or so villages are grouped together to form a zone, which makes decisions about how external resources will be allocated among the villages based on informal project proposals.[7] Zones are represented at the area level, and area representatives in turn meet in national assemblies. DESEC in Bolivia has a similar structure with village, zonal, regional, and national levels of organization, with higher levels intended to provide essential coordination and support services to lower ones.

Not all programs have such an amplified structure of local organization. Whether such a structure is needed and feasible depends on the objectives and the situation. The integrated pest management program in Indonesia was conceived mostly as a training program, stressing human resource development. Farmer groups that already existed (often just on paper) were brought into the program, and the training was conducted through group exercises rather than being provided to collections of individuals. The program has not tried systematically to strengthen organizational capacities, leaving this up to whatever enthusiasm and skills its trainees exhibit. It is apparent, however, that the impact and spread of the program have been greatest where farmers have worked in groups after completing their courses and have organized others into groups that can carry out farmer-to-farmer training (Krishna, Uphoff, and Esman 1997, 296).

The Agroforestry Outreach Project in Haiti was designed to provide tree seedlings to individual farmers to plant on their farms based on private incentives. Local work groups were used as channels to reach farmers and encourage planting, but no effort was made to build local institutional capacities for maintaining agroforestry initiatives. Getting 60 million trees planted in a decade shows that a program can achieve major programmatic success without investing in local organization, so long as some social structures exist to work with and through. In this case, it is also evident that the program's sustainability was compromised by not having developed an institutional base in the countryside that could continue producing seedlings and promoting their planting.

Plan Puebla in Mexico started out essentially as an extension program, aiming to build a bridge between agricultural researchers and farmers. Its initial individualistic approach was replaced fairly quickly by a group-based strategy. Staff helped form farmer groups and gave them every encouragement, but no higher level of organization was promoted to speak for farmers or act on their behalf, even though staff later helped one regional farmers' organization get access to credit and technology.

The user committees formed in Rajasthan for each microwatershed being conserved and developed are, by topographical definition, independent of one another. The committees could and should be federated as the program gets better established and as local organizations gain more confidence and interest. This will enable watershed residents to share experiences and innovations. A federation could also become a political force supporting the program, which the government may or may not want to sustain.

That no effort was made to federate farmer associations in Mexico can be attributed partly to the government's disinterest in having any autonomous and effective peasant organizations, which has been the case in Indonesia as well. This is one reason that national or even state federations are uncommon in most countries. But a federated structure can go up to whatever level is sustainable and useful, and it need not become politicized in ways that invite partisan infiltration, conflict, or subordination. More will be said on this in Chapter 9.

Small base-level groups, which can improve programs' coherence and motivation while reducing transaction costs and problems of free riding, gain from being joined together in a larger structure. Our comparative study of rural development experience in sixteen Asian countries over a twenty-year period identified this as a key factor for success, in that such a structure of organization combined the advantages of solidarity with the advantages of scale (Uphoff and Esman 1974). Likewise, a quantified analysis of local organization experience found strong evidence that small base-level groups that are linked horizontally and vertically contribute much more to rural development than do larger ones.[8] A nested organizational structure with small groups at the base is more likely to be successful than larger, one-tier associations at the local level.

Having horizontal linkages among base-level organizations and with other kinds of institutions contributed even more to success. Those having horizontal linkages had average performance scores of 146 if they were linked vertically to one higher tier of organization and 166 if they were part of structures that had three or more tiers. The average score for those with no horizontal linkages was only 41, whereas those with occasional horizontal linkages scored 143 and those with regular links had the highest average scores, 200 (Esman and Uphoff 1984, 152). Thus, although vertical linkage is an important factor contributing to success, horizontal links are even more significant. This is consistent with Putnam's (1993) proposal that horizontal networks be considered a particularly productive form of "social capital."[9]

ORGANIZATIONAL PROCESS

Our analysis should not give the impression that merely establishing a desirable structural form of organization is a guarantee of success. *How* local organizations operate is crucial, such as whether they proceed in a learning process mode (Chapter 2) and what kind of leadership and personnel they have (Chapter 3). The potential benefits of solidarity and scale deriving from a multitier structure may not be realized if experimentation and revision are not encouraged and if motivation is lacking or misdirected.

Organizations are formed for the attainment of certain purposes, but these may change and can fade if memories attenuate and if procedures come to dominate purposes—a process that is all too common. Organizations, as well as their members, benefit from purposefulness and consistency. At the same time, there needs to be flexibility in how goals are attained, maintaining intelligent pragmatism in the pursuit of organizational purposes. This sets the stage for a discussion of organizational process, where two important and apparently contradictory principles—predictability and adaptability—need to be jointly optimized.

Predictability is, in important ways, a defining characteristic of organization. Situations that lack predictability are said to be disorganized or unorganized. At the same time, situations are continually changing, and different persons have different needs and capabilities, so always insisting on the same routines or performance is not necessarily the most cost-effective way to attain goals. Adaptability is a desirable characteristic, provided it does not become "ad hocracy." One can try to reconcile these two conflicting factors that contribute to success by maintaining purposefulness as the overriding norm, so that the form of action does not subordinate the substance of results. Programs need to evaluate continually their means in relation to their ends and to assess whether their ends remain valid.

It is often proposed that rural development programs build on existing or traditional organizations to the extent possible. Traditional modes of organization offer a number of advantages (Blunt and Warren 1996; March and Taqqu 1986). Since they are already in place, they can, at least in principle, be engaged quickly and with little start-up cost. They are familiar and meet existing expectations, so compliance should be easier to obtain. Since they are for the most part informal, they usually offer a pragmatism that is the envy of persons bound up in formal organizations. They are legitimate in the eyes of many if not all local people. They usually have well-established precedents and are not averse to starting new precedents, since they are not preoccupied with legal prescriptions for every subject.

As noted already, some successful programs such as DESEC in Bolivia and the Orangi Pilot Project in Pakistan adopted the policy of simply working with existing groups. But often this is not feasible, as suitable groups for large-scale development work may not exist or would not support equitable as well as participatory processes. In such situations, the catalyst approach, as discussed in Chapter 3, becomes more appropriate than trying to base programs on existing organizational structures. The process of development becomes one of creating organizational capacity, not just capitalizing on what exists.

Even when building up such capacity anew, however, some echoes and resonances of traditional practices and values can strengthen new initiatives. Although the participatory irrigation groups in Gal Oya, Sri Lanka, were started from scratch, the organizers were able to draw on the traditional practice known as *shramadana*. This institution justified people's contributing voluntary labor for agreed-upon community purposes by suggesting that they would gain religious "merit" by doing so. Although this practice was mostly moribund in Gal Oya because this was a resettlement area, it could be appealed to as a precedent for mobilizing work parties to improve water distribution by repairing and restoring irrigation channels. Collective action initiated on an informal basis helped create the sense of solidarity needed to undergird organizational efforts to institutionalize local problem solving. Similarly, involving the traditional roles of village elders when forming user committees helped legitimate and accelerate the formation of such organizations for watershed conservation in Rajasthan, India.

One of the most important process variables is the recruitment of leadership for local organizations. The kinds of persons who come to fill the responsible roles in these organizations have as much influence on performance as the structuring of these roles—their authority, their control over financial resources, and so forth. To the extent that local leadership is oriented more toward public-serving than self-aggrandizing outcomes, the whole climate of operation is more favorable for rural development, and those who are attracted to leadership positions will be similarly disposed. Conversely, having persons who are mostly self-serving or corrupt tends to bring in others like themselves as allies or as competitors, while potential leaders with more altruistic inclinations are repelled.

High standards for leadership start at the top, but rectitude gives only partial protection against rottenness at lower levels. Deliberate and consistent efforts from above are needed to recognize and reward "virtue" and to respond quickly and preemptively to any signs of "vice." This will set the tone for the whole organization. Leaders of successful programs understand this and act vigilantly, though as organizations grow large, it becomes more difficult to ensure that standards are uniformly maintained. Deviations cannot be monitored from the center as well as they can be policed from the periphery. This makes it important to have "transparent" operations that even uneducated members can follow and understand, with procedures for weeding out malpractice and nonperformance. Members' determination and ability to supervise internal operations can be reinforced by external checks and controls, but the latter should never be allowed to weaken members' resolve to maintain responsibility for the integrity of their own organization.

By creating opportunities for public-serving leaders to gain positions of responsibility, more capable and well-motivated persons emerge than was previously thought (Uphoff 1992a). The rural leadership cadre often looks rather thin because prominence is monopolized by a few well-connected or well-born persons. Leadership skills may be similar to musical aptitude or mechanical talent. More people have the potential to become excellent leaders than we know, because few are given a chance to demonstrate and develop their capacities.

The traditional Japanese system of rural local organization is one of the most intriguing in this regard. As in other countries in East Asia, rural society in Japan has been quite structured for perhaps 2,000 years. Traditional rulers clustered six to ten households in groups called *kumi*, which had a sense of collective identity and responsibility. Leadership of the *kumi* rotated annually among the respective heads of member households. This meant that all household heads (invariably male, given the era and the culture) were given a turn at demonstrating what, if any, leadership skills they had. If someone was incompetent, only a small group suffered at any one time, and for a limited period of time. Those persons who showed leadership skills, aptitude, and initiative were chosen for leadership roles within the village and at higher levels. Systematic testing of all persons who might have talent for leadership meant that rural life could be rather effectively self-managed, as was consistent with the feudal social system prevailing up to the modern era in Japan (Aqua 1982).

Such a system can be adapted elsewhere if organizations are structured with small base-level groups. The cost of having poor management for some groups at any one time can be more than compensated for by having a larger pool of leadership to fill higher-level positions throughout the organization. This principle of rotation has been adopted for the five-member borrower groups participating in the Grameen Bank. BRAC similarly rotates the position of secretary in the small groups within its village organizations to get more membership involvement.[10]

A general observation from successful programs is that they have avoided unnecessary formalization of their operations and procedures, keeping these as simple and transparent as possible. The Grameen Bank, for example, has minimized the use of legal instruments in its lending operations, keeping transactions simple and basing them on trust and mutual responsibility among borrower-members. It seeks to maintain openness in its operations, describing them as containing "no secrets." Six-S similarly emphasizes simplicity in its regulations and decision-making processes, talking about "accounts in the sunlight" so that there will be a high degree of transparency in financial operations. The Rajasthan watershed conservation program likewise stresses openness, accountability, and representative management for all resource transactions. Conducting all business in full public view, a "goldfish bowl" approach, is important for overcoming the distrust and skepticism that local populations with limited literacy have developed toward programs that are offered from outside. A little time is required to gain credibility and acceptance, but once it becomes clear that this will be a consistent policy, the responses are likely to be positive and constructive, as seen from the experience of the Self-Employed Women's Association (SEWA) in India (Rose 1992).

The matter of time is important. Progress need not be slow, but it should not be rushed. Putting a nominal organization in place does not accomplish much unless the processes that it seeks to institutionalize acquire a vitality of their own. In the Gal Oya program, a decision was made to start informally, recognizing that government-created formal organizations in rural areas had been mostly unsuccessful, usually disappearing after a few months of induced activity. Farmers were quite aware of the deficiencies of such an approach, whereby an organization was said to exist if a ready-made constitution had been approved and a slate of officers elected. Farmers preferred a structure that was simple and informal, especially at the lowest levels, but that became more complex and formalized toward the top, where larger amounts of money, contracts, and policy representation were involved. The idea of starting work on an informal basis and then creating more formal organizations later had not occurred to officials, who were interested in having the organizational equivalent of "body counts." But it made sense to farmers, who had seen much effort wasted and many hopes disappointed by programs that had settled for nominal rather than committed and effective participation.

There is a need for local organizations to acquire legal status and recognition at some point, to have certain rights and powers that enable them to act legally on behalf of their members. Starting on an informal basis, as suggested above, is intended to avoid situations in which a "supply" of organization is offered to people before there is "demand" for it. But groups that have become a social reality also need a legal personality, through incorporation according to the law or through government recognition and enrollment that entitles the group to defined rights. This subjects organizations to certain regulations, some of which can be constraining, but having certain regulatory processes also provides some benefits. Although organizations need to be vigilant against financial and other irregularities and not delegate all control and responsibility to government agencies, it is helpful to have outside scrutiny as an additional check and deterrent. Organizations need registration or recognition to be able to open bank accounts, make contracts, take loans, and go to court to uphold their interests. Without such authority, encroachment of political and bureaucratic interests can destroy what members are trying to achieve. Acquiring legal status, although never a sufficient condition for success, is a necessary part of the process of organizational development.

ENCOURAGING PARTICIPATION

Participation in all its aspects, including participation in benefits as well as in decision making, implementation, and evaluation, is perhaps the most central feature of successful rural development (Cohen and Uphoff 1980). Organizational structures and roles should be fashioned to support ongoing processes of participation that enlist people's ideas and ideals as well as their material contributions and management skills.

The rhetoric of participation often calls for maximum involvement of people in all aspects of program design and operation or, in the words used for the U.S. War on Poverty, "maximum feasible participation." Participation, however, has costs as well as benefits, so maximum participation is not likely to be desirable. These costs in terms of time, forgone income opportunities, and money and other contributions and in tensions with neighbors can become excessive relative to their associated benefits. Besides, whenever there is more than one objective, it is better to seek optimizing outcomes rather than to try to maximize any single goal.

Policy makers, planners, and program managers thus should think in terms of *optimum* participation, because this is how rural people, conscious of the costs that they bear, regard their options.[11] Deciding what is optimal should itself be determined in a participatory way, based on the assessments of rural people about how much involvement in what kinds of decisions and activities would best serve their needs. In fact, since few programs have approached an optimal level or extent of participation, we should consider how to increase and make effective people's involvement in the many tasks of rural development.

Although there are different ways in which rural people can participate in their own development, the process best begins with decision making, which is the essence of empowerment. What are the principal needs and problems? What are promising and reasonable solutions? How should costs be apportioned? How would responsibilities be allocated or shared? What technologies are likely to be effective and accepted?

There is increasing appreciation of the value of having local or indigenous knowledge inform development plans and decisions.[12] Better decisions should be possible if local people add their knowledge to that which more formally and technically educated persons can bring to development efforts; local and outside ("expert") knowledge each become more effective when they are combined.[13] Also, it is more likely that local people will accept responsibility for carrying out plans and programs if they have been actively involved in shaping these decisions. A successful program is one that becomes truly "localized" in its operation.

Beyond initial decisions to carry out a localized activity as part of a larger program, such as programs for credit, agricultural improvement, or watershed conservation, there will be important ongoing management decisions to be made. Practically all the successful rural development programs reported in *Reasons for Hope* stressed the importance of participatory management. They also support the finding of our earlier study that the most beneficial decision-making system is a combination of some kind of assembly that involves all the membership and some form of committee structure, where responsibility for management can be fixed with a few selected and accountable persons (Esman and Uphoff 1984, 144–6).

A variety of arrangements can support a participatory system of rural development. The irrigation associations set up under the NIA in the Philippines have a decision-making structure that explicitly aims to ensure participation as well as accountability. There is a general assembly that serves as a watchdog over the work of the officers and the executive committee. Local traditions in that country support fairly elaborate structures of organization, with many roles and much division of labor. For example, there is a special committee set up during construction projects to monitor quantity and quality of materials to ensure that members and the government are getting their money's worth.

More generalized duties and roles are found in places with stronger traditional institutions, such as in the West African Sahel or the South American Andes. Organizations working under Six-S auspices at various levels operate mostly in the general assembly mode, with broad participation in all decisions on the use of funds. DESEC in Bolivia similarly reports that all important decisions are left to the membership at large so that oversight is maintained and a critical mass of leadership skills is developed in the membership as a matter of institutional capacity building.

Although it is often thought that democratic processes of participation should culminate in voting, often by secret ballot, to determine the majority view, we are impressed by the extent to which decision making by consensus seems more satisfactory, accommodating various local interests and avoiding divisions and polarization. The interests of poorer or weaker sectors may not be well served by a voting system, because majority decisions, especially those made by a narrow majority, are not easily enforceable in the rural periphery. When a matter has been discussed openly and all stakeholders have publicly given assent, implementation becomes easier, since this decision becomes the operating assumption for all concerned.[14]

Some rural development programs, more often in Asia than in Africa or Latin America, have fairly formalized systems of management. But even a huge organization such as BRAC, with an annual budget of $86 million, builds participation at local levels into its operation. Its management information system, which keeps the center apprised of what is going on at various levels outside Dhaka, can also provide information that is useful for local decision makers, thereby helping to maintain local accountability.

The SANASA credit cooperatives in Sri Lanka have a process for continually querying their base-level organizations, called primary societies, about needs and performance so that members can initiate SANASA policies from the grassroots level. In 1993, SANASA undertook a systematic effort to formulate a five-year plan from the bottom up. Primary societies contributed the initial ideas, which were combined and refined as the planning process moved up through cluster, divisional, and district organizations. The final plan was formulated and approved at the national level by delegates from the levels below. One purpose of such a structured process was to activate the membership and to identify more persons who could and would assume leadership positions at all levels in the years ahead.

SANASA is unusual in that it invests significant resources in education programs for members at various levels, as discussed in Chapter 6. Its programs aim to provide more than technical skills such as bookkeeping and the ability to run meetings. Their purpose is also to encourage independent assessments and awareness, getting people to think more systematically about the future. SANASA is one of the few organizations that has been able to institutionalize on a large scale the democratic principles of cooperative philosophy and organization. This does not happen without considerable planning and experimentation, backed by systematic investment of both leadership time and organizational finances. Assistance from overseas nongovernmental organizations has been important for SANASA, as much for its flexibility and ideological support as for the monetary amount. This is an example of where the quality of aid matters more than its quantity, as considered in Chapter 8.

Participation by Women

Just as special provision needs to be made for educational programs that give members more skills and motivation for participation, special efforts are called for if there is to be substantial participation by women. It is encouraging to see that astute program leadership has been able to enhance women's roles and opportunities, even in countries where women's autonomy and public participation have been disparaged (Abed and Chowdhury 1997; Khan 1997; Lovell 1992; Yunus 1997). In Bangladesh, over 90 percent of the Grameen Bank's borrowers are women, despite traditional exclusion of women from access to credit. To surmount gender barriers in that country, BRAC often requires a community to form a women's village organization before support will be given to a men's village organization. This may cause some initial opposition, mostly from men, but once the groups are formed and functioning, the fact that women's education and income opportunities also benefit the rest of the household undercuts most lingering resistance. Women make up between 10 and 80 percent of participants in different BRAC programs. The Orangi Pilot Project in Pakistan has faced some fierce resistance from conservative religious leaders because it elicited active participation by women, despite their history of social segregation and lack of education.[15] In Sri Lanka, a South Asian country where women's opportunities have become greater over the past fifty years, 3,000 of the 7,000 savings societies in SANASA are made up of women.

This raises the question whether women's participation should be separate or segregated. The answer should come from working with rural people, letting them determine what arrangements will be culturally feasible and socioeconomically beneficial. The fact that a program supported from outside is concerned with women's status and advancement helps start that process, but working out a strategy for implementation is a matter for those who must live with its consequences. Some of the most successful rural development programs started promoting women's opportunities twenty or even thirty years ago, before there were conferences or decades devoted to women's issues.

There are some good pragmatic reasons for making sure that women have equal access to program benefits and take leadership positions. In many rural communities, women are considered more trustworthy when it comes to handling money and are chosen as treasurers, as reported from the Philippines (Bagadion 1997, 159). The National Dairy Development Board in India has made a series of efforts to increase the quantity and quality of women's participation in dairy cooperative management, because women do 85 percent or more of the work involved in milk production (Thomas Carter, personal communication).

The integrated pest management program in Indonesia started out with mostly male participants, accepting the prevailing notion that religious beliefs militated against women participating in the same training programs with men. But women also need training in pest management, because they perform a significant share of crop production tasks, so separate classes were started for them. Still, few women were brought into the training effort. When mixed classes were started, the results for both men and women were better than with separate training, provided there were more than a few women; there needed to be at least five women in a group to keep them from being marginalized in discussions. Earlier fears of social problems have been replaced by satisfaction that the program is strengthened—for men as well as for women—by integrating women into it.[16]

In areas such as health and family planning, women's participation is obviously essential. The Population and Development Association in Thailand, the Iringa nutrition and health program in Tanzania, and the Posyandu/women's program in Indonesia have depended largely on the efforts and local leadership of women (Mechai 1997; Jonsson, Ljungqvist, and Yambi 1993; Rohde 1993). This would be expected, because women are expected to have more responsibility for raising and nurturing families. But the self-help rural water supply program in Malawi, which required substantial mobilization of physical labor to install pipelines from mountainsides down to villages, was also carried out mostly by women; for them, saving time and effort when acquiring domestic water was a great incentive.[17] Women often have a great stake in improving returns from agricultural production, so they should be entitled to participate in any and all sector activities as fully and at as high a level as sociocultural circumstances—and their own time and energy and interest—will permit. We have observed that the success of rural development programs appears to correlate positively with the active participation of women, though we do not have quantitative evidence of this.[18]

A continuing controversy concerns whether local organizations should be segregated by gender or integrated. This is similar to the question of whether group membership and services should be restricted to persons below the poverty line or open to all who will share in the costs as well as receive the benefits. We accept the compelling arguments made by Ela Bhatt, founder of SEWA in India, for separate women's organizations justified by the particularly impoverished and oppressed circumstances of those women who have been brought into SEWA (Rose 1992).

For similar reasons, the Grameen Bank and BRAC in Bangladesh have limited participation to the poorer sections of rural communities, with most of the organizations being all women. But it is not clear that this will be universally the best strategy for developmental change, because of the importance of large-scale solidarity and cooperation among disadvantaged persons. As seen below, it can be argued that under some circumstances the poor, like women, may benefit more from heterogeneous associations. We are persuaded that under most conditions and for many if not all developmental purposes, integrated organizations are likely to have more long-term impact. But even at the end of the twentieth century, in many parts of the Third World, structures that are devoted exclusively to the opportunities and advancement of women are still necessary and justified.

Participation by Other Disadvantaged Groups

A similar conclusion applies regarding participation for the lowest strata of the rural poor or minorities suffering some social stigma and economic deprivation. The experience of BRAC argues against having heterogeneous organizations so that the interests of all group members will be more compatible. BRAC started its rural development efforts in 1972 working with village organizations encompassing the whole community. Within a few years, it found that richer elements were monopolizing benefits intended for the poor, which led BRAC to adopt an "exclusive" strategy whereby it works only with homogeneous groups of the poor, generally separated between women and men as well.

An opposite strategy was developed by the SANASA savings movement, which makes special efforts to bring the poorer elements of rural communities into its primary societies. Its educational programs seek to orient all members toward the advantages of collective action and to support poverty alleviation efforts. A study found that 52 percent of SANASA members were below the poverty line established by the government, compared with 46 percent of the rural population as a whole. So although it may not include all of the poorest of the poor, SANASA has brought many of them into a self-financed program for economic improvement. Since loans are available to all members, and not just in proportion to savings accumulated, SANASA gives poorer members access to the resources of richer members, a reversal of the usual direction of flow.[19] The head of SANASA suggests that if only the poor could belong to the savings groups, these would have less management capacity (Kiriwandeniya 1997, 67). As long as the rules governing savings and loans are equitable— indeed, somewhat biased in favor of the poor—an "inclusive" approach can benefit the poor. The crucial thing is to hold leadership—of any social class—accountable. This is done through educational programs and through transparency in transactions, as already discussed.

Disadvantaged groups, being generally less educated, have the greatest need for such openness. Along with transparency, it is important that procedures be kept simple and easily comprehensible. Otherwise, participation by the poor can be discouraged or made ineffective by various manipulations. Once disaffected, their active involvement becomes much less likely. The factors of organizational structure and process discussed in the first part of this chapter are important influences on participation, particularly by marginal and disadvantaged groups.

Participation by Youth

Any rural development programs that expect to be successful into the future need to give attention to the roles that young people, both male and female, can play in them. Although the world has been dragged, often unwillingly, to confront and redress the disabilities of sexism, a similar kind of discrimination, ageism, remains largely ignored. Most cultures require the young, even persons in their twenties and possibly thirties, to defer to their elders. Until they are married, young men and women have to be content with low status and little voice in community affairs.

Yet if rural development programs are to be sustainable, they need a continuing infusion of new leadership and energy as time takes its toll on present leaders. There is a pervasive and expanding "world culture" that is attracting young people out of rural areas and into towns and cities, usually to an uncertain but potentially glamorous future. Often the most enterprising and ambitious youth are leaving, so the future cadre of leadership in rural communities is likely to be less capable and energetic than at present, which would represent a real loss in human capital. Alternatively, if young people can find opportunities for respect and achievement at home, they will be more likely to seek their fortunes locally, making their natal communities as productive and pleasing as possible.

Few of the successful programs we have surveyed have made much of an attempt to enlist the best efforts of the youth. An exception is Six-S in the Sahel, which was built on the opportunity that the movement's initiators saw for putting to good use the underutilized time and talents of village youth. During the long annual dry season, young people had the choice of migrating to find work elsewhere or idling away their time. Although elders appreciated and supported the new initiatives that Six-S supported, it was the youth who grasped the opportunity to demonstrate their capabilities by making their home communities more productive year-round.

The SANASA savings societies in Sri Lanka take an active approach to youth participation. They sponsor youth clubs, and children's savings societies, and preschool facilities are also supported by primary societies. This is intended partly to encourage values and habits of thriftiness and good management, but it also grooms a cadre of young leadership that can carry forward the tasks and ideals that SANASA was established to further.

Some other programs have made provision for youth participation, but few have given this priority. As we look ahead to the next decade or two of rural development, we anticipate that there could be a kind of cultural struggle, a Kulturkampf, as the values of present rural societies come under attack by the aspirations and expectations of a new generation whose imaginations and appetites have become enlarged in an age of satellite communication and video. Elders will find that the values they respect, and often they themselves, will be rejected as young people strive to find fulfilling identities and promising futures in a world that the elders will never see.

It is not a certainty that the spread of modern and commercial values will displace traditional and more national ones, but this outcome is more likely to the extent that community management and leadership remain the property of the older generation, with the next one having to wait its turn. If the younger generation is not incorporated into rural development efforts in meaningful and fulfilling ways, it will not wait. The average age of rural populations is already moving steadily upward as youth relocate to urban areas. If this continues, the possibilities for significant and sustainable rural development will be lost, not dramatically, but over time.

CREATING THE RIGHT ENVIRONMENT

Encouraging participation is something that practically by definition comes from above or outside. One should not assume that participation will automatically or easily "bubble up" from below. The situation in developing countries represents a current equilibrium between forces that would promote participation and those that would inhibit or even repress it. A significant complex of factors, varying from country to country as well as community to community, maintains a political, economic, and social status quo that keeps the large majority of rural people from having much voice in or control over their lives. Poverty, prejudice, despair, paternalism, local power structures, legal and regulatory restrictions, adverse past experiences, and other forces commonly discourage people from playing more active roles in changing their circumstances and opportunities. Yet there are encouraging examples of emergent local activism and institutional development that can change the participation equation.

Programs such as those highlighted in *Reasons for Hope* have offered many rural people ways to gain more benefits from their participation, so that the costs involved—and there are always some costs to be considered—appear worthwhile. Indeed, participation that is costless is unlikely to produce much long-term benefit, because there will be no investment of local resources in making it succeed. Successful rural development is not about "free lunches" but rather about being able to grow one's own food and prepare it, to have sufficient nutrition of one's own making and liking. The analogy, of course, is not just for food and nutrition; it encompasses other sectors such as education, health, infrastructure, and public services. The challenge for rural development programs is to create opportunities whereby participation by local people in various facets of economic, social, and political advancement will yield sufficient benefits—and reinvestment—that present and future generations may exercise greater control over their lives and the resources they create.

NOTES

1. We do not use the standard term *beneficiaries*, because this designation assumes that people will necessarily benefit from particular development initiatives, when in fact, this is an open question. Not all good intentions get fulfilled. The term has self-congratulatory, even patronizing implications that it is best to avoid. If the word *beneficiaries* is used, it should be accompanied by the adjective *intended*.

2. The concept of *social infrastructure* is applied here in a micro sense to explain the effectiveness of local planning and implementation. It also has macro implications for concerns of equity and democratization. The managing director of the National Dairy Development Board in India speaks of the need for institutions that the poor can hold accountable and that are responsive to their needs. Cooperatives represent "real growth in the nation's social and political capital as a plurality of local institutions is created and strengthened" (Kurien 1997, 106). Such organizations can have systemic benefits for what is increasingly referred to as "civil society" that go beyond their membership or technical performance.

3. These are similar to the traditional labor-exchange groups that were enlisted for watershed conservation work in the Massaide region of Haiti, analyzed by White and Runge (1994). This project was remarkably successful under adverse conditions, but the work was done with no aim of creating long-term, sustainable local capacities. So although the Massaide case was very productive, it was not included in our selection of successful cases, since the local efforts are not ongoing. About 40 percent of the labor for soil conservation structures was contributed by persons residing outside the particular watershed and thus not "beneficiaries" of the collective action. The performance of these *groupmans* is an indication of the potential in traditional organizations. Whether these can (or

should) be engaged in development efforts depends on many factors, as discussed by March and Taqqu (1986).

4. In a previous study of local organizations' contribution to rural development, we calculated overall performance scores to be 45 for local organizations that were unlinked (autonomous, isolated), 84 for those in two-tier structures, 117 for those in three-tier structures, and 143 if federated in structures with four or more tiers (Esman and Uphoff 1984, 149). Jain (1994, 1366) argues, correctly, that the goal is not to create a large number of autonomous, independent local organizations but instead to develop an apex organization that works through the grassroots. However, he incorrectly sees his conclusion as different from previous work done at Cornell on this subject. Although he cites Uphoff and Esman (1974) in his references, he appears to have missed its central argument in favor of multiple levels of organization (discussed later in this chapter).

5. This has not been encouraged by advisers who helped form the organizations, because of the danger that a national structure could be captured by partisan political leadership, undermining its ability to meet all members' needs.

6. In a previous analysis of local institutional development, ten levels at which decision making and action can occur were identified, ranging from the individual level up to the international level. In between are the household, the group, the village or community, the locality (a set of communities), the subdistrict, the district, the province or state, and the nation (Uphoff 1986b, 10–4).

7. Lecomte says that this structure was developed to avoid the "parochialism and egotism" of the village, which would likely judge in its own favor. When larger numbers of villagers convene to decide financial allocation matters, they act as constructive checks on one another, seeking to raise overall zone performance (Lecomte and Krishna 1997, 82).

8. Other things being equal, larger groups had a somewhat higher average net performance score (87) compared with smaller groups (73). But when small groups were linked to several higher levels in a federated structure, their average net score was 134, compared with 108 for large groups having such linkage (Esman and Uphoff 1984, 150).

9. Putnam (1993), unfortunately, equates vertical linkages with clientelism and subordination, which are asymmetrical and nonaccountable. Vertical relations can be more reciprocating and equitable. We interpret the data as meaning that vertical linkages can be almost as productive as horizontal ones if accountability is maintained.

10. One can ask whether requiring such rotation is not an infringement on local groups' right and responsibility of self-determination. Farmers in Gal Oya rejected our suggestion that representatives for their field channel groups be rotated, saying that such a decision should be left to each group—a reasonable justification. They did, however, decide to rotate annually the farmer-representatives who served on the District Agriculture Committee, an official body chaired by the district minister, to which they were invited to send four members. This decision was made by farmers in order to broaden their top leadership

cadre and to keep any individuals from becoming too close to officials, also a reasonable consideration.

11. We have quantified evidence of this from surveys and experience in the irrigation sector in Sri Lanka, where farmers' preference for more participatory management is a clear function of the net gains that could be achieved in agricultural productivity from their direct (versus indirect) involvement in water management (Uphoff, Wickramasinghe, and Wijayaratna 1990).

12. Although the term *indigenous knowledge* has become widespread in the literature, we favor the concept of *local knowledge* because that does not prejudge its origins. Knowledge provided by rural people may be contemporary rather than primordial, implied by the word *indigenous*, or it may have been brought from some other place—by migrants, for example—and thus not be indigenous to the area. *Local knowledge* is a more inclusive term and usually more apt.

13. From the literature, we know of cases in the Philippines, Nepal, and Mexico in which design engineers planned diversion dams for irrigation systems that local residents said would not be suitable for that particular location, given the placement and the materials proposed for the dam and considering the occasional high flows of water there. The technicians insisted that their scientific calculations provided sufficient basis for proceeding with their design, and construction went ahead. But in all three cases, farmers' objections were confirmed when the dams washed out within a year. If local knowledge should have been factored into decisions as technical as designing a dam, incorporating it into program designs in which human factors are involved is surely advisable.

14. When it comes to the election of leaders, however, secret balloting may be the only way that the interests of the vulnerable and disadvantaged can be effectively expressed.

15. Akhtar Hameed Khan, the initiator of the Orangi Pilot Project (OPP), was arrested and charged with blasphemy in 1993. The fabricated accusation, which carried a possible capital penalty, was eventually dropped. What most aroused conservative ire and precipitated the action against him was apparently the economic and educational opportunities that the OPP had opened up for women and girls.

16. Smyth (1995) reports on a 1993 study of 200 farmer field schools: 169 had only men, 3 had only women, and 28 were mixed. In general, women were found to be more active and creative in discussions, and their observations were more detailed compared with those of men. They were also more willing to ask questions and to include consideration of economic issues. Despite earlier fears that women's social and household obligations would interfere with their participation, women had a higher attendance rate (96 percent) than men (87 percent). In mixed groups, men were more argumentative, and women worked to create harmony and thus arrive at decisions more easily. In all-male groups, decision making was more contentious and implementation more difficult. "In all cases, women's participation in IPM [farmer field schools] was found to be of benefit to the entire group process and has been strongly endorsed [by the national program]" (Smyth 1995, 11).

17. Such predominance of women can be a matter of exploitation more than of participation. Especially when it comes to heavy labor, programs should be concerned with gender equity.

18. Although correlation does not establish causation, the National Dairy Development Board in India has found that the rate of growth in the procurement of milk by district unions is positively correlated with the growth of women's membership (Thomas Carter, personal communication).

19. The very richest persons in communities are not likely to join SANASA, partly because of its egalitarian ideology, but also because they have other, more lucrative options for using their surplus income. Many middle- and upper-middle-class rural residents do become members, however. They are paid a reasonably attractive rate of interest on their savings, and they enjoy greater flexibility and convenience when saving with SANASA than when they put their money into a bank.

5 Management, Planning, and Implementation

S uccessful rural development programs are distinctive for their philosophy, their leadership, and their engagement of local people's energies
and abilities, as seen in preceding chapters. But more is needed than inspiration and participation. A close look at successful experiences shows
much attention being paid to factors such as operational routines, incentives, delegation of responsibility, management of finances, and information systems. Although opportunities for individual initiative and local
adaptation are built into such programs, much thought goes into achieving
predictability, reliability, efficiency, and effectiveness. In seeking to avoid
the disabling effects of becoming bureaucratic, programs do not go to the
other extreme of simple spontaneity. If those who provide leadership do
not relish the tasks of managing increasingly large and complex operations, they need to get assistance from others who can contribute such
skills.

Program managers are responsible for mobilizing, allocating, and utilizing available resources in ways that achieve the objectives of the organization most reliably, quickly, and efficiently. The kinds of resources
involved are many. Most can be categorized under the headings of human,
financial, and material resources—people, money, and physical inputs.
Financial management receives the most attention, because funds often
appear to be the most constraining resources, inasmuch as various other
constraints can be alleviated with sufficient budget, and because financial
accountability has damaging legal consequences if breached. But as will
be argued, personnel management is even more important, because it
influences all other aspects of performance. Management of material
resources, usually referred to as logistics, is less complex than the other
two, but breakdowns in this domain can have adverse consequences for
both personnel and financial management. So it should not be derogated,
although it can be delegated. It is important to fashion and maintain an
effective team effort, while at the same time attending carefully to mun-
dane things such as scheduling and maintenance.

Along with the application of incentives, discussed later in this chapter, there are two widely used ways of increasing the productivity of material and human resources—use of improved technology and provision of training. These are addressed in a chapter of their own (Chapter 6), drawing implications from successful rural development programs for how these means can be employed most effectively. A resource for management left out of the usual "manpower, money, materials" formulation is information. Because it has rather special characteristics as a resource and is not usually considered in resource terms, it is given a chapter of its own (Chapter 7), which covers the role of monitoring and evaluation in creating sustainable organizational capacities.

The responsibilities of managers can be analyzed in terms of their dealing with internal and external task environments. The internal task environment includes those persons, roles, and relationships over which a manager has some degree of control, being able to decide on personnel, budgets, delegation of authority, and information flows; the external task environment contains actors, institutions, and resources that a manager can only hope to influence, not having any direct means of control. In this chapter, we consider lessons learned about dealing with the internal task environment, setting up systems and processes that facilitate execution of the diverse tasks of program implementation. We reserve for later chapters the consideration of strategies for dealing with the external task environment—forging supportive linkages with other organizations (Chapter 8) and mobilizing or mitigating political forces (Chapter 9).

Such forces surely play an important part in organizational success, but external support derives at least as much from good and efficient performance as from the political skills of top leadership. Although efficient and honest management does not guarantee success, failing to meet expectations in this regard will surely undermine a program. Especially in socioeconomic settings where efficiency, equity, and honesty are not widespread, demonstrating these qualities gives a program great advantages with the publics it intends to serve. This even gains the grudging if not enthusiastic support of politicians and bureaucrats who might not be persuaded to cooperate simply on the grounds of helping the disadvantaged. Reservations and resistance can be weakened by a statistic such as the one the Anand-model dairy cooperatives can boast of in India: 70 percent of the consumer rupee spent for milk and milk products gets back to their small producer-members. This efficiency helped the Anand cooperatives when they had tens and hundreds of thousands of members; now that there are 9.5 million, the ability of these cooperatives to stand up to political pressure is great, though still dependent on continued good management.

Like any other organization, a development organization must recruit, deploy, train, and motivate staff; it must assign tasks and ensure a dependable flow of resources to sustain operations; it must monitor performance, rewarding that which is good and diminishing that which is poor; and it must continually adjust strategy and tactics to deal with changes in the environment, both internal and external. These management tasks are thus very similar to those that must be performed for other types of enterprises in the private or the public sector. But the manner in which each of these tasks is performed differs substantially.

More than the health and well-being of the development agency itself, the prospects of and the progress made by the publics it serves provide the main measure of its success. The critical characteristic of rural development management that sets it apart from most other kinds of management is that authority and responsibility must be shared not only with rank-and-file staff members but also with program members or clients. This goes beyond merely consulting with them to determine their needs and preferences. It requires passing over some roles traditionally played by management. With a participatory approach, members and clients become closely associated with the program, sharing its goals and providing some part of its resources, as well as contributing to their management.

DEVOLVED MANAGEMENT

Given this realization, the tasks of management should be seen as *co*-management, where the objective is not to operate a program for rural people and communities so much as to set up a program that will be managed with them, devolving significant authority to local institutions. This is quite a radical idea. How many commercial banks in the world allow their borrowers to decide among themselves the amount of loans and the conditions under which they will be made? Any bank foolish enough to adopt such a practice seems a good candidate to go out of business. Yet one of the most successful programs of rural credit, the Grameen Bank in Bangladesh, does this. It has 2 million borrowers, with a recovery rate of more than 95 percent. Its success has resulted largely from handing key operational decisions over to borrowers, having created acceptable incentives that enhance the probability of repayment.

Utility companies do not usually expect and assist their customers to co-manage the facilities that deliver water or dispose of sewage. But the self-help rural water supply program in Malawi and the Orangi Pilot Program in Pakistan do just that, as do the national irrigation programs in the Philippines and Sri Lanka, which share with water users the financing and management of the irrigation systems' operation and maintenance.[1] Effectiveness and cost-effective performance are achieved not by the program managers trying to make all the decisions themselves or even attempting to please their customers. Rather, a system is created with incentives and support from higher levels whereby persons at local levels take responsibility and use it productively.

This mode of operation resembles what Peters and Waterman (1982) found in their study of successful U.S. corporations—what they call a "loose-tight" approach to management. With agreement on goals, congruent incentives, and a shared set of values that bind persons operating at all levels of the enterprise, control from the top can be relaxed, delegating much decision making to lower levels of the organization and giving them the opportunity for initiative and innovation. Consistency in organizational performance is achieved not by detailed management from above but by dispersed problem-solving efforts guided by widely shared norms and goals.

Grameen Bank borrowers want to improve their economic and social positions at least as much as the bank wants to see their situations enhanced. Five-member groups determine which members will get loans and for what purpose, and they know that if the loan cannot be or is not repaid, the rest of them will lose their access to Grameen Bank credit. The members—most of them poor, illiterate women—know one another, their characters, capabilities, and intentions better than any bank officer could. They also know their local economic environment firsthand. Bank staff do what they do best, such as handle paperwork and provide training to group members. Staff cannot make better decisions than members about which individuals are creditworthy and which investment opportunities are worth pursuing. The bank staff concentrate on doing well those tasks for which they have comparative advantage.

Similarly, in the Orangi program, efforts to develop more appropriate technology were undertaken by the central technical team, while supervision and collection of funds for projects on each lane were devolved to lane committees. Neighbors along a lane in a squatter settlement all have an interest in each of them getting effective sewerage. If any household fails to join the program and to meet its obligations in maintaining waste removal, its neighbors suffer in terms of aesthetics, health, and economics. There are good reasons why everyone on a lane should join the program and make contributions to it once it is shown to be technically and economically feasible. The program developed a system for installing and maintaining sewerage facilities based on local ideas and evaluations, working out appropriate technologies, as discussed in Chapter 6. Once the system was developed, major decisions could be left to local residents, such as whom to hire to supervise construction and how much payment would be in cash and how much in kind. This made overall management easier than if the central program management attempted to plan and implement all the local details of the sewerage system.

This is a different approach to management from that conventionally proposed; to achieve their objectives, managers are usually advised to maintain control over as many resources and decisions as possible, not jeopardizing their success by letting others take initiative. The approach we see again and again with the successful cases of rural development is the evolution of a shared understanding among all partners of their respective roles, rights, and responsibilities. The term *evolution* is used because these roles are not planned in advance and laid down from above, although there are usually some initial assumptions made. The Grameen Bank requirement that the base groups of borrowers have five members looks like a rigid requirement. But it was arrived at after several years of experience, when the conclusion was reached that group formation and maintenance were facilitated by focusing on who would be reliable fellow members rather than on how many members would be too few or too many. The latter question could be needlessly divisive, and having a fixed number has not proved to be an impediment to forming effective groups.

An advanced example of co-management, taken to the extreme that the central organization does very little managing, is the Six-S association in West Africa. All planning starts with small groups at the village level. They bring plans to a zonal assembly where thirty to fifty villages are represented. Proposed activities are discussed, and the funds provided to the zone by Six-S from donor grants are allocated among proposed village projects according to assessments of need, capability, equity, and any other criteria that members of the local assembly think important. The groups monitor and discipline one another as they seek funding from the same pool of money to combat the constraints of the long dry season in the Sahelian region. Any group's project can be selected if others can be convinced of its merits. The central office has no need to police the use of funds when member groups are competing in terms of viable and valuable activities that they are in the best position to assess. Management of activities is left to the respective villages. This greatly reduces the workload of the central organization and has made it possible for a very small staff to assist hundreds of thousands of villagers spread across the Sahel, achieving more efficient and adaptive use of resources over a large area.

Several arguments support a strategy of co-management. In rural development, viable and sustainable solutions need to be location-specific to get the best and most cost-effective use of resources, a conclusion now being affirmed in the development administration literature.[2] Moreover, since the aim is to achieve long-term self-management and maintenance of programs, local people might as well learn from the outset how to take on and carry out responsibilities. The concept of turnover, in the sense that out-side agents create a capacity and then hand it over to local communities to be maintained, is generally fallacious, because of the need to learn by doing and to acquire a sense of ownership in the process.

There is also a practical consideration that delegating decisions to local bodies can produce better outcomes even in the short run, because of more complete knowledge and more opportunity for self-policing. It has been feared by many that local politics and favoritism would produce a less desirable distribution with delegated decision making, but data from Rajasthan show that locally made decisions met the state's criteria better than it had been able to do itself with regard to electricity distribution. Once allocations were made closer to the grassroots and in open meetings, and the claims of applicant villages could be scrutinized and challenged in public, the allocation of connections was significantly more congruent with productivity and equity objectives than when decisions were made by officials, who were more susceptible to behind-the-scenes manipulation by influential political actors.[3] Contributing to this success was not just trans-parency, important though that was, but also the operation of devolved management, whereby agreed-upon criteria pointed out the directions for decision making and set parameters within which decisions should be made. With such a system in place, local knowledge could be mobilized and well utilized.

PARTICIPATORY MANAGEMENT

As noted previously, we do not find a contradiction between strong, active leadership and widespread, empowered participation in successful rural development programs. Leadership should be sought and evident at all levels of the organization. The National Irrigation Administration (NIA) in the Philippines follows the rule of thumb that there should be at least one leader for every ten members, so that leadership is diffused through-out the program. There is a need to stimulate the input of ideas and the assumption of management functions among all members to achieve a widespread sense of responsibility for the program and its success. The French concept of *responsibilization* would be a useful concept to have in English. An important role of leadership is to create a framework of roles, procedures, and expectations within which this process can occur.

Participatory management applies not only to the local organizations to which authority for program operations is devolved but also to the staff of the central organization, particularly its field staff. A number of programs have independently developed the concept of a team approach to decentralized management. Both the Gal Oya irrigation project in Sri Lanka and the Rajasthan watershed and soil conservation program in India delegated responsibility for planning, implementing, and evaluating work to multidisciplinary groups—of organizers in one case, of technicians in the other. Individual members of the team each had specific geographic areas of responsibility, while the whole team was collectively responsible for a combined area. This made them interdependent, as each needed the help of other members with different competencies from time to time. In the Rajasthan case, each official was in charge of working with the user groups in a particular microwatershed, while team members collectively looked after the whole watershed. Satisfaction came from both personal and group accomplishments. Any deficiencies in performance were noted and remedied more quickly than if the whole area had been divided among individual staff for separate supervision. This system of organization, which contrasts with the usual hierarchical one in which subordinates report to superiors, created a regime of self-management within the staff that adopted a problem-solving posture. This produced both higher morale and better results (Wijayaratna and Uphoff 1997; Krishna 1997).[4]

In the Iringa child nutrition program, at the district level, both line and sector agencies placed their relevant staff under a district coordinator for child survival and development who was chosen from among the personnel of the participating agencies. Under such "horizontalization," the coordinator's position could rotate among the staff of different agencies. This person reported at the national level to a planning officer who exercised supraministerial authority to coordinate the contributions of all line agencies involved with the program. Staff at the district level became an operating unit with shared interests and identity, which would not have happened if they had merely been members of a coordinating committee. They were authorized collectively to make decisions on behalf of the program so that actions would be initiated closer to the field than if left to the center. This made management participatory as well as devolved.

In rural development, a participatory style of management is necessary, because personnel are so dispersed and because, unlike in most factory settings, local differences among program sites may be important. There are logistic as well as staffing limits on how much field supervision can be exercised, so more depends on the initiative and judgment of the personnel operating at the grassroots. If they have been able to shape the program of activities themselves—and especially if the program has been devised by and with rural people who are then committed to its fulfillment—the likelihood of achieving objectives is increased.

Another practical reason for stressing a participatory mode of management was suggested in Chapter 3. A conclusion from organizational theory is that organizations tend to replicate in their environment—that is, among those with whom they interact—the same values and social relationships that they display internally. As VanSant and associates (1982, 4) suggested:

> People tend to deal with others as they are dealt with themselves. An agricultural extension agent who must function according to typically rigid bureaucratic procedures, rules and precedents is unlikely to approach farmers with the flexibility and responsiveness needed to encourage meaningful responsibility [on their part] for project initiatives.

The Gal Oya and NIA programs to improve irrigation management demonstrated how important it is, if participatory and egalitarian farmer organizations are to be fostered, that the agency promoting them exhibit such values and modes of operation. It needs to project into its surroundings both visible examples and mental attitudes that support the kinds of relationships it expects to emerge. If local organizations are to become self-managing, the personnel working with them should likewise be to a significant extent self-managing. The best way to propagate responsibility is to diffuse it.

Devolution does not mean abdication but involves a higher level of management in supportive and facilitative roles. To make this approach succeed, field staff must be motivated, if not self-motivated, to serve organizational objectives. Shared values are an important source of motivation, but regular supervision and sensible monitoring also contribute to long-run performance. This kind of role was played by personnel appointed as "link officers" in the Rajasthan watershed program. They served as liaisons between the central staff and the interdisciplinary teams working and living in the subwatersheds. Everyone could proceed more comfortably and confidently with a decentralized strategy knowing that there were actively facilitated communication and feedback in both directions.

INCLUSIVE MANAGEMENT

In our review of successful rural development programs, we found a wide variety of organizational forms. Basically, however, they have similar structures that look different because of the various designations attached. This basic model is sketched in Figure 5.1., tracing a line from program leadership (A) to village or group organizations (E). In between are the program staff (B) and field staff (D), with possibly some affiliated agencies (C) operating in between.

Figure 5.1 Basic Organizational Structure of Rural Development Programs

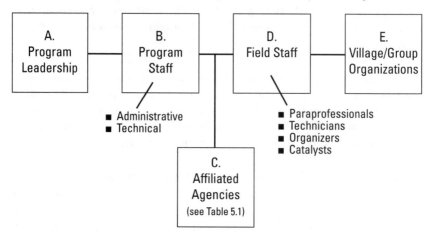

The Anand-model cooperatives in India and SANASA savings and loan associations in Sri Lanka encompass this whole structure organizationally, with their primary societies represented by E in the diagram and several tiers of organization between E and A aggregating cooperative units at levels such as the cluster, division, district, and state. The Institute of Rural Management at Anand (IRMA), a training and research organization established by the National Dairy Development Board in India to train a new generation of managers for rural organizations, is an example of C; so is SANASA's National Training Campus. In a cooperative's structure, A is accountable to E through a set of intermediate levels that are responsible to the one below. In most other kinds of rural development programs, the links between the center and the field are less direct and democratic. The Anand cooperatives have an extensive field staff (D), including veterinarians and other personnel; SANASA has thousands of village cluster and divisional staff, many of them volunteers from the primary societies (E).

At the other extreme, in World Neighbors' program with Guatemalan farmers in San Martin Jilotepeque, the program leadership (A) consisted of only three expatriates for the first two years, after which Guatemalans took over leadership responsibility. B and D were essentially the same, as this was a relatively small program. The Kato-Ki cooperative was an affiliated organization (C). Although some remarkable progress was made in the region around San Martin in only a few years, the program did not spread throughout the country. This very limited and loose organizational structure could have inhibited its expansion to other communities, although this cannot be verified, because the program was operating in the midst of a civil war in the countryside. The methodology of farmer-to-farmer research and extension was disseminated to many countries beyond Guatemala after the project formally came to an end in 1979. The Six-S association in the Sahel draws its central staff from its village federations so that B is more accountable to E than to A.

More typical are programs such as the Bangladesh Rural Advancement Committee (BRAC), Plan Puebla, and CAMPFIRE, where there is a clear distinction between D and E, with program leadership reaching down to rural communities through its field staff to help them get organized and to take advantage of the technical, financial, and other opportunities that the program provides. Some overlap is possible between D and E, however, especially when paraprofessionals are extensively employed. Programs such as BRAC, CAMPFIRE, and the Grameen Bank have built in some structured accountability to the local organizations they serve by creating mechanisms such as general assemblies or boards of directors, where local proposals and criticisms can be voiced on a regular and formalized basis. But there is not the same kind of membership control in such programs as in cooperative organizations, with explicit accountability of officers and managers to the membership. In the cases in which an irrigation department helped establish water user associations, institutions for joint management were established. In such a situation, farmers cannot control the department's professional staff, but to the extent that the agency is financially dependent on water users, their views carry more weight.

The purpose of delineating these differences is to underscore that the boundary between the internal task environment for program managers and their external task environment is not clear-cut. Legal relationships of accountability and control differ, but functionally, the program leadership (A) is responsible for catalyzing, motivating, and coordinating the whole system of organization from B to E, even if formal authority extends only to B and possibly also to D. One can hope and work for a system of planning and implementation that is so oriented to the needs, wishes, and capabilities of E that, over time, the whole operation becomes controlled by representatives of rural communities. Top-down impetus can in this way become inverted, with bottom-up responsibility through an organizational structure in which interactive upward and downward communication and cooperation are the norm.

PLURALISTIC MANAGEMENT

One aspect of inclusive management that may seem paradoxical is that many successful rural development programs spin off a number of independent subsidiary organizations to serve particular functions. This has the effect of reducing overall management burdens by delegating tasks to sets of decision makers who are organizationally autonomous (C in Figure 5.1) but who continue to be motivated by the same aspirations, values, and objectives. Examples of such affiliated agencies are given in Table 5.1.

BRAC, the Center for Economic and Social Development (DESEC), and the Self-Employed Women's Association (SEWA) have had ambitious strategies in this regard. BRAC has devolved many functions to separate but affiliated organizations, to keep the central organization lean. Its founder has not discouraged some of his staff to leave BRAC and start new nongovernmental organizations (NGOs), believing that the NGO sector will be stronger for having more centers of initiative. BRAC, as a very large organization with over 17,000 staff members and a budget of nearly $90 million annually, would rather not become a more inviting target for political interference or antagonism. DESEC has similarly sought to achieve both stability and sustainability by spinning off enterprises that can become self-supporting in different sectors and for various purposes (see Table 5.1).

SEWA has established a great variety of affiliated organizations to simplify management tasks and enlist a broader network of leadership and participation. As noted in Chapter 2, it combines both trade union and cooperative organizational forms. The original SEWA in Ahmedabad has sponsored over thirty unions for garment stitchers, *bidi* (cigarette) rollers, cart pullers, used garment dealers, vendors, and other groups of poor women who can benefit by having some collective bargaining power and more favorable access to raw materials and selling opportunities. The various unions undertake negotiations, lobbying, protests, legal defense, and other functions that are often of a confrontational nature. At the same time, almost forty cooperatives have been established in and around Ahmedabad for vendors, artisans, and other producers to purchase better supplies and get more favorable marketing conditions. Child care providers, wastepaper collectors, industrial cleaners, and community health workers have also formed service cooperatives under SEWA auspices.

SEWA members are supported by a bank for savings, credit, life insurance and mortgage recovery. A community health service and a maternity protection scheme have also been launched (see frontispiece). Such a proliferation of organizations gives the overall organization a diversification and depth of leadership that permit it to carry on despite weaknesses in any particular area. Such a complex structure might appear unmanageable, but it can proceed because the leadership from the top does not try to make decisions for all different activities or for all levels. In this way, SEWA has mobilized some truly remarkable talents from among groups that are otherwise considered totally dependent and debilitated (Rose 1992).

Table 5.1   Agencies Affiliated with Rural Development Programs

Program	Country	Affiliated Agency
Anand Cooperatives	India	Institute of Rural Management at Anand
Bangladesh Rural Advancement Committee (BRAC)	Bangladesh	Research and Evaluation Division Rural Enterprise Project Rural Credit Program Non-Formal Primary Education Program Health and Population Program Ayesha Abed Foundation
CAMPFIRE Collaborative Group	Zimbabwe	CAMPFIRE Association Wildlife Trust (Nyaminyami)
Center for Economic and Social Development (DESEC)	Bolivia	AMERINDIA (artisan cooperative) ARADO (regional association) ASAR (service organization) ICE (campesino education institute) VIPO (housing association) SEPSA (public health service) SEPA (potato seed production unit)
Grameen Bank	Bangladesh	Grameen Trust (health insurance) Grameen Agriculture Foundation Grameen Fisheries Foundation Grameen Enterprise
Orangi Pilot Project (OPP)	Pakistan	Orangi Charitable Trust Karachi Health and Social Development Association OPP Research and Training Institute Women's Work Centres (13)
Population and Development Association (PDA)	Thailand	Thai Business Initiative for Rural Development (TBIRD)
Plan Puebla	Mexico	Regional Credit Union Family microenterprises
SANASA	Sri Lanka	National Training Campus
San Martin Jilotepeque	Guatemala	Kato-ki Cooperative
Self-Employed Women's Association (SEWA)	India	SEWA Bank Vendor Cooperatives Service Cooperatives Artisan Cooperatives Video SEWA SEWA Polytechnic Trade Union Groups Community Health Program

Such a strategy of spin-off does not guarantee that devolved agencies will be successful or self-sustaining, but it reduces the vulnerability of the overall enterprise to economic or personnel setbacks. Some spin-offs will fail, but they can do this without jeopardizing the overall program. A function can be given a separate organizational base when the systems and processes supporting it have demonstrated both capability and stability, when necessary competencies in the staff have been acquired, and when appropriate incentives have been arrived at. Giving a function operational autonomy too soon can lead to failure, as DESEC discovered in its relationship with one subsidiary regional organization (Demeure and Guardia 1997, 96). Withholding autonomy too long, however, can lead to dependence and stasis.

A strategy of pluralistic management recognizes that both rural people and staff are more likely to take initiative and responsibility if given a substantial degree of authority and autonomy. This permits the overall enterprise to expand and evolve in accordance with both needs and opportunities. Program leadership can reach out to encompass both more people and more functions as program competence increases, but its touch is light. It is willing to let go of the reins for diversified activities as people with talent and commitment emerge, and as experience with activities leads to learning appropriate processes and refining organizational roles.

FINANCIAL MANAGEMENT

Good financial management has been a hallmark of successful rural development programs, though many have run into some difficulties in this area from time to time. Considerable investments are made in training local staff to handle financial transactions and records for several reasons: it lowers costs, diffuses knowledge of finances within rural communities, and enhances confidence in the program both among donor agencies and among clients. A program such as SANASA in Sri Lanka, which has accumulated over US$40 million in savings, achieves high efficiency and low overhead costs by relying on local people to handle its funds, which turn over constantly in savings deposits and loans. Having a large number of volunteers staffing the lowest rungs of the organization need not mean amateurism if there is extensive training and if competence, reliability, and accountability are emphasized, along with occasional audits.

Two cardinal principles of financial management are seen again and again in programs that grow and retain the support of their members: simplicity and transparency. The first is important so that less-educated members of the community can help manage their own programs, and both are important to build up trust and confidence. The Grameen Bank, BRAC, and SANASA have all adopted simplified banking rules that are easy for their villager members to carry out and that also ensure high recovery rates. The NIA in the Philippines has put much effort into simplifying its financial and management procedures so that farmers can assume more responsibility for improving, operating, and maintaining irrigation systems. Some amount of complexity is unavoidable at the central management level, especially if a large number of activities or diverse donors are involved. Simplicity is most important at the field level, where most of the funds are (or should be) spent.

Rules and procedures for sharing costs and benefits need to be worked out with and among local residents, as well as between them and the development program. This was done very purposefully in the Rajasthan watershed program, accepting that different formulas for local resource contributions would be arrived at in different locations, so long as the overall local share was at least 10 percent for all villages. A participatory process of reaching agreement on financial formulas and criteria ensures that they will be widely known and makes their fair implementation easier. Communities should have the option of establishing different principles and formulas for allocation that serve local needs and correspond to local values. One of the localities participating in the CAMPFIRE program in Zimbabwe decided, for example, that when the agricultural harvest is good, it will put more of the village's share of funds received from wildlife revenues into investments, and when the harvest is poor, more of these funds will be used to augment household incomes. Complexity at the local level is an acceptable deviation from the rule of simplicity, because meeting people's needs and expectations enhances their assumption of responsibility.

Our endorsement of simplicity in rural development programs differs from that of Jain (1994), who proposes that only the simplest tasks be allocated to the lower levels of any organization. We agree that it is a mistake to assign complex duties to local organizations or, worse, to impose such duties on them. But in fact, as seen in the Grameen Bank case, lower levels can carry out major responsibilities, such as deciding on the amount and repayment conditions of loans, if there is concurrence from participants and if the structure of incentives conduces to effective, fair, and efficient performance of these tasks. Participants need to have sufficient knowledge with which to proceed, but in rural development programs, much of the information needed is available locally, and rural people may have better access to this than do project staff.

To make such devolved financial management work, the program may set some requirements, such as a certain period of training (BRAC requires at least three to six months of educational sessions before it gives credit to village organizations) or evidence of seriousness and solidarity (Six-S will not accept a local organization until it has carried out a self-help project with its own resources). Managing funds is not simply a technical task but something grounded in the social setting and in the bonds among rural people.

Money flows can be a mixed blessing. If they are mishandled, they become a leading cause of organizational failure. This danger can be reduced by working as much as possible with in-kind contributions of labor and materials. The San Martin program in Guatemala minimized flows of money as a matter of principle (Krishna and Bunch 1997). The Orangi Pilot Project decided not to handle any money in the construction of water and sewerage facilities, leaving this to lane managers selected by their neighbors on the basis of a reputation for honesty and efficiency; the project provided only technical advice and materials (Khan 1997). This way, any malfeasance would be limited to individual lanes and would not be attributed to the whole program. In addition, communities quickly learned how to handle finances, which was important for the sustainability of program benefits.

Program designers who approach financial management from above (and from afar) are likely to misread local situations and capabilities. A case study of water point development in the semiarid areas of Botswana by Roe and Fortmann (1982) found that rural communities were not following, for good reason, the prescribed process for mobilizing funds to maintain facilities built by the government—charging all water users a fixed amount of money per head of cattle watered at the water point. The prescribed amount was considerably greater than necessary if users contributed their labor, a resource that is more available than cash in rural areas. Taking up a collection of money when needed to purchase spare parts or other materials was more realistic and convenient. Also, not having a fund in someone's hands (banking facilities were not easily accessible) meant that temptations for misuse were avoided, and the group's solidarity was thus more maintainable. An evaluation of water point maintenance and functioning found that most facilities were serving users' needs in an efficient way with such an improvised system. That these communities were rather isolated and poorly educated confirms the feasibility and desirability of working out consensual systems for financial management that are tailored to particular tasks and situations.

Whether systems should be as informal as in this Botswana case is a different question. This method of resource mobilization supported a single function, water supply. Most successful rural development programs, however, diversify to serve a variety of needs as participants gain experience

and confidence. Some formality in procedures and an increasing accumulation of funds become important as a program progresses. As larger
amounts of financial resources are involved, it is necessary to have more
well-defined and legally sanctioned roles and accounts, although the
amounts that base-level organizations are handling will be thousands of
dollars, not the hundreds of thousands or millions of dollars that the overall program is responsible for.

Simplicity and transparency are essential operating principles at all levels. Backing such principles up with formal or legal requirements, audits,
inspections, and reporting gives everyone more confidence, detects and rec-
tifies errors, and reduces temptations to misuse funds. It is worth noting that
Six-S, which has perhaps the most decentralized and informal procedures
for allocating large amounts of money, has a Swiss chartered accountant
review the books on a regular basis and prepare a financial report that is
freely and widely available. Some degree of formality can make the informal procedures work better, without compromising the potential for local
control of the program. This is another example of loose-tight management style.

DIVISION OF RESPONSIBILITY

An important principle that emerges from reviewing successful programs'
management is that of having each unit contribute what it can best provide, recognizing that what constitutes comparative advantage is not static but changes over time. The self-help gravity water supply program in
Malawi is a good example of a well-thought-out sharing of responsibilities. Labor is provided by the communities; it is organized and supervised
by community leaders, together with the program's technicians. The program provides these technical services and overall management, and pipes
and other material supplies come from donor sources.

Similarly, a bridge-building program in Nepal worked out a division of
responsibility that enabled a rather disadvantaged district in a mountainous region to construct sixty-two bridges in five years, some up to 300 feet
in length. This was accomplished several times faster than the government
could build bridges and at as little as one-quarter of the cost (Pradhan
1980). Planning and management at the village level were undertaken by
local organizations, linked only loosely to the local government system,
which was fairly lethargic and fraught with partisanship and corruption.
Communities were asked to propose bridges that would most improve
their economic and social conditions. The criteria for selection were cost
of the bridge (how much outside resources would be required, giving com-

munities an incentive to pledge substantial contributions), economic value (amount of traffic and savings of time), and social benefit (saving of lives, which could be lost when people attempted to cross swollen rivers during the rainy season).

The district government chose half of the 125 bridges proposed for construction under a five-year plan. The government provided small block grants, and UNICEF provided steel cable to hold up the suspended bridges, a different and simpler technology than suspension bridges. Local materials were used (stones instead of concrete), and local technicians were employed with the funds provided from outside. Because local materials and skills were employed, the bridges were constructed more rapidly and more cheaply and have also been better maintained over the last twenty years than government-built bridges. Many factors contributed to the success of this program, but the appropriateness and complementarity of the division of responsibilities in Baglung district were critical.[5]

Under the Agroforestry Outreach Project in Haiti, a system of complementary responsibilities, discussed previously, was devised that made sense and used each party's available resources to best advantage. Farmers who were willing to contribute some of their land and labor were given the capital needed for reforestation in the form of free tree seedlings from the project, which was funded by the U.S. Agency for International Development (USAID). The cost per participant was one-tenth as much as when the project was reformulated in 1991 and operated in a more conventional manner, nominally unsubsidized but in fact becoming much more costly per unit of output. It was also much less effective in getting trees planted.

The division of labor worked out during the 1980s limited the project's financial management responsibility to overseeing the nurseries that produced seedlings. These were operated by NGOs, which could be monitored simply for the number of trees they produced and whether this was sufficient to justify the grants they received. Although there could have been some leakages or diversions of funds (certainly not as much as if the project had been operated through the government of the day), this system of financial management achieved remarkable cost-effectiveness in terms of area replanted and respectable survival rates. The incentives for all involved were conducive to each playing the expected role successfully.

INCENTIVES

As the agroforestry project in Haiti shows, it is essential to get the incentives (not just the prices) right. This applies to all the actors whose efforts contribute to success, not just to program management. The NIA in the

Philippines, when required to support its operations with water user fees, established a sliding scale that would give farmers' irrigation associations some strong incentives to increase collections. If more than 50 percent of the total amount due was collected, a share stayed with the association collecting the fees: 2 percent was retained from collections up to 60 percent, 5 percent from collections between 60 and 70 percent, 10 percent from collections between 70 and 90 percent, and 15 percent from any collections over 90 percent. This was a positive-sum arrangement for everyone involved, as NIA revenues went up at the same time as those of farmer associations increased. When more farmers paid their fees, the agency and associations were both better able to carry out their operation and maintenance responsibilities, and this helped boost farmers' production and income, improving their ability to pay irrigation fees.

Incentives can be moral as well as material. Although successful programs generally undertake to "do right" by their personnel in terms of conditions of service, promotion opportunities, and training, most emphasize that theirs is not a commercial operation but rather one devoted to public service and advancing the interests of the underprivileged. The satisfactions from contributing to a successful operation that tangibly and visibly improves the lives of disadvantaged men, women, and children can themselves be substantial and motivating (Tendler 1997). Relying only on material incentives or only on moral satisfaction would be either expensive or uncertain, whereas combining these sources of motivation in some optimizing effort produces operations that are both performance-effective and cost-effective.

To induce staff and communities to work together fruitfully, it is good to provide for some *interdependence*. Standard management theory endorses division of labor (not the same as division of responsibilities). It would assign tasks to separate groups of persons, expecting each to have under its control the means necessary to accomplish them, so that they can be held accountable for any shortcomings. Since rural development requires cooperation and the creation of capabilities more than specific outputs and products, one needs to fashion working relationships. The Philippine government's requirement that the NIA become self-financing—mobilizing payments by water users, for example—forced the agency to become more responsive to farmers' ideas and suggestions (Korten and Siy 1988).

In Sri Lanka, the introduction of farmer organizations under the Gal Oya project encountered initial difficulties because the donor funding that supported it was routed through the Irrigation Department rather than coming directly from USAID. Although implementation could have proceeded more quickly with the latter arrangement, the fact that budgets had to be negotiated with the department eventually led to more integration between "software" and "hardware" and helped engage the department to accept the new system of participatory irrigation management. Although interdependence, financial or otherwise, can create obstacles, it can lead to a more integrated program if the parties will negotiate solutions to mutual advantage. Losses in short-run or narrowly conceived efficiency can be more than compensated for by forging stronger organizational linkages as a result of the need to proceed interdependently.

Within an overall framework of cooperation, it can be useful to introduce competition to provide specific incentives for better ideas and performance. The Six-S system of allocating funds among village groups in the Sahel requires each to formulate, present, and defend proposals, justifying how they would make the best use of available funds. Success with previous initiatives is considered a point in favor of subsequent proposals. In the Rajasthan watershed program, rewards were offered to user groups and communities for technical innovations. Since the competition was open and fair, and many could benefit from the best ideas that emerged, its effect was more unifying than divisive.

STANDARDIZATION

Our discussion has stressed adaptive management strategies, tailoring programs to local conditions and needs. Yet an essential feature of management is some degree of standardization—formulation and enforcement of core procedures and routines that give predictability to operations and economize on time for decision making. What we find in successful rural development programs is that procedures and criteria are developed empirically, through testing and with consultation, rather than being decided centrally in a deductive manner and implemented in an authoritarian manner.

General roles, rights, and responsibilities need to be spelled out, but in ways that do not interfere with making local adaptations and variations. Appropriate solutions to local needs are likely to be location-specific and only imperfectly known in advance. As Rondinelli has said, "Organizational solutions can no more be designed and universally prescribed for all rural areas than they can for all developing countries" (1983, 138). But this does not mean that no standard rules or routines are feasible. Some general provisions should be established for all participating persons and groups, but with latitude for local initiative that can further the overall goals of the program. The rules and routines that are most valuable are the ones that band people together in a shared effort and reinforce standards of efficiency, equity, and honesty—core values that are especially important in programs working with the rural poor.

The dairy cooperatives in India and the Kenya Tea Development Author ity (KTDA) show the importance of having standards linked to incentives that support both increased quantity and increased quality of the commodity being produced—milk in the first case, and green tea leaf to be converted into processed tea in the second. KTDA is a parastatal organization that has worked with committees of smallholding growers that are similar to the primary societies that constitute the base of cooperative federations (Lamb and Mueller 1982; Paul 1982, 51–62).

In the dairy program, a processing plant will dump a whole shipment of milk from a village, thereby forfeiting that day's income for all the producers in that primary society, if their milk is diluted or contaminated. This provision has enforced discipline and honesty in an industry that is notorious for spoilage and contamination. By ensuring high quality, Anand products marketed under the AMUL trade name command a premium price, the benefits of which are passed on to cooperative members who accept and meet its standards. Quality is tested in the village to avoid such problems and again at the processing plant as a check on village scruples. By having a rigorous system that can detect shoddy products, temptations to abuse the system are minimized, and millions of persons have benefited, consumers as well as producers.

Efficiency, equity, and honesty can all be served by clear and well-enforced standards. KTDA tea factories similarly inspect loads of green tea leaf brought in from various locations. If the weight has been bulked up by including branches or stones rather than just the tender bud leaves, the whole truckload will be refused, and all the producers along the pickup route will lose the value of their plucking for that day. Having high standards and stiff collective penalties is accepted because, as with the dairy co-ops, premium prices are received when high quality standards are met. Participatory rural development programs oriented to helping the poorer segments of society can operate with high standards; indeed, members may be keen to enforce these standards themselves if there is sufficient reward for meeting them.

The system for picking up milk from Anand-model village cooperatives, like KTDA's collection of green tea leaves, is very organized, since a tight schedule must be kept to prevent deterioration of their highly perishable products, which need quick processing. But do all members have to bring their products in standardized containers? No, that is unnecessary. The milk is tested to ensure that it has not been watered down or contaminated, just as the tea is inspected so that only high-quality bud leaves are purchased. As long as hygienic and quality standards are met, what difference does it make how the milk or tea is brought to the collection point? But as dairy operations face stiffer competition and need to meet higher quality standards, it may be necessary to standardize containers, among other things, in the future to serve farmers' interests. The burden of proof for change should be on those who want to standardize, having to justify this in terms of benefits to the organization and its members.[6]

Standardization produces benefits only when consistency in performance is more important than innovation or enterprise. Any standard prescriptions, patterns, or criteria need to be reconsidered as more is learned in a program. The Iringa nutrition program provides some good examples, in that it standardized the reporting formats to make aggregation and comparison of data on children's nutritional status easier and more valid. It did not, however, standardize the solutions that people at the village level and officials at higher levels should use to redress instances and concentrations of malnutrition. Similarly, in the Orangi Pilot Project, costs of construction were reduced by standardizing the sizes and designs of pipes and manholes, but each lane committee had to decide how it would finance the sewerage improvements and how it would undertake the construction. Thus, local options can coexist with standardization, seeking to get the most benefit from each management principle when appropriately applied.[7]

LOGISTICS

The general lessons for personnel and financial management also apply when dealing with equipment, supplies, vehicles, and other material matters. The best approach is to delegate responsibility to lower levels as much as possible, relying on simple rules, criteria, and procedures that have been discussed with program staff and participants to achieve a needed minimum of standardization and reliability in performance. The reasons that justify certain rules, criteria, and procedures should be evident and widely known so that they are viewed as facilitating program objectives rather than as being arbitrary impositions.

This is an area where considerable effort can usefully be devoted to ensuring that material bottlenecks, such as no spare parts to repair machinery, do not hold back programs when finances and personnel are available. Such planning was one of the things contributing to the success of the Malawi self-help water program. Once work schedules for constructing the systems were agreed on with communities, program managers made certain that the necessary supplies and equipment were at the agreed-on places ahead of time, so that community labor would be well utilized. The integrated pest management program in Indonesia likewise put considerable effort into planning for the facilities and logistics of its training activities at different levels, from the national center in Yogyakarta down to farmer field schools in the rice paddies. This is how 650,000 farmers could be trained in six years (Oka 1997).

There will always be material scarcities in rural development programs. Anticipating material needs such as spare parts requires forethought. When material resources have to be conserved and used sparingly, it is tempting to ration their use by never having enough on hand. This is especially true in government programs. But the opportunity costs of lacking "the needful" must be considered. "Just-in-time" procurement is still decades off in most rural areas of developing countries. This means that equipment or building materials should be procured and prepositioned as systematically as possible, given financial and informational constraints.

Material resources such as vehicles, building materials, and telephones need to be assessed in terms of how they can make a program's other resources as productive as possible. The Orangi Pilot Project in Pakistan concluded that by making tools and instruments available to residents of neighborhoods who wanted to install water and sewerage facilities, the use of local labor and management skills could eliminate the need for private contractors, with whom there was much unhappy experience. Of course, to the extent that already available materials and equipment can be utilized, management requirements are considerably reduced, as seen in the case of the Baglung bridge-building program in Nepal, discussed earlier. This suggests that technology should be rethought and redesigned when there is a shortage of tools and materials rather than taking technology as a given and seeking simply to get more inputs.

Disaggregating materials and responsibility for their management is a good idea in rural development, seeking economies of detail when efficiency comes from careful rather than massive use and application.[8] Smaller packages of materials are easier for people to manage. Although keeping track of resources is more difficult because there are more units to be monitored, this responsibility can be delegated, to draw on as much public knowledge as possible. Any mismanagement or malfeasance should be characterized as hurting not the program so much as the communities that the materials were intended to benefit. Handling all transactions within the public purview will probably deter misuse more than hiring a number of accountants, although, as suggested earlier, having some external auditing is an appropriate check to reinforce proper local management. The operational principles of simplicity and transparency, ensuring that how resources are used is easily evident to all, apply to logistics as much as to finances.

This discussion underscores that even when dealing with material resources, the objective in rural development management is to use them in ways that build and strengthen local management capabilities as much as it is to utilize these resources efficiently. This is what makes personnel management, broadly conceived, the most important aspect of management. Even handling logistics should contribute to capacity building for persons whose actions will help achieve a program's social and economic aims if it is successful. The "battle" to produce certain outputs with material and financial resources should be won in ways that improve prospects for winning the "war" for long-term, self-sustainable development.

NOTES

1. Thomas Carter, adviser to the National Dairy Development Board in India, has reminded us that rural electric cooperatives in the United States operated this way too, until they became large and financially "successful" (personal communication).

2. "Detailed pre-implementation planning presupposes that future economic, institutional and political conditions can be predicted. . . . Yet unpredictability, environmental or institutional, and lack of knowledge and operational information are typical of the project experience" (Porter, Allen, and Thompson 1991, 130–1). "The question of what combination of ways and means would avoid *particular* difficulties and make best use of *particular* assets is one that is given too little consideration by the designers of projects. Virtually every project proposes a single method, as though it were obviously the best, indeed the only one conceivable. This over-hasty restriction lessens the chances of success for those projects which need to be conducted in a complex and changing environment" (Lecomte 1986, 29). See also Rondinelli (1983).

3. One of the few rigorously quantified evaluations of the effects of devolving decisions to local bodies is Hadden's study (1980) of rural electrification in Rajasthan. Funds were available to connect only about 2 percent of that state's villages each year to the main power grid. Rather than continuing to have the state electricity board decide which villages should get hooked up, these decisions were delegated to local government bodies, with criteria for allocation specified by the state government. To get more economic benefit, priority was to be given to villages with the hydrological potential to pump groundwater, since agricultural production could then be increased through the installation of tubewells; also, village proximity to the main distribution grid was to be considered, because more villages and villagers could be connected each year if the total distance for hookups was minimized. Politicians often used their influence to get favored but more distant villages connected, which reduced the number of persons who could be added to the electricity network.

4. It is important that the incentive system be modified so that rewards and recognition are given on a group basis, not just to persons for individual accomplish-

ments. Jain (1994, 1370) suggests from his study of successful rural development programs that "functional" integration of team members is not as important as "associative" elements (team feeling and a sense of brotherhood). The latter contributes to members sharing information, filling in for one another, and making mutual adjustments, things that we have observed in the Gal Oya and Rajasthan cases.

5. Unfortunately, this bridge program did not spread to other districts, indicating that another crucial factor, leadership, was not as readily transferable as was the technology and the organizational model. This program was initiated by a member of parliament, Om Gauchan. His leadership helped buffer decisions and implementation from petty kinds of political manipulation and maintained a districtwide perspective that transcended purely local interests.

6. On irrationalities and diseconomies that can result from standardization, see Chambers (1997, 63–70).

7. We would not go as far as Jain (1994) does in advocating standardization of operating procedures, though as argued here, we support considerable standardization as long as it serves to strengthen program performance at the grassroots. Standardization is not desirable for its own sake so much as to give more coherence and predictability to decisions and action, providing frameworks and contexts for decentralized decision making. Tendler, in her study of the performance of development programs in Brazil, found support for all of Jain's findings except the one on standardization; she found much flexibility among the more successful government programs (1997, 173–4).

8. This is one aspect of what Leibenstein (1976) characterized as "X-efficiency," discussed by Thorbecke (1990) in relation to development.

6 Technology and Training

The most important factor operating in development is knowledge, which can be manifested in various forms. It might appear that we are concerned in this chapter only with material investments and technical skills, two factors often stressed in development literature and policy. But we regard both as reflections and expressions of knowledge. Technology and training represent, respectively, advances in knowledge about how to take better advantage of the world's resources—natural, physical, and human—and means for transmitting such knowledge and putting it to practical use. In Chapter 7, we consider information as a factor for improving management in rural development programs. Our focus here is on knowledge as it can be generated and imparted for the sake of increasing people's productivity and well-being.

The coping and advancement strategies adopted by rural residents are pursued in variable, uncertain, and often unfriendly environments (Chambers 1997, 162–87). Caution in the acceptance of new techniques is a rational response to the insecurity of resource-limited households for which the difference between a good harvest and a bad one is not merely a temporary setback; the effects are more serious and long lasting. Uncertainty and risk avoidance are not simply technical considerations; they are often the result of weak or nonexistent institutional support. Poor farmers are largely dependent on themselves when using traditional practices. Newer, more market-oriented techniques of production involve them in relationships with outside agencies, which are typically not responsible to or even easily accessible by the poor.

Given that technological changes invariably have institutional concomitants, programs seeking to improve the lives of rural people by introducing more productive technologies must take account of those factors in their environment that inhibit risk taking and innovation. Either they have to deal with or compensate for these factors directly or they must limit the scope of technical change to initiatives that can be sustained within existing institutional capacities. Sustainable introduction of technology for rural development involves local capacity and control, not just invention and adoption as focal activities. Technology as a factor in rural development thus depends on corresponding alterations in organization and management. Appropriate program design seeks solutions that fit technology and organization together (Korten 1980).

TECHNOLOGY

Successful rural development efforts can proceed without inventing or popularizing new technologies. Some make improvements in hundreds of thousands of people's lives by improving organization and management, utilizing whatever technologies are available and using available resources better. Programs such as SANASA in Sri Lanka and the Grameen Bank in Bangladesh provide loans for investing in whatever technologies appear promising to their members individually or in groups. Irrigation management programs as in the Philippines and Sri Lanka can benefit from improved "hardware," but most of their contributions come from the "software" of water user associations. Health programs such as Iringa in Tanzania and the Posyandus in Indonesia make existing medical services more widely available, emphasizing what parents can do for their children's health and well-being (Rohde 1993). The CAMPFIRE association in Zimbabwe and the Nepal-Australia Forestry Project both worked with local communities to change natural resource management practices and policies. These initiatives, given their opportunities and objectives, were able to produce benefits without far-reaching or sophisticated technological interventions.

Other programs seek to spread and upgrade existing technologies, without particularly investing in invention and experimentation. Focusing efforts on the functioning of village organizations and on giving access to sound technical advice can produce some good results, for example, the Center for Economic and Social Development (DESEC) in Bolivia, Six-S in Burkina Faso, the Program for Integrated Rural Development (PIDER) in Mexico, the Small Farmer Development Program (SFDP) and the Nepal-Australia Forestry Project (NAFP) in Nepal, the Aga Khan Rural Support Program (AKRSP) in Pakistan, the Khorat Integrated Rural Development Program in Thailand, and the Organization of Rural Associations for Progress (ORAP) in Zimbabwe. Similarly, there are cases in India and Haiti—the Self-Employed Women's Association (SEWA) and the Agroforestry Outreach Project—in which very disadvantaged groups, low-caste and marginally employed women and poor hillside farmers, were benefited by new organizational mechanisms, and technological advances were mostly incidental.

In nearly half the programs that we reviewed that made significant contributions to rural well-being, there were active efforts to create, acquire, or otherwise utilize new technologies—actually, sometimes old ones that had not previously been used in this way or in this location. In all these cases, the technologies were judged appropriate by their users after testing and evaluation under local conditions in the context of supportive organization and management. Brief sketches of these cases are presented in Table 6.1 to characterize the range and variety of ways in which technological innovation was promoted.

Developing and Diffusing Appropriate Technologies

It is appropriate at the start of any program to begin with a set of simple technologies addressing identifiable problems that local people are encountering. The innovations should be relatively easy to handle and should provide early visible results (Bunch 1982). Even when program managers are reasonably confident about a particular technology, they cannot be sure of its acceptance by local people until success has been tangibly demonstrated and people feel confident that they themselves, not only trained technicians, can put the new technology to good use. Programs of technological change thus need to proceed in a gradual way, first testing and demonstrating some simple techniques, and then waiting until these are accepted and adapted by a critical mass of people before starting to experiment with more complex techniques. There will be more popular confidence in and support for the process as a result of the improvements already attained.

The benefits of a step-by-step approach are illustrated by World Neighbors' program for agricultural development in San Martin Jilotepeque, Guatemala (Bunch 1982; Krishna and Bunch 1997). Program managers set for themselves the ambitious short-term objective of doubling the yields of corn and beans, which together accounted for over 80 percent of the area's agricultural production. Their strategy consisted of identifying and finding techniques to deal with the two or three most important limiting factors responsible for low productivity. Action research revealed soil erosion and consequent nutrient loss as the main limitations. To deal with these, program staff, working together with farmer extensionists, began to search for suitable techniques, ones that people could implement with the means that they already owned or could easily afford.

The technique that was finally selected for controlling erosion—building contour trenches on hillsides reinforced with forage grasses—was cheap, easily understood, and readily reproducible by large numbers of farmers. It required raw materials available locally, with little cost to the farmers,

Table 6.1   Technological Innovations in Rural Development Programs

Program	Core Idea

Bangladesh Rural Advancement Committee / BANGLADESH   Created Rural Enterprise Project to improve technological options for village organizations' income-generating activities; technology expected to be relevant and realistic, addressing a felt need and an available opportunity; has to be accessible by the poor and relatively cheap and easily usable by villagers

North Potosi Program / BOLIVIA   Engaged farmers in experimenting with and evaluating use of an indigenous legume as a green manure; able to double or triple the yields of subsistence crops without using chemical fertilizers; farmers extending simple research methods to other areas

San Martin Jilotepeque / GUATEMALA   Enlisted farmers in experimentation to raise agricultural yields and conserve soil; forage crop as perennial cover plus contouring increased yields sixfold within seven years; farmers oriented to such innovation doubled yields again on their own after the project ended

Anand Dairy Co-ops / INDIA   Applied modern technology for milk collection and processing to benefit small farmer members who now market 10 million liters of milk daily; also utilized artificial insemination; member-producers get 70 percent of consumer price for milk products due to use of efficient processing and marketing technologies

Rajasthan Watersheds / INDIA   Working with user groups at the village level, developed methods to reduce erosion and raise incomes; production of fodder grass and cereal crops increased 50 to 150 percent by simple methods

Integrated Pest Management / INDONESIA   Trained over 650,000 farmers in principles and methods of ecological farm management to protect rice crop with little or no chemical pesticides; farmers improved and did not just routinely apply integrated pest management methods; imports of pesticides cut by $150 million a year without reducing yields

Kenya Tea Development Authority / KENYA   Improved the technology of growing and processing tea within a well-structured organizational framework, so that smallholders, previously thought incapable of competing in quality with tea grown on plantations, were able to outproduce commercial plantations in both efficiency and quality

Self-Help Water Program / MALAWI   Devised low-cost, easily manageable techniques for installing and maintaining gravity-flow potable water systems within well-organized management systems serving over a million people

Plan Puebla / MEXICO   Focused efforts on improving production technologies for small farmers growing rain-fed maize; able to get more adoption when the whole farming system was considered and farmer groups were more involved in the research and evaluation process

Baglung Bridges / NEPAL   Utilized indigenous technologies and local materials to construct suspended bridges in difficult mountain terrain more quickly than the government could and at much lower cost

Orangi Pilot Project / PAKISTAN   Created better low-cost technologies for installing self-help sewerage in huge squatter settlement and for building low-cost housing; purposefully invested in finding appropriate technologies that could be managed locally

Population and Development Association / THAILAND   Developed rainwater storage technology so that households and groups could live better during the long dry season; first step in integrated rural development was seen as improving technology for villagers and it employed skills that could readily be passed from farmer to farmer. Once they had seen the benefits achieved by the first adopters, other farmers could easily implement the new technique for themselves. A cooperative society was set up concurrently with the technical experiments to help farmers obtain credit and remunerative prices for their crops. Enhanced confidence in their own abilities and support from the newly established organization assisted farmers in taking up more and newer technical innovations. Maize yields went up from an average of 400 kilograms per hectare in 1972, when the program was launched, to over 2,500 by 1979, when external assistance was withdrawn in the face of mounting civil strife. The program's cost was only about $50 per household.

Even projects focused on technological change need to proceed slowly, not just to prove lab-tested technology under field conditions but also to build up essential organizational scaffolding and institutional incentives. Plan Puebla, based in Mexico, was initially conceived as an agricultural extension project, but field implementation quickly ran up against constraints that had to be dealt with before the new technology could become a viable option to poorer farmers (Diaz Cisneros et al. 1997). Banks had to be persuaded to change their lending procedures and to advance credit to farmers' groups without insisting on individual guarantees. Before that could happen, farmers had to be organized into solidarity groups. Coordination had to be arranged among disparate government agencies that dealt separately with input supply, transportation and warehousing, crop insurance, and grain pricing. The need to get all these pieces in place limited the pace at which technical advances could be achieved.[1]

Indonesia's program for integrated pest management (IPM) could not take off until the national government reduced or removed subsidies for chemical pesticides (Oka 1997). Removal of subsidies could have been predicted as a precondition of program success in this case; if chemical means of control were made artificially cheaper, manual means would be less attractive. But usually the factors that facilitate technological change are not known in advance; they are discovered or discerned gradually during program implementation.

Pilot programs or initial phases of implementation provide information about appropriate organizational arrangements and management principles that can best support the new technologies. In some cases, organizational forms arise naturally from technical considerations. For instance, projects that deal with water, such as irrigation or water supply projects, need organizational structures that closely follow the pattern of hydraulic flow. The Gal Oya program in Sri Lanka and the National Irrigation Administration (NIA) program of participatory irrigation management in the Philippines both organized farmer groups to coincide with the pattern of irrigation channels. Primary groups were organized along the field channel, the lowest level of water distribution. Field channel groups were federated upward into higher and higher levels, with organization at the distributary, branch, and finally main canal or project levels. Similarly, in the Malawi rural water supply projects, villagers organized themselves into tap committees, branch committees, and, in large projects, section committees, with a main line committee responsible for overall planning, operation, and maintenance.

Technology's influence on organization is not limited, however, to hydraulic groups. Any activity in which users are divided by clear-cut physical lines has its own "natural constituency," which may differ from units defined by political or administrative boundaries. Thus, watershed programs in Rajasthan have worked with user groups formed separately for each hydrogeologically defined microwatershed and not by village or hamlet (Krishna 1997). New forms of local organization are necessary to accommodate the subdivisions that work best with the preferred technology.

As noted above, technology is not a critical component of all programs. Those concerned mostly with resource allocation may succeed with little or no technological change. But when resource creation is an objective, technical factors assume more importance. Organizing user groups to manage forests and share forest products can proceed with little technical innovation, whereas if such groups are getting credit to finance production activities or are seeking to increase forest products, suitable technological improvements will assist them in achieving these goals.

As its first program intervention, the Bangladesh Rural Advancement Committee (BRAC) made credit available to its members. Members of village organizations were assisted by program staff as they organized themselves into self-disciplining savings and credit groups. It was not long, however, before members began to look for ways to employ more productively the affordable credit that was being made available. BRAC set up a special technical research and design wing "to improve technological options for use in BRAC-sponsored, income-generating activities" (Abed and Chowdhury 1997, 49).

Not all these technologies were introduced at the same time. The development and dissemination of new techniques followed a reinforcing sequence of activities that enabled BRAC's members to capture the benefits of forward and backward linkages. BRAC's inquiries among destitute rural women revealed a potential for introducing poultry-rearing activities. To supply day-old chicks to women participating in the poultry program, BRAC supported other women who were prepared to operate hatcheries. Still other women were trained to administer vaccinations, collecting a small fee for their services. A similar sequence of activities was followed in BRAC's sericulture program. Realizing that a shortage of mulberry leaves was limiting the production of silk cocoons, BRAC encouraged farmers to plant mulberry trees. One or two farmers in each village were assisted in setting up nurseries. A central facility was set up with machinery for reeling silk thread and producing cloth; cloth production was linked with marketing by establishing sale outlets in the cities.

The Anand dairy cooperatives in India similarly added technological functions to reinforce economic gains made through each preceding innovation. Each step has been preceded by organization, accompanied by adaptation, and followed up by training and local capacity building. The Anand cooperative movement started humbly in the Kheda district of Gujarat state as a milk collection operation. It took some years to improve and stabilize these activities. Once these were established and profits were accumulating, a pasteurizer and a milk powder plant were added. Along with this construction activity, organizational capabilities were improved to ensure that milk would be collected hygienically and delivered quickly and reliably to the processing plant. To do this efficiently on a twice-daily basis over an entire district, the organization trained village-level workers to test the purity and fat content of milk delivered by tens of thousands of individual suppliers, to keep accounts and give out payments, and to keep the village collection centers in good repair. Liaison with the district level ensured that the entire process would flow smoothly and reliably.

To its milk procurement functions, the organization later added the provision of improved cattle feed to farmers, followed by veterinary services and artificial insemination to upgrade animal health and productivity. The strategy was based on these premises:

> Unless farmers are assured of higher incomes, they will not invest in improved cattle feed, and until they improve the feed, there is no point investing in better breeds of cattle. Thus, it is futile to introduce a component of artificial insemination until the first two stages have been achieved and there is both an opportunity and a felt need for genetic improvement. (Kurien 1997, 116)

New activities were added step by careful step, initially conducting small-scale experiments, learning from mistakes, refining the strategy, and only then extending it to involve larger numbers of producers. Each new technological initiative, once learned and widely practiced, opened the door for the next stage. Newer technological interventions were presented to farmers only when the farmers and their organizations were ready to receive and utilize them.

To perform these new functions well, the organization adopted a two-tier staffing pattern similar to the one it had for milk collection and processing. Village members chosen by their peers are trained to undertake basic management duties; they are complemented and supported by more highly qualified professionals employed at the district, state, and national levels. These professionals—the best that can be recruited—work according to the policies set by cooperative members, who own the organization and manage it through the directors they elect. Appropriate technology need not be simple; the Anand cooperatives use technology that is state of the art. Sometimes quite advanced technology is best suited for a particular task. The lesson learned from the Anand experience in India is that even when some parts of the technical chain are controlled by nonmembers, these persons should be accountable to the local members whom they are expected to serve.

Participatory and Renewable Technology

In none of the successful programs we reviewed has a community been just a recipient of technology, simply adopting the practices and advice handed down by specialist technicians. A few technologies, such as vaccination against disease, may be so effective almost everywhere and so self-contained that they can be extended, transferred, applied, or adopted—to use the verbs that commonly describe the spread of technology. But for the most part, the technologies relevant for rural development need modification and adaptation, even serious revision, before they can be productively and confidently used in a variety of locations. The concept of *extension* taken literally can obscure the complexity of this process. Determining "recommendation domains" for a given crop variety or technology begins to address this problem, but for most technological innovations, the domain is limited, and conditions change and fluctuate. People need to manage their lives from day to day, without always looking to external agencies, which may or may not be responsive. What is effective today may not be beneficial a year or more from now. There thus needs to be capacity for continuing technological innovation.

Participatory technology development helps generate among local people a sense of confidence in their use of the new technology. It builds up local capacity that is congruent with the technology, and it facilitates the melding of local knowledge with what professional technologists have to offer. Acceptance of the new technology becomes easier when it is demystified and made easily comprehensible (Jiggins 1989; Haverkort et al. 1991).

DESEC's programs in Bolivia engage in participatory testing in which farmers come together to share knowledge and experiences. Scores of local-level tests are undertaken each year on farmers' fields, and the results—there for all to see—are analyzed in group discussions (Demeure and Guardia 1997). The World Neighbors program in Bolivia and other Andean countries takes a similar approach, even teaching farmers who are barely literate and numerate to understand and do statistical testing to verify the reliability of good results. Evaluating the productivity of specific potato and barley varieties under highly varied local conditions, controlling for different ways to increase soil nutrients (green manure, animal manure, chemical fertilizer), has helped increase yields dramatically. What is so impressive is not just the higher production but the farmers' own understanding of the process of technological improvement and their ability to share this with peers (Ruddell, Beingolea, and Beingolea 1997).

In such a process, technical professionals also learn a lot about the logic of traditional practices, which helps them develop other suitable techniques. Technical specialists need to be sensitive to the conditions of local communities if they are to devise techniques that people can easily and affordably accept. Neither local knowledge nor outside scientific knowledge should be privileged over the other, as each can contribute to the improvement of practices and production, and each is more beneficial when complemented by the other.

The Orangi Pilot Project (OPP) began its search for a suitable urban sanitation system by working for three months with the residents of just one lane (Khan 1996, 60–9; 1997). From interacting with lane residents, OPP staff learned how much capacity for implementing self-help solutions was nascent. A critical element in convincing people that they could construct the sewerage system on their own was the development of simple technologies that could be easily understood and were affordable given people's meager resource base.

There were three components to this strategy of participatory technology development: first, research was conducted by OPP engineers using a variety of designs and materials; second, the engineering staff explained and defended their designs in open lane meetings, in several instances revising their designs and estimates after gaining a better understanding of problems and solutions; and third, local skills were upgraded by training and education, which also generated much public discussion and understanding. The technology that was developed cost less than one-fourth of what municipal authorities charged for an equivalent level of service. It has now been extended to cover most of the Orangi squatter settlement, with a population of nearly a million.

OPP's low-cost technology was grounded in a variety of local institutions and roles. Lane committees and lane managers were selected by residents from among themselves, and the latter were trained in surveying and basic engineering, as well as financial management. Designs and prototypes were given to local contractors to help them produce the materials, manhole covers, and so forth that were needed for installing the new low-cost technology. Tools and equipment were centrally purchased and made available to any group of residents so that they would not need to hire (often untrustworthy) contractors. Any apprehensions and misconceptions about the technology were removed through hundreds of meetings where people learned about the problems of waste removal and about technical solutions. They were taught techniques as specific as the proper way to mix cement. In this way, a very physical process of construction was also a very human one.

The watershed conservation and development program in Rajasthan, India, started by focusing on activities that could deliver early visible results with the help of simple-to-adapt technical advice (Krishna 1997). There was an acute shortage of fodder for livestock in these areas, and program staff believed that growing quick-maturing grasses would overcome the "inertia of disbelief" they encountered among village groups. As attention to soil nutrients and other practices dramatically boosted yields, farmers' confidence grew in their ability to find and implement solutions to the problems they faced. They have come forward to offer locally devised technical solutions for various problems or have asked program staff for assistance in refining appropriate techniques. Field staff are encouraged to devise low-cost solutions, and they are rewarded for the innovations they contrive.[2]

Unusual for a large-scale government program, there has been little prescriptiveness and little standardization of technical content. This varies from watershed to watershed, resulting in a mix of traditional practices and ones proposed by scientists and technical staff. Although some practices may be suboptimal in a purely technical sense—that is, other techniques could possibly result in somewhat higher yields—they are chosen because they are self-regenerating in the hands of farmers. Apart from learning the "how to" of these techniques, most farmers also learned the "why." Within the first few years of the program, they were already becoming quite self-reliant. Vegetative inputs, rather than costly mechanical structures, are used to control erosion, relying on plants that are either native to the area or grown in village nurseries. Technical advice is provided by fellow villagers, paraprofessionals who have been trained by the program and linked with technical institutes. Outside expertise has diminished, increasingly playing a supportive rather than an instigating role.

A menu of improved practices has been developed within the program, responding to variations in farmers' problems and preferences. Offering farmers alternatives enables them to select techniques that are best suited to their own particular mix of economic objectives, pursued under certain environmental conditions, balancing risk and opportunity in some desired proportion. The Rajasthan program offers a variety of activities concerning agriculture, soil conservation, forestry, and pasturage rather than a single, set technological package. This is also appropriate in projects that deal with fewer sectors. The Agroforestry Outreach Project in Haiti started by encouraging farmers to plant fast-growing trees on their land (Murray 1997). But after farmers had become actively engaged in tree planting, the project began to offer different ways in which farmers could combine trees with field crops. Border planting along cropped fields, rows of trees planted as windbreaks or erosion controls, and intercropping of nitrogen-fixing trees with other crops were offered as alternative techniques of plantation, each serving different needs. A program that started mostly for reforestation evolved into more complex activities of agroforestry.

Another aspect of a renewable technology is that it should periodically be modified. Actually, unless innovations are discouraged by persons in positions of control or influence, they are likely to emerge continually as people find ways to improve on the elements of any technological advance. Systematically discussing the results of innovations and disseminating those that appear most promising is one way in which technical knowledge can constantly be upgraded. Too often, however, programs constrict the scope of technical choice to the few alternatives that are laid down in approved technical manuals. We do not suggest that technical manuals be done away with, but they should be more like periodicals than like books. At the same time that they provide users with state-of-the-art knowledge, they should encourage further innovation and provide space for entering more and new knowledge, encouraging people to experiment and evaluate. This will ensure that many can benefit from the practices developed by a few among them.

The best result of a program of technical change occurs when persons participating in it develop a capacity for continuing innovation. We have already mentioned the remarkable achievements of farmers in Guatemala's San Martin Jilotepeque region. Fifteen years after program assistance was withdrawn, farmers were continuing to innovate and improve their production. The principles formulated and followed in San Martin were:

- Start where the people are.

- Discover the limiting factors.

- Choose simple, limited technologies.

- Test ideas on a small scale, to avoid exposing people to the risk of major failures.

- Work to attain early visible results, to maintain the momentum of enthusiasm.

- Evaluate results.

- Train trainers (Krishna and Bunch 1997, 151).

This step-by-step method of participatory technology development, accompanied by complementary developments in organization and management, gives concrete expression to the principle of assisted self-reliance (see Chapter 2). Technology without local capacity is like a well with no water. It looks inviting from a distance, but up close, it is dry and worthless. The essential lesson of several decades of rural development experience is that most technology, to be successful, has to be embedded in local institutions, in structures and systems that are accountable to the people they serve and responsive to their concerns.

TRAINING

Training is an important aspect of capacity building, but like technology, it is more a process than a thing. It is not something undertaken to start a process of technical or organizational change, but rather a continual effort to upgrade human resources by sharing ideas and concepts and disseminating techniques, methodologies, and skills. Indeed, the process should be one that contributes to and enhances knowledge, so that knowledge is not simply being transferred through training any more than it is conveyed through the transfer of technology. We use the term *training* with some unhappiness, being mindful of a saying in the Philippines that one trains only dogs and water buffalo. People become educated, not trained. But the term has its uses, distinguishing generalized human resource development from that which is goal directed, aiming to enhance people's capabilities for solving various problems and attaining higher levels of productivity. Leadership training needs to be part of all programs, not just a specialized course for a preferred few.

Program implementation and training should each build on the other. Training curricula have to be relevant to carrying out day-to-day tasks, but in turn experience needs to feed into training activities as new problems are discovered and new solutions developed to deal with them. Training should not, therefore, proceed separately from the rest of a program's efforts or be tacked on as an afterthought, as happens when training is seen as something less glamorous and less appreciated than design and implementation.

Training should knit together the separate tasks and personnel of the organization and unite them in a shared understanding of philosophy and objectives. In addition to providing specific tools, training is important for fostering attitudes and group motivation.[3] It needs to employ appropriate methods—formal, informal, on-the-job, or peer training—for each purpose. A guiding principle when designing training programs is that knowledge of context and content should complement each other. Whereas the theory behind technical applications can be taught formally in the classroom, issues of technology application and dissemination are best learned less formally through demonstrations under field conditions and by actually using the technology firsthand. We discuss below various training focuses that support the diverse tasks of program staff and suggest some methods to address these needs. A representative set of training strategies is summarized in Table 6.2.

Training in Technology

Because technological adaptation needs to proceed from the simple to the more complex, training in technology works best if it follows a gradual learning curve, starting slow and then accelerating. The initial intention is not to impart a fixed amount of knowledge about some set of technological applications so much as to inculcate among rural residents attitudes and skills for experimentation and evaluation that will help them continue to innovate. Rather than being completely dependent on outside expertise, as we mentioned earlier, they should feel equipped to control and adapt the new technology. This requires that technological training be participatory, with residents understanding both the "why" and the "how to" of any technique. The IPM program in Indonesia follows a methodology of participatory learning-by-doing that is exemplary in this regard. The trainer assigned to a group of farmers does not teach them so much as encourage them to identify and discuss problems, to experiment and discover, and to derive from these experiments some actionable recommendations.

Farmers enlisted in the IPM program conduct small-scale experiments on their own fields. When they meet in groups, they discuss the results of their experimentation, learning from one another and devising new ways to solve common problems. Training in groups is helpful in several ways: mutual learning is encouraged, solidarity is built, and a base is created for further technological discussion and problem solving. To facilitate participation, the training cohorts of twenty-five farmers are divided into

Table 6.2   Training Strategies of Successful Programs

Program	Program Focus	Training Approaches
OPP PAKISTAN	Urban waste disposal and health, housing, and income generation	Artisans and suppliers of building materials were trained to provide services and inputs for low-cost technologies; lane residents were trained in basic surveying and engineering techniques
BRAC BANGLADESH	Multiple income-generating activities	Training includes courses on social awareness, leadership, and organization and management and in various technical skills; organized training is provided for both full-time staff and paraprofessionals; sixteen Training and Resource Centers (TARCS) provide training of trainers; TARCS are self-financing, as program managers and field offices pay to have their staff trained
SANASA SRI LANKA	Savings and credit societies	Educational programs in philosophy and operations are organized at the village level for almost 200,000 persons a year; a national training facility, the Campus for Cooperative and Development Studies at Kegalle, holds courses in financial management, banking procedures, leadership, and gender analysis
DESEC BOLIVIA	Agriculture, forestry, handicrafts	Instituto Campesino de Educacion was set up to provide training in organization and management, as well as technical training in agriculture, animal husbandry, forestry, and other techniques
Anand Cooperatives INDIA	Dairy development	The Institute for Rural Management at Anand (IRMA) was set up to impart specialized management skills for rural producer associations
San Martin Jilotepeque GUATEMALA	Agriculture, soil conservation, health	Methodology for farmer-to-farmer training was pioneered, linked to farmer experimentation with new technologies
NIA PHILIPPINES	Farmer-managed irrigation	Training for community organizers and for leaders of irrigator associations is comprehensive, including components on leadership development, simplified financial management, and irrigation systems management
Gal Oya SRI LANKA	Farmer-managed irrigation	The Agrarian Research and Training Institute set up training of institutional organizers and farmer-representatives in subjects covering organization, communication, and water management techniques
IPM INDONESIA	Integrated pest management	A widespread system was set up to support farmer-to-farmer spread of methods; 650,000 were trained by 1996

subgroups of five persons. Each subgroup is assigned a common problem and works separately from the others to devise solutions, which are then discussed by the full group. The trainer assists in keeping the discussion flowing without dominating it. In this way, farmer groups develop the ability to assess and analyze problems, adopting a scientific procedure that consists of observation and analysis, followed by recommendations. Their rice fields become "the blackboard on which the lesson is written" (Oka 1997, 194).

The process is quite similar to what we find in the Triple-A cycle developed in the Iringa nutrition program in Tanzania. Both programs encourage participants to think for themselves, not to absorb passively some predefined solutions. "Once they learn to practice and understand what they are doing . . . they will not easily forget what they have learned" (Oka 1997, 194). More than just helping retain the lessons of training, a participatory methodology evokes in rural people a spirit of innovation and a concurrent capacity to experiment and evaluate. This is more important that any particular knowledge acquired from training.

World Neighbors' program in San Martin Jilotepeque similarly focused its training efforts on developing local technological capacities. Village leaders were prepared to perform the role of teachers. They first practiced the new agricultural techniques on their own plots, adapting and refining the techniques in the process. Then, with visible results to point to, they went on to train interested neighbors. Each round of extension was accompanied by further adaptation and improvement. The effort was not so much to extend a given technology as to bring forth a process of demonstration and learning that would later enable grassroots groups to innovate on their own.

The farmer-to-farmer extension method developed in San Martin illustrates an effective way of diffusing technological capacities. Rural people quite often live in dispersed, hard-to-reach locations, and they find it difficult to sacrifice several days' work to come to training institutions. This is particularly true in the case of women, who find it hard or impossible to get away from their homes. Instead of expecting them to come to central training locations, trainers often have to go among the people and train them in or near their homes. Scarcity of good trainers limits the extent of training, so a diffusion method of training through fellow farmers can multiply the numbers of trainers, sustaining a process that we call *horizontal diffusion*.

Long-run success in any diffusion model depends on the ability of the system to learn and adapt through a strong, built-in feedback loop. Not only should trainees learn from trainers; trainers need to be sensitive to local conditions and to absorb and utilize knowledge coming from the communities. Training efforts have to be adapted as needs or conditions change and to match the pace of local capacity building. The entire system should evolve, reframing its messages and responding quickly and appropriately to farmers' concerns, which change as they learn more during the course of program implementation. Indonesia's IPM program keeps its methods and content relevant and popular partly through refresher courses that keep trainers in touch with lessons from field implementation to be incorporated into the next round of training. Learning from experience encourages the development of new methods, the extension of these methods to new crops, and new research studies to deal with problems for which no solutions have been found using available methods.

Training in Organization

Rural development programs work best when people participate through their self-managed organizations, as discussed in Chapter 4. Such community organizations may not exist, or they may exist only in rudimentary form, not immediately suitable for the program at hand. Appropriate organizations will then have to be created or modified by a program's participants, often with assistance from program staff. Anand in India developed specialized "spearhead teams" to assist villagers in forming dairy cooperatives and to train them in the organizational as well as technical skills required for successful dairy operations at the village level. BRAC in Bangladesh and DESEC in Bolivia assist village groups in forming working organizations among themselves. Group members build solidarity around an understanding of common problems and through agreement on solutions arrived at by means of group analysis. Skilled facilitators participate in problem-solving sessions without attempting to influence the agenda or to impose any decision.[4]

Program managers and others who are prepared to work in tandem with community organizations are often dismayed to find weak organizations at the village level or none at all. For community participation to become significant and effective, considerable effort may be required from program staff to assist in the formation or revitalization of community organizations. In Chapter 3, we discussed the role of catalysts, specially trained staff who are able to evoke local initiative and amplify local manifestations of responsibility. Such catalysts need to be trained to assist communities in organizing themselves, not imposing any predetermined formats on community organization.

Some programs have developed systematic methodologies for assisting group formation and action. Tanzania's child survival and nutrition program developed the Triple-A methodology to facilitate village groups' discussion of problems and solutions, focusing attention on assessing, analyzing, and acting on problems. This develops a shared conception of problems' causes and of the effectiveness of possible solutions. Facilitators are trained to use the Triple-A cycle with groups and, at the same time, to train each village group to develop its own diagnostic process. Once facilitators have gotten communities engaged in this process of identifying, diagnosing, and solving problems, both remedial and proactive efforts flow almost integrally therefrom.

Training in Management

We discussed in Chapter 5 the need for responsible financial management, but this is not the only aspect of management in which local organizations need competence. To be sure, even the best of programs can get derailed by sloppy accounting or financial mismanagement, arising due to lack of knowledge or from dishonesty. Careful audits can rectify errors, but sound knowledge of account keeping is required to prevent sloppiness and deter dishonesty. Programs that rely on decentralized and participatory management must devote considerable attention to training those persons who keep track of their organization's money, since misunderstanding or malfeasance is a predictable way to undermine local organizations.

Among the programs we know, the Six-S program has the most decentralized structure for financial management. Every village group is in charge of its own finances, including funds that are passed down to them as grants or loans. Treasurers of the village groups are extensively trained in a standardized but simple-to-operate system of single-entry bookkeeping. The program expects that with well-kept accounts, along with a record of successful project implementation, donor agencies will continue to provide funding on a flexible basis, without prior submission and approval of detailed plans and budgets. If this process can continue to function satisfactorily, it could become a model for other rural development programs. Success depends on well-trained and conscientious treasurers, backed up and kept honest by functioning local organizations.

But not all management is of money. Material resources also need to be inventoried and deployed in ways that are most productive. In the self-help water supply programs in Malawi, during the construction phase, communities are shown how to organize work teams and how to handle pipes and joints. This is important not just for construction but also for managing the system and maintaining the pipelines. Leaks can be fixed and faucets repaired in a prompt and effective way because knowledge is broadly distributed. Although the paraprofessionals have more technical knowledge than most villagers, there is no monopoly. This is another example of how technology, organization, and management need to be combined in ways that fit together.

As programs expand, villages that subscribe to the program later can learn from the experiences of pioneer communities. They can see the benefits of the new technologies for themselves, and they can build on the organizational forms and management methods developed among the pioneers. This potential for communities to learn from one another was explicitly built upon in the Malawi project. Village leaders were taken to Chingale, the site of the first project, to inspect the results and to discuss the process of construction and related problems with the local water supply committees. Acquainting themselves with the organizations that had successfully implemented the technology in Chingale, leaders could propose this system to fellow villagers, not as a model for imitation, but as an example for starting up operations in their own villages.

Just as village communities participating in a program can learn from their predecessors' experience, program staff can also be trained by their peers. Staff who are highly motivated and sufficiently experienced can serve as trainers for new recruits into their cadre. Such training, in addition to acquainting fresh staff with the practical aspects of their duties, helps develop camaraderie among new and old members of the cadre. Peer training was utilized in the Gal Oya irrigation management program in Sri Lanka initially as a stopgap arrangement to deal with high turnover rates among the cadre of organizers. This form of training helped in the development of rapport and team spirit among new and old organizers (Wijayaratna and Uphoff 1997). Similarly, NIA employed experienced community organizers to train new entrants. Although peer training has often been used for the purposes of organization and management, peer group sessions are also helpful for promoting understanding of technology. The Rajasthan watershed development program picks out field staff with a record of successful innovation to lead discussions with colleagues in refresher training sessions that are held every year. Staff learn from one another's experience, thus enabling new developments to be disseminated through the organization.

Training for Support

Persons at all levels of a program's structure are likely to require some sensitization to the needs of program implementation. Senior persons can best assist in the provision of policy support and programmatic inputs if they are fully aware of both the purpose and current directions of the program and the needs and aspirations of client groups. This is likely to require keeping critical decision makers abreast of program developments on the ground and involving them regularly in feedback and policy discussions, supplemented by visits to participating communities. The Iringa child nutrition program in Tanzania adopted both these methods. A regular system of monitoring kept policy makers aware of what was happening in the field. Crucial policy decisions were made only after senior ministry personnel had gone into the field and held discussions with local staff and villagers. This way, policy decisions could be most helpful in dealing with the practical concerns of field implementers (Jonsson, Ljungqvist, and Yambi 1993).

Another good example of involving senior staff in participatory decision making was PIDER, a program for integrated rural development in Mexico assisted by the World Bank. The novelty of this approach was to get planners to see development needs and opportunities through farmers' eyes, rather than viewing them remotely according to technical or financial considerations. The program developed a methodology for participation that relied on iterative programming to facilitate accommodation between the needs and priorities of local communities and the technoeconomic concerns of senior officials (Cernea 1983).

Sensitization to the overall goals of the program need not be confined to senior officials. Staff at lower implementation levels also work best when they are aware of the "big picture" rather than being informed, as is more often the case, only about particular tasks and targets that each of them is separately expected to achieve. Community organizers in the NIA's irrigation programs in the Philippines are trained in technical matters as well as group management techniques, but they are also instructed in the concepts and objectives that guide overall development. This helps them develop more innovative approaches to solve problems and to spot new opportunities for action that could assist in the achievement of organizational goals.

Technical staff in the Rajasthan watershed are trained to implement the new low-cost technologies, but before that, they take part in group sessions where the philosophy of the program and its long-term objectives are discussed. This makes them more productive in the field. Regarding themselves as essential parts of the larger organizational endeavor—rather than feeling like insignificant or bit players, a role to which they were accustomed—enables them to recognize and report new opportunities. A shared understanding of larger organizational goals thus facilitates the flow of relevant information up and down the organization's channels, an issue considered in the next chapter.

Group Training and Timing

Training and deploying staff in groups, wherever possible, is preferable to individual training and placement. As mass production is being reconsidered and reorganized the world over to take account of concerns about quality management, assembly-line methods of industrial production are being supplanted by problem-solving teams. The benefits of goal-oriented teamwork are likely to be even greater in the diverse, changing, and uncertain environments that characterize rural development programs than on factory floors.

Group training helps members become aware of problems that other members have faced and solved but that have not yet occurred in their own areas. This enables all members of the group to anticipate problems and generate solutions. We have seen how this dynamic worked in the Indonesian IPM program. In the Gal Oya irrigation management program, too, the benefits of group training for organizers were realized when these persons went on to form tight-knit teams in the field, helping one another solve problems and develop more effective solutions than they could have if each had acted alone.

Another consideration is the timing of training. Training has been organized in the most successful programs to suit the work calendars of trainees and the cropping calendar when agriculture is involved. For farmers, training needs to be organized at times when they can get away from their agricultural duties. Similarly, full-time field staff are best trained when they are relatively unburdened with the activity of field implementation.

Knowing that farmers were unable to spare a long stretch of time for training all at once, trainers in the San Martin Jilotepeque program designed training programs that could be given one day every week for nine weeks. Farmers who took part in these training sessions could do so without having to neglect their agricultural and other tasks. This also gave them time to fully absorb what was learned after testing it at home. Other programs, such as the Malawi rural water supply program, have scheduled training activities to coincide with the agricultural off-season, when farmers have more time on their hands. Of course, taking time out for training is almost always somewhat disruptive of schedules and normal work flows. There is therefore often a disposition to postpone it, but since there is seldom a convenient time for training, it might as well be done sooner rather than later.

Training as an Ongoing Concern

Since it involves learning, training is something that is never fully accomplished. Retraining and in-service training are necessary to ensure that knowledge does not become dated or stale, and it should be provided in ways that encourage trainees themselves to experiment and innovate rather than just apply what is being taught. As program concerns evolve or as better technical and organizational recommendations are developed, there need to be periodic refresher training programs. BRAC's administrators regularly call together teachers in that NGO's nonformal primary education program to participate in review and training sessions. Held at the end of every month, these one-day sessions enable teachers and trainers to learn from one another's experiences. Within the NIA's programs in the Philippines, ongoing reviews of training facilitate the development of refresher training curricula that are most relevant to the developing concerns of staff and farmers.

Just as it is never complete, training does not provide any final solutions to the problems it addresses. What training can best provide is a set of concepts and tools that enables program staff and participants to approach problems with trained though still open minds. The test of successful training and technology diffusion lies in the continuing ability of program staff and participants to appreciate and assess new problems and opportunities as these arise from day to day, to devise innovative solutions for these problems, and to make good use of new opportunities. Thus, rural development is knowledge driven, whether that knowledge concerns technology, organization, or management.

NOTES

1. Another requirement was that the technical problem be redefined. Smallholders in Puebla State depended as much on beans as on maize, and "improved" maize varieties that did well in monocrop situations produced less than local varieties when intercropped with beans. So the effort shifted from introducing high-yielding varieties, the initial solution offered to farmers, to providing fertilizer and making other improvements in the existing farming system (Whyte and Boynton 1983, 36–40).

2. Providing incentives was made difficult by systemwide civil service rules concerning pay, promotions, and placement. Thus, somewhat unconventional incentives had to be devised. Good workers and their teams were selected for visits to other parts of India that had outstanding programs in natural resource conservation. These visits came to be seen as a sign of recognition in the department. Also, by sending the best staff to these programs, they could see how much further they had to go compared with the best in the country. Asking people to contribute articles about their innovations for the department's technical manual and to lead training sessions was another way of recognizing and rewarding achievement in nonmonetary ways.

3. One of the important elements of institution building is *doctrine*, a shared understanding of the institution's or program's purpose and approach (Esman 1972). Some of the most successful rural development programs have set up special training institutions that impart knowledge about objectives and philosophy

as well as more technical subjects: the Institute for Rural Management at Anand created by the National Dairy Development Board in India, which grew out of the Anand dairy cooperative movement; the sixteen training and resource centers operated by BRAC; the Campus for Cooperative and Development Studies set up at Kegalle in Sri Lanka by SANASA; and the Asian Center for Population and Development established by the Population and Development Association in Thailand. The latter two carry out training for persons and organizations in the Asian region.

4. In neither of these programs are villagers offered any financial assistance until they have demonstrated that the group has matured into a functioning organization.

7 Information as a Management Tool

The present era is heralded as an information age, in which many advances are made possible by the acquisition, dissemination, and analysis of information through various electronic technologies. Although this is most dramatic for high-tech enterprises, we find that many of the most successful rural development initiatives have also tapped into the power of information. Thus far, there has been limited use of or benefit from computers or satellite dishes. But as such hardware becomes cheaper and more accessible, we expect to see it adopted usefully in rural development programs, provided that appropriate software and programming are available.

In the previous chapter, we considered what benefits could be derived from information and knowledge when used in the form of technology and when transmitted through training to improve skills, motivation, and coordination. Here we focus on uses of information that can lay the foundation for systematic utilization. Already, computers are starting to be employed in managing various rural development programs, enabling these to operate larger and more complex activities.[1]

What is information? In the broadest sense, almost everything can be reduced or attributed to information. It can be understood in the hierarchical terms suggested by this verse from T. S. Eliot (1934, 7):

Where is the wisdom we have lost in knowledge?
Where is the knowledge we have lost in information?

To this, we would add the question: And where is the information we have lost in data?

Data are the most elementary descriptors of physical or social reality. By themselves, they make little sense unless and until they are organized into information, which in turn needs to be integrated and structured into knowledge to be really useful. The transformation from knowledge into wisdom, which is the highest achievement, is something for which we still have no rigorous or reliable methods, unfortunately.

For practitioners of rural development, there are two steps: creating information from data, and using information to change behavior and outcomes based on some knowledge of how these can be affected. In recent years, increasing attention has been devoted to management information systems (MIS), enabling practitioners to handle more efficiently the large amounts of data and information that programs generate and require. We consider such systems in this chapter, along with others for using information to achieve development goals more effectively and reliably.

Information as a resource has some special qualities that set it apart from funds, personnel, incentives, and materials, considered in Chapter 5. Operating outside the law of the conservation of matter, information is not diminished by being given away. Indeed, the value of what information one already has can often be enhanced by sharing it more widely (except in the case of matters that derive their value from secrecy, which is not common in rural development). Information can be shared almost indefinitely, with the process of dissemination producing mutations that can either enhance or degrade the information in circulation.

There are, however, costs associated with information generation, storage, retention, retrieval, analysis, and application. Not all sorts of information are worth having, considering the resources and effort required. Many agencies, especially government agencies, waste much staff time accumulating mounds of information, piles of paper that usually lie around in the head office and gather dust. The following discussion is not an unqualified endorsement of information gathering. Rather, there should be some concept of "need to know" that compares the cost of having information with its expected value for improving decisions and making better use of resources.[2]

There can be substantial costs, widely underestimated, associated with not having certain information. In this chapter, we consider how information has been and can be used as a management tool that enables programs to get more benefit from the other resources at their disposal, provided these tools do not acquire autonomous lives and imperatives of their own. Some of the strategies and systems used are familiar concepts within the field of management, though they have been applied more often in urban than in rural settings, and with industrial production more than agriculture. Later in the chapter, we consider innovative information systems developed in Tanzania and Thailand for participatory rural planning, implementation, and monitoring. These two experiences offer useful ideas for employing information to affect the behavior of both villagers and officials. We also consider strategies for communicating information within development programs.

MANAGEMENT INFORMATION SYSTEMS

As the information age was emerging and managers had to cope with increasing amounts of information, MIS came into vogue. Because these systems were quite demanding of trained personnel and finances, however, few development programs adopted them. More appropriate is the kind of system called a programming and implementation management system (PIMS), developed to manage rural programs in Kenya (Chambers 1985, 43–54).

Among the cases considered in *Reasons for Hope*, the most extensive and formal MIS are operated by the Bangladesh Rural Advancement Committee (BRAC) and the Anand-model cooperatives. As noted in Chapter 5, BRAC values its MIS in part for its bolstering of a system of participatory management (Abed and Chowdhury 1997, 55). Having extensive information detailing resources expended, staff deployed, village organization performance, and program outputs has enabled persons with management responsibilities at all levels to engage more knowledgeably in evaluations and decision making. Operation Flood, implemented by the National Dairy Development Board in India, collects data from more than 70,000 dairy cooperative societies, aggregating these for the 160 participating district unions and then for the states and the entire nation.

The MIS approach as developed for large-scale business enterprises has not generally been adapted for rural development, although various less formal versions have been put in place. Credit operations such as the Grameen Bank in Bangladesh and the SANASA savings and loan cooperatives in Sri Lanka have set up quite detailed information systems, as these are necessary for financial record keeping and accountability, intended to deter any misuse of funds.[3]

A distinction between information for the management of programs, on the one hand, and information on the programs themselves, on the other, is not easy to operationalize in rural development. Systematic acquisition and review of information about operations are essential, however, and become more important as the operational scale grows. We find particular merit in information systems based on data that originate from and are understood by program participants. Rather than have a specialized flow of information for program managers, the program itself should operate in an information-rich environment, as seen in the Tanzanian and Thai cases discussed later. It is also important that the MIS be designed to serve management requirements rather than simply suit donor agencies' ideas of what is appropriate.[4]

MONITORING AND EVALUATION

Widely employed by successful rural development programs are systems of monitoring and evaluation (M&E) that feed back to program managers and participants relevant information on progress, performance, and problems. M&E should improve management decisions by focusing on improving processes as well as achieving objectives determined by program leaders and members. The Center for Economic and Social Development (DESEC) in Bolivia, a nongovernmental organization (NGO) that supports a wide variety of rural local organizations and initiatives, has made M&E a central function of its organization. Initially, most monitoring was done informally, but following guidelines of the United Nations' Administrative Committee on Coordination, it established a permanent system of M&E:

> Formal monitoring and evaluation force us to make detailed analyses of projects and to gain a clear definition of our objectives, expected outcomes, associated activities and indicators of success. The experience gained so far has allowed us to fine-tune our working methodology and provided valuable information as we expand our activities to neighboring zones. The formal system is complemented by periodic meetings with staff and people's organizations. . . . A system of periodic joint evaluations has been established alongside some of our bilateral donors. This has proved to be an interesting learning exercise on both sides. (Demeure and Guardia 1997, 99–100)

DESEC's system of M&E was developed incrementally. It was started with work in the forestry sector as a pilot effort and then extended progressively to other activities. The mode of evaluation is participatory, with local-level testing and assessment of innovations. Six-S, a similar program for rural development in West Africa, has developed continuous M&E involving rural communities not only in evaluation but also in self-evaluation (Lecomte and Krishna 1997).

Making M&E participatory and introducing self-evaluation are trends that we see in a number of programs. The Gal Oya farmer organization program in Sri Lanka started with systematic record keeping involving over 500 farm households, which contributed to seasonal reports on performance and progress in improving irrigation management. These more objective assessments were subsequently complemented by a methodology of self-evaluation that could best be translated into Sinhala language with a word meaning "self-strengthening," an appropriate concept. This methodology elicited subjective views from farmer-members and converted these into systematic information that could help the organizations and program managers identify areas that needed some bolstering of institutional and technical capabilities (Uphoff 1988, 1991).

In anthropology, a distinction is made between more subjective interpretations (emic) and more objective assessments (etic). Although these internal and external perspectives can differ, both have validity within their respective frameworks, and together they give a more complete understanding of phenomena than either can by itself (Uphoff 1992b). When evaluation is undertaken, the usual advice is to make it as objective as possible, preferring that it be done by outsiders who have no stake or vested interest in the program or its outcomes. Both Plan Puebla in Mexico and the Gal Oya program, having considered the limitations of taking a purely detached approach, found advantages in combining both internal and external views.

In the Mexico case, there were long debates when the program was planned whether to carry out evaluation as a function separate from operations. It was decided to develop in-house evaluation capacity so that mutual confidence could be built up between evaluators and field staff, and so that there would be quicker feedback than if a separate agency or division were making all the assessments. This arrangement is judged to have contributed much to program success. It was kept reasonably rigorous by having specified objective measures that were continually assessed by operational staff and by involving outside specialists in periodic data gathering and analysis (Diaz Cisneros et al. 1997, 125–6).

In the Sri Lanka case, an end-of-project evaluation by a team from the U.S Agency for International Development (USAID) estimated a much higher benefit-cost ratio (47 percent) than that which researchers from the Agrarian Research and Training Institute and Cornell University had calculated (between 16 and 24 percent). This showed that evaluators from outside are not necessarily more critical, or more correct.[5] The external end-of-project evaluation was also amiss in other ways (Uphoff 1992a, 221–3, 227–9). An important lesson that applies to rural development programs anywhere is that if institutional capacity building is a central objective, the criteria by which progress is evaluated need to change over time, since capacity building is itself an evolving process. The initial criteria may not be appropriate for assessing more advanced levels of institutional capacity.[6]

How much information as well as what kind should be gathered depends on how it will be used. If rural communities derive benefit from an M&E system, they have some reason to assist in the effort. The CAMP-FIRE program in Zimbabwe, which encourages local communities to help protect wildlife in return for a share of the economic benefits generated thereby, has a sophisticated monitoring system set up with support from the World Wildlife Fund for Nature. This monitoring system enjoys support from the communities because, in addition to keeping track of the number and status of wild animals in the respective regions, it maps crop damage caused by animals, for which villagers can be compensated.

The degree to which M&E can and should be quantified depends on the nature of the task. Programs may gather and report data because donor agencies expect such quantification. But there can be benefits for both program management and program participants from knowing things like changes in crop yields, use of purchased inputs, fragmentation of landholdings, school attendance and dropout rates, nutritional status of children under five years of age, and survival rates of tree seedlings planted for reforestation. The significance and meaning of such numbers are seldom self-evident, however. Data like this should be treated as indicators that require analysis and evaluation to determine whether they signify better achievement of program objectives. Numbers should be used, rather than merely believed.

Many elements of program performance are not amenable to quantification. The Aga Khan Rural Support Program (AKRSP) in northern Pakistan has developed one of the most thorough M&E systems. It monitors 120 indicators concerning participatory social organization, dependence of village organizations on project funds, management performance at the village level, linkages with other organizations, and improved natural resource management. Such measures were used to construct an institutional maturity index. The conclusion of AKRSP after several years, however, is that it is difficult to measure the process of institutional development quantitatively. Gathering the required data is quite time consuming, and at best, it gives a snapshot of a moving picture. The program has also adopted a qualitative case study approach to provide more insight into the progress being made for institutional development.[7]

The degree to which M&E should be formalized is partly a function of the size of the program. In a small program such as World Neighbors' agricultural development initiative in Guatemala, no systematic M&E was needed, so long as program managers were working closely with the people. In San Martin Jilotepeque, there were frequent meetings that included villagers, and the whole management style was participatory, with plans based on consensus. Given the amount of direct involvement, both participants and managers knew the status and progress of program activities. Still, even a small program benefited from periodic evaluations that brought in some perspectives from outside (Krishna and Bunch 1997, 148).

A rural development initiative at the other end of the size continuum is the Rajasthan watershed conservation program, which had similar objectives of reducing soil erosion while helping to raise production. It had to start up quickly before any M&E system could be put in place, so it utilized extensive and systematic debriefings at the end of the first year. The meetings focused on local practices that had demonstrated potential for wider application. As the program expanded with this initial knowledge base, it developed an M&E system that involved NGOs and university research stations. When trying to cover a very large area, hundreds of thousands of hectares, there is no alternative to instituting an explicit and extensive system of M&E. This is also seen in the Iringa child nutrition and survival program in Tanzania, which now covers the entire country. What was most significant about its M&E system was the extent to which it was participatory and designed to promote community education and action, as discussed later. A main message from experience with M&E is that it is worthwhile to give up, if necessary, some speed or precision in M&E to gain more local involvement.

Process Documentation

Monitoring can be done entirely in quantitative terms, with data being gathered and reported for a variety of selected variables. But by themselves, these do not inform managers very well about how and why their efforts are succeeding—or lagging. One of the major innovations in rural development management has been a form of qualitative M&E known as process documentation. This was devised as a methodology to enable the participatory irrigation management experiment launched by the National Irrigation Administration (NIA) in the Philippines, with Ford Foundation support, to be self-correcting (Korten 1982; Bagadion 1997). The Institute of Philippine Culture at the Ateneo de Manila was contracted to put specially trained social scientists into the field to observe community organizers as they interacted with farmers and officials. Their fortnightly narrative reports, called process documentation (PD), included whatever numbers and statistics appeared relevant, such as number of farmers contacted, meeting attendance, and dues collected. Qualitative assessments of things such as the pace of organizational development and emerging problems were, however, the main focus.[8] Reports were reviewed each month by a high-level committee in Manila, which was established to oversee the program. PD enabled it to make suggestions and give guidance on a timely basis (Korten 1988).

This system for M&E proved to be a well-justified investment in the view of both donors and managers. Although certain comparable data were assembled and analyzed by this process, more valuable were the

comments and insights of observers who monitored the activities of organizers and their interactions with farmers in the field. This methodology
has been assessed and refined by Philippine social scientists so that it can
be adapted to a variety of rural development initiatives (de los Reyes 1984;
Volante 1984; Veneracion 1989).

In the Gal Oya case in Sri Lanka, there were neither financial resources
nor personnel available to establish a separate cadre of process documenters to monitor and provide information for evaluating the program
as it evolved at the field level. Accordingly, a few of the organizers were
assigned responsibilities for PD on a part-time basis, being given only half
as large an area to work in as other organizers. This could be faulted for
possibly reducing the objectivity of the M&E process, but there were actually greater compensating benefits, supporting the view that the Plan
Puebla organizers expressed about evaluation, noted earlier.[9] More important than keeping M&E personnel independent and separate from operating staff is ensuring that the latter maintain a self-critical attitude. If
evaluation is seen as helping everyone associated with the program make
it more effective, staff will be more supportive of this function.[10]

Surely M&E information should be as correct as possible, but this will
not ensure the acceptance of findings and the modification of policies and
practices accordingly. Having cooperative, even interdependent working
relations between those who carry out programs and those who monitor
and evaluate them is important if the program is to explicitly and eagerly
learn from its experience. Some of the current canons concerning evaluation are thus misconceived. The process of M&E should be both detached
and engaged, concerned with knowing the factual situation as much as
possible, not preoccupied with assigning blame but rather seeking to make
improvements. After the government took over responsibility for the program, Plan Puebla suffered when the main objective of evaluation became
measuring "progress" rather than diagnosing limiting conditions and
taking action to correct deficiencies (Diaz Cisneros et al. 1997, 136).

RESEARCH AND EVALUATION

A more sophisticated use of information than monitoring and evaluation
is research and evaluation. This aims to create or acquire knowledge that
will improve program performance, not just keep track of what is happening. Research can explain why something is happening, or why not.
Some successful rural development programs have gone beyond MIS and
M&E efforts to engage in knowledge generation, although an explicit
commitment to research is not yet common. Perhaps this is because

"research" is often regarded by practitioners as impractical and costly. We propose, however, that there is nothing so practical as a good idea, and few things are more costly than ignorance.

The most ambitious effort to undertake and apply research for rural development is by BRAC, which has created its own Research and Evaluation Division. Over 100 BRAC staff members undertake a variety of research activities, including contract research for other agencies, which earns revenue to support program activities (Lovell 1992). Indian dairy cooperatives have similarly established the Institute for Rural Management at Anand (IRMA). Its professional staff number around thirty, and in addition to doing degree and nondegree training, they carry out research on a wide range of subjects bearing on rural development. The Orangi Pilot Project (OPP) approached most of its activities as a form of action research (Khan 1997, 26). Once effective technologies, organization, and incentives had been worked out, solutions that were devised and grounded in community-based organizations were spun off to be carried forward by separate but associated programs.[11]

DESEC is an example of a program that is increasingly involved in participatory research and evaluation, actively involving members of communities (Demeure and Guardia 1997, 99–100). World Neighbors' program in the Andean countries, expanding on the action research tradition it started in Guatemala, has established a community-based system of field experiments managed by paraprofessionals and other villagers to improve soil fertility through the use of cover crops and green manures (Ruddell, Beingolea, and Beingolea 1997). Yields of potatoes and barley are being doubled and tripled with minimal outside inputs.[12] The Rajasthan watershed conservation project devised a variety of new technologies and methods in consultation with communities. Once they were field-tested by staff, who acted on their own initiative in working with local user groups, these innovations were disseminated to other communities. They were presented as suggestions rather than solutions, however, since villagers would have to satisfy themselves in each situation that the new practice was suitable (Krishna 1997). There is much more scope for participatory research than has been seen so far in rural development programs. To some extent, there needs to be some demystification of what constitutes research, to satisfy farmers and researchers alike that research can generate useful knowledge.

Operations Research

Operations research is the adaptation and application of rigorous research methodologies to understanding and improving management processes, focusing on behavioral aspects of system performance. It has been used mostly for business and military purposes, but we find it employed by BRAC to refine its implementation of major national programs, such as for oral rehydration therapy (ORT). This program, which explicitly adopted a learning process approach, is well documented and assessed in Chowdhury and Cash (1996; see also Lovell and Abed 1993). In ten years' time, BRAC staff educated over 12 million mothers in rural Bangladesh on how to save the lives of their children afflicted with diarrhea. The technology involved was simple—mixing salt and sugar into a solution of prescribed proportions—but the task of getting millions of mostly illiterate women scattered in tens of thousands of villages to do this correctly and use it with therapeutic effect was massive.

Bangladesh has no detailed data on the causes of death among children, so evaluation of impact cannot be precise, but diarrhea is the leading cause of death among children under age five. This source of mortality among children aged one to four has been lowered by 35 percent, indicating considerable impact. BRAC researchers studying the ORT program assembled data that enabled them to compare impacts on a household and village scale to improve the design of the program as it proceeded. The message communicated to mothers—how many points were taught, and how they were worded—was changed several times in response to research findings, and it was determined that teams needed to stay in the villages longer to build up trust. Through experimentation, it was learned that mothers could produce a solution within prescribed limits by using "pinches" of sugar and salt rather than measuring out spoonfuls, which caused some confusion. Inclusion of men as part of the village training team was also tested and validated by operational research methods.[13]

Success was rigorously evaluated by testing whether, some months after training, mothers could mix solutions that met medical standards. Laboratories were set up for this purpose in rural areas, and a system of incentive payments to trainers was linked to this independent evaluation of program effectiveness. When operations research determined that program expansion during a second phase was too rapid to maintain training quality and the commitment of mothers to use what they had learned, modifications were made in the strategy (Chowdhury and Cash 1996, 86–7).

No other rural development program that we know of has made such extensive and detailed efforts to determine the extent and causes of its effectiveness, with corrective measures built into the process of knowledge generation. Data are gathered systematically and converted into information, and this, in turn, is transformed into knowledge that can guide program efforts. BRAC provides a good example of how operations research can strengthen a program by the application of research methods in a goal-oriented, problem-solving way. As rural development efforts expand, and especially as they venture into unfamiliar areas of activity, programs are well-advised to invest human and financial resources in this kind of knowledge generation. This is what has helped BRAC grow into the largest indigenous NGO in the Third World. It creates and uses knowledge purposefully and imaginatively to ensure that scarce resources have their intended benefit.

COMPREHENSIVE SYSTEMS OF INFORMATION

The functions of management, monitoring, and evaluation can be combined into a comprehensive program of rural development if the task of planning is also included, especially if all these activities are carried out in a participatory way. We have been impressed by two cases in which information was used for comprehensive program development and implementation: in Tanzania for improving child health and nutrition, and in Thailand for integrated rural development. The Iringa child survival and development project, reported in *Reasons for Hope* (Krishna, Jonsson, and Lorri 1997; see also Pelletier 1991; Jonsson, Ljungqvist, and Yambi 1993), and the Khorat rural development program (Uphoff 1986b, 348–50; Piyaratn 1993) are different in appearance, but their uses of a nested hierarchy of local organizations generating information from the bottom up are both similar and exemplary.

In both cases, there was a small organizational unit at the base: a ten-household cell (Iringa) or a ten- to fifteen-family cluster (Khorat). In the Tanzanian case, the project built on the system of political organization that the ruling party already had in place, whereas in Thailand, the program grouped households together within neighborhoods. In both cases, these groups were subunits within established villages, and there was a second tier of organization at that level. Then there was a level of organization at the locality level, called a ward or a *tambon* in the respective countries. It reviewed needs identified and initiatives taken at village and group levels. Above this, there were district levels and then regional or provincial levels of organization before getting to the national level. The point of this analysis is that above the household, there were five levels of organization (group, village or community, locality, district, and region or province) through which information passed upward and downward to and from the national center. The generation, flow, and evaluation of information had the effect both of changing attitudes and behavior at various levels and of mobilizing and directing resources to meet prioritized needs.

In the Tanzanian case, the objective was fairly simple: to reduce malnutrition among children, measured biometrically in terms of weight for age, as well as disease and mortality among infants and children. In Thailand, the goal was integrated rural development, as defined by villagers themselves using the concept of basic minimum needs (BMN) rather than by development experts.[14] The core of both programs was regular and quantified assessment of status and progress according to a number of measures. In Tanzania, village health days were held every three months, when every child under five years of age would be weighed and measured by health paraprofessionals in the village square, with measurements recorded on the child's growth chart. Every parent, but also health workers and local officials, could see which children were falling below developmental norms. This would trigger efforts—starting at the household level but moving upward to the cluster, village, or ward—to mobilize resources for food availability, employment opportunities, sanitation improvement, or whatever else was diagnosed as being necessary to remedy lagging development.[15]

In Thailand, the process was more complex. Clusters assessed their status annually according to the thirty-two basic minimum needs agreed on. Percentages were established below which a cluster or village would be considered unacceptable, for example, more than 40 percent of infants born underweight (less than 3,000 grams). Cluster data were aggregated to the village level to be reviewed by a village council, chaired by the village headman. Everyone in the village was made aware of which clusters were not up to expectations, and in what specific ways. The village considered what could be done to correct the situation so that by the next annual review, the problem would be within more acceptable limits. Village data, in turn, were passed on to and reviewed by a subdistrict council. Then the district and provincial governments determined where there were concentrations of poverty and social disorganization that warranted action from higher levels. The process is described as one of:

> problem identification, planning, prioritizing the types of activities and supports needed, implementing and evaluating by re-survey of the BMN status of the village. As a result, villagers, by themselves, are aware of their own problems and levels of achievement. At the same time, the district and provincial administrations are able to effectively carry out their supervisory and supportive tasks and closely interact with villagers in trying to respond to their needs.
>
> An evaluation of the BMN in Khorat province showed that significant improvements in participating villages' BMN status were observed for 1983–1985. Moreover, a comparison of villages over time revealed that the longer the period of people's/villages' involvement, the higher the achievement in terms of BMN indicators. (Piyaratn 1993, 69)

As in Iringa, there was observed change in the behavior of both villagers and officials once systematic evaluative information was available to everyone at the village level and above. Special incentives were not needed; simple, reliable information about the true conditions was enough. Although initial measurements could be wrong in either case, having a system of repeated measurement meant that over time, inaccurate figures (or purposeful under- or overreporting) were corrected. In Thailand, it was found that about 80 percent of the problems identified could be handled by local action, without resources or policy changes from above.[16] Similarly, in Tanzania, village health committees followed up on any children whose weight put them into the "red zone" of concern.[17] Such a system of information mobilized and directed resources both at local levels and from above. Higher-level bodies were able to direct their discretionary development funds to those communities and to those problems that most needed targeted investment.

Most of the villages in Thailand began using BMN indicators to gauge their own developmental status and achievement. There have been some modifications as the process has continued, sometimes adding new indicators and sometimes raising the criteria for success to a higher level. "However, long-term success still needs constant and persistent government supports" (Piyaratn 1993, 70). The process described from Thailand applies almost verbatim to what has been established concurrently through the Iringa project in Tanzania:

> [The program] entails people assessing their own achievements and situations, analyzing the causes of problems, and taking action to correct these through their own resources or with government support. Equally necessary for ensuring community participation and intersectoral collaboration are decentralization of planning and resource support, improvement in community organization, and the training of local officials and community members in areas relevant to community development (for example, community financing, manpower development, etc.).
>
> Tactically speaking, the application of BMN indicators in searching for problems, priorities, and the ways and means to solve them at the village level by villagers themselves has proven successful in releasing untapped village resource potential. Introduction of the new planning process using BMN indicators by direct involvement of village leaders has created awareness regarding the priority needs and development issues. It has also motivated them to take an active part in development activities because of direct benefits arising from their participation. (Piyaratn 1993, 70)

The usual explanation for behavior is framed in terms of motivation, and the prescription for changing behavior is to offer new or different incentives. What we see in these cases are far-reaching changes in behavior attributable to information. Parents in Tanzania already wanted to improve the nutrition and health of their children, and Thai villagers wanted to live in communities that provided better for their basic needs. Producing information on deficits in a fully participatory manner—identifying deficiencies and their incidence—had a considerable motivating effect. People were uncomfortable about their cluster or village being below what had been agreed was a reasonable norm. Moreover, they could now know when progress was being made, and how much. This information altered not only the behavior of villagers but also that of local officials. The latter were enjoined by the facts of the situation and by villagers' expectations—as well as by their superiors' concern—to become engaged in problem solving.

In both cases, there was conversion of raw data—children's weights, school attendance numbers, incidents of home garden theft—into information, summarized data in a form that was intelligible. This was put within a framework that called for some initiative when the indicators of performance were outside the range judged acceptable. What ensued was a problem-solving process involving local people, in their roles as parents or as village residents, together with any paraprofessionals, technicians, or administrators available. The information now publicized begged for corrective action, but it did not prescribe any particular course of action.

Solutions were to be contrived that would most effectively redress the undesirable situation, drawing on the resources and personnel at hand—private and individual if possible, but public and community if needed. If some action had to be taken that was beyond local means, this was possible and more likely if local capabilities had already been activated and utilized. The program established a system for reporting and reviewing information that went upward, engaging higher-level decision makers on a regular basis with facts about what existed at ground level.

The existence of systematic data gathering, with regular, periodic conversion of these data into information that was widely known and understood, created dynamics of its own. The information provided its own reinforcement, enabling people to accomplish things that they already wanted but could not achieve otherwise due to lack of concerted effort and support. Having baseline information gave all parties a sense of accomplishment whenever progress was made. Although there was some increase in the input of external resources, these were used to create a system of information generation and distribution, linked to a nested structure of decision making empowered to take remedial action.

Most of the resources required to improve child survival or the quality of village life were mobilized from local sources, or they were resources that higher levels of government would have expended anyway but could now target better. Information in this way became a factor of production that was not used up in the process, one that made other factors—money, materials, and human resources—more beneficial. The highly participatory and public ways in which the information was elicited and processed contributed to the impact that these local development information systems could have.[18]

COMMUNICATION SYSTEMS AND STRATEGIES

Information by itself is inert. It does not possess any intrinsic means for its own diffusion. There need to be channels, means, and motivations for getting information to those who need it and can put it to use. Very few rural development projects ever design an explicit strategy for communication so that everyone in a "need to know" position receives appropriate information. Increasingly, however, projects include mechanisms such as inception workshops to inform all stakeholders (or, more likely, representatives of stakeholders—not everyone can participate) about objectives, programs, timetables, and the like. Newsletters, periodic public meetings, posters, suggestion boxes, and other means are fairly common, but seldom do they add up to an effective strategy for ensuring that all relevant parties are kept informed. When a communication process is purposefully planned, it is likely to be stronger for downward than for upward information flows. Communication, practically by definition, needs to be two way, however.

Plan Puebla in Mexico, one of the first major integrated rural development initiatives in Latin America, took a proactive stance in this regard:

> The production and dissemination of information were seen as a continual process, with constant interaction among staff members and feedback of information, from the planning of research through the delivery of findings to farmers to the evaluation of results. . . . The members of the team lived in the project area, cooperating closely in conducting the field trials and demonstrations and attending farmer meetings. (Diaz Cisneros et al. 1997, 122)

There had to be a system of communication set up to deal with other institutions in the rural sector that affected the ability of rain-fed maize farmers to adopt and benefit from the new technologies, such as rural banks and marketing agencies. The project coordinator was assigned to manage these linkages:

As information flowed in from the field work, he communicated new findings to the institutions. After each harvest, the coordinator was in frequent contact with representatives of these institutions, explaining the plan of operation for the following year and working to obtain their approval and support. When a problem arose due to the operating procedures of an institution, information on this was prepared by staff and communicated by the coordinator to the responsible people. (Diaz Cisneros et al. 1997, 126)

Reaching members of the public is more difficult than communicating with institutions, because the public is more diffuse. Standard advice from the advertising profession is that multiple channels of communication should be used, and used repeatedly, since no single channel or single exposure will reach all who need the information. There is no substitute for face-to-face communication, but this should be supplemented by other media. The Orangi Pilot Project, for example, held hundreds of meetings to reach people in their neighborhoods, and posters and pamphlets were concurrently used to explain OPP objectives and plans (Khan 1997, 31).

Culturally appropriate and innovative means of communication have been useful. Both SANASA cooperatives in Sri Lanka and the Population and Development Association (PDA) in Thailand found it advisable to use Buddhist venues and teachings to get their messages across (Kiriwandeniya 1997, 65; Mechai 1997, 206). In Indonesia, the integrated pest management (IPM) program used a wide variety of means to supplement and diffuse the information provided through its farmer field schools:

After the field school, a number of follow-up programs have been organized by program field workers, including IPM field days for horizontal communication, IPM people's theater, farmer-to-farmer training, farmer seminars, training in participatory planning, and farmer field studies. The field school program is just the entry point for developing a farmers' network, linking local organizations and improving their access, leverage and capability. (Oka 1997, 193)

The entertainment value of communication is not to be disregarded, since people have to attend to a message before it can be conveyed. Films at the village level are more attractive than spoken messages, although as the video technology spreads, it will increasingly lose its novelty value. The Iringa nutrition project found that a film it produced called "Hidden Hunger" provided a good way to engage villagers' interest (Krishna, Jonsson, and Lorri 1997, 218). The Rajasthan watershed conservation project used a film provided by the World Bank to get discussions started in village meetings; even a movie on farmers' use of vetiver grass in Fiji served this purpose (Krishna 1997, 160). Part of the success of the PDA's program to change thinking about family planning in Thailand was due to the public-relations skills of its director, who had been an actor on television before starting an NGO. The PDA's approach to communication appealed to people's sense of fun; blowing up condoms like balloons before audiences and on TV helped to demystify something otherwise kept hushed up (Mechai 1997, 205).

The content of communication needs to be varied. Facts are the kind of information most explicitly conveyed, but to reinforce the kinds of activities and changes in behavior a program aims at, there needs to be some impact on attitudes and values, not just on people's knowledge. Ideas and concepts, more than just facts, should be disseminated. This requires imaginative formulations that are culturally appropriate, as noted above, and that are easy to grasp—simple, succinct, attractive, self-evidently legitimate, and enhancing of self-esteem.

Ideas were used very purposefully in the Gal Oya irrigation management program. Explaining to engineers the proposed transition to a more participatory system in terms of going from "retailing" water to "wholesaling" it made sense. It justified their no longer trying to allocate and deliver water to individual farmers, providing instead an agreed-upon volume of water to the head of a distributary canal, where farmer groups took responsibility for its distribution. This concept reinforced engineers' status as responsible professionals; it legitimated their doing less and extricating themselves from the most controversial and least successful part of their jobs (Uphoff 1992a, 360–3, 373–5). Ideas, well conceived and communicated, can propagate themselves, with both beneficial and detrimental mutations in the process. In addition to thinking about means of communication, therefore, much thought should go to crafting messages that will be self-propagating and robust, with more positive than negative embellishments as they spread.

The more public the processes of communication, the better. The village health days that the Iringa project in Tanzania instituted at the community level not only encouraged the transaction of specific health and nutrition-related information. This event also created a public climate of interest and discussion that raised people's consciousness about what was desirable and achievable to improve children's possibilities for survival and success. Successful rural development programs have increased the volume of information transactions at many levels concerning the purpose of their efforts—for girls' education, savings and loans, milk production and processing, family planning, tree planting, or wildlife conservation. Initiatives to achieve rural change have to be concerned with communication as a complement to whatever they are doing on the technical and organizational fronts.

Farmer-to-Farmer Dissemination

Not all diffusion of information needs to be through program efforts or under program auspices. Indeed, one mark of a successful program is that its messages regarding technology, incentives, and organizational structure get diffused through the efforts of local people. One successful rural development initiative that did not have an explicit communication strategy was the Agroforestry Outreach Project in Haiti. It decided to let its technology and incentives do the talking. In fact, there was rapid acceptance of replanting; "as news of the project spread, peasant demand for the seedlings kept increasing" (Murray 1997, 246).

It is possible that some innovations can be simple and attractive enough that they do not need deliberate efforts by program designers and implementers to deal with the communication dimension of rural change. But it is also unlikely that programs' impact could not be improved, hastened, or extended by some attention to communication means and strategies. This does not mean that project planners design such methods by themselves; rather, they work with program participants at the grassroots to devise intelligible and effective ways of engaging the attention, interest, and inputs of local people like themselves.

There is increasing interest in farmer-to-farmer extension, what can be described generically as horizontal diffusion of information and innovation. This methodology has been promoted by NGOs such as World Neighbors and the International Institute for Rural Reconstruction (Bunch 1982). We find it in various versions in most of the programs reported in *Reasons for Hope*. In assessing the Indonesian IPM program, Oka says:

> The second stage of the strategy—farmer-to-farmer extension—has begun to occur, enhancing the impact of the initial government-led thrust. Those farmers who have been trained in IPM are training their neighbors. The IPM program has also contributed a new learning methodology to the toolkit of our extension workers. The participatory learning process practiced in the IPM farmer field schools will now be used to accelerate other extension programs. (1997, 197)

This is a pattern that one hopes to see in most initiatives for rural development. One hopes that participants in a program will begin fairly quickly to diffuse innovations to their peers because they have confidence in the new technology or mode of organization. To the extent that they appreciate the opportunities that the program has given them, they should be willing to expend some effort to share their new knowledge with others like themselves. This may sound idealistic, but we have seen this occur in programs that we have been personally involved with—farmers taking the time and making the effort to help spread the benefits of which they are partaking (Krishna, Uphoff, and Esman 1997, 296–8; Wijayaratna and Uphoff 1997).

Willingness to participate in farmer-to-farmer extension can be enhanced by program design. The earlier model of extension associated with conventional diffusion theory was that "progressive farmers" be identified and given access to the most modern technological information and the subsidized credit and inputs. Their example—higher yields in the fields—was supposed to persuade other farmers, less well endowed and less educated, to follow suit. What typically happened was that the success of "advanced" farmers was attributed in other farmers' minds to their privileged status and access, with the result that little diffusion took place, partly due to resentment and rejection.[19]

One design feature that can facilitate farmer-to-farmer dissemination is for those farmers receiving training or managing demonstration plots to be chosen by their peers, not by the program or its field staff. This way, the training and experimentation are undertaken on behalf of the group, rather than particularly for the individuals involved. They will get some benefit by being the pioneers if the innovation is successful. In some programs, the project or the group insures the innovator, guaranteeing that any losses will be made good because the time and resources spent in training and experimenting were for the sake of the group, not just the individual. Such an arrangement gives the group reason to take an interest in the training or experimentation, to follow its progress, and to offer opinions on how it might be best applied. There is no reason for others to be envious—often a barrier to the spread of innovation—since they agreed that the person would take the initiative. (It is not uncommon for the flourishing crops of a "progressive farmer" to get sabotaged by jealous neighbors.) The spread of successful improvements is more assured, because the training or trials are really a collective endeavor.[20]

This system is not simply a communication mechanism. It is concerned with the substance of rural development, improving what can be done and how it can best be done. As with other successful methodologies, it integrates substance with process. Communication means are designed into the process of devising and testing innovations. This breaks the linear sequence of research first and then extension. Although this organizational model has contributed to many advances in agriculture, nutrition, and home economics in the United States and elsewhere, it is increasingly outmoded in the contemporary world, where resources are scarcer and where rural people are more educated and able to take responsibility for improvements adapted to their own conditions. We conclude this chapter by referring back to the preceding one, noting how technology, training, and communication should all be linked as part of a single enterprise, keyed to improving productivity and living conditions rather than being separate and parallel functions.

NOTES

1. When Uphoff visited BRAC's handicraft sales outlet in Dhaka in December 1996, he found that the cashiers had a very efficient computerized system that helped BRAC manage inventory and credit the makers of the handicrafts purchased, as well as produce a correct and legible sales slip. The Agricultural Development Bank in Nepal (ADB/N), which launched the large and impressive Small Farmer Development Program in 1975, decided in the late 1980s to introduce computers to expedite managing and tracking all savings and loan transactions. The gains in efficiency made over 100 employees redundant. These staff, rather than being dismissed, were redeployed to open up and operate more ADB/N branches in rural areas. The gains in efficiency permitted the bank to raise the interest rate it paid on savings by 1 percent, thereby attracting more savings. The net effect of computerizing operations was to increase the volume of deposits in urban areas and to expand the number of loans made in rural areas, with the same labor force as before. Whereas too often Third World banking systems funnel money from rural to urban areas, imaginative use of information technology by the ADB/N reversed this flow (S. K. Uphadyay, personal communication).

2. Recognizing this, we proposed some years ago the principle of "optimal ignorance" (Ilchman and Uphoff 1969, 260–2), which Chambers (1985, 153) has endorsed in his proposals for rural development planning and management.

3. Jain (1994, 1368) proposes detailed information gathering at the grassroots level to enable easy tracking of local events, including the pinpointing of individual mistakes by staff. This approach to MIS is not in the spirit of "learning process," inasmuch as it is intended to deter or punish rather than embrace and learn from errors. In addition, Jain does not consider how this much information would be monitored and used without paralyzing information overload at the top.

4. The Operation Flood MIS mentioned earlier, set up in response to donor requirements, is probably too elaborate. Obtaining information has become an end in itself, with limited analysis and use of that information.

5. A postproject evaluation done by researchers with the International Irrigation Management Institute calculated a benefit-cost ratio of 24 percent (Aluwihare and Kikuchi 1991, 45).

6. The USAID end-of-project evaluation reported that although measures such as improved water-use efficiency and channel maintenance indicated that the organizations were performing well, as did the personal assessments of engineers, local officials, and farmers, the organizations' capacity appeared to be declining according to two criteria: (1) the percentage of channel cleaning done by voluntary group labor rather than by individual efforts, and (2) the frequency of group

meetings held at the field channel level. Both measures had declined from about 80 percent to 50 percent between 1981 and 1985.

Farmers and organizers rejected this inference from the data, because they were satisfied that the organizations had gotten stronger during the life of the project. However, it was pointed out that these criteria were ones that the program itself had used when it started assisting farmer organizations in 1981. Once the system of organization was well established, they were no longer good measures of organizational strength. Maintenance by individual effort was more feasible once canals were in better conditions, and it was often more convenient. It could be effective because of group sanctions. And once problems soluble at the field channel level had been taken care of, regular meetings were less important, and efforts were directed toward problem solving above the field channel. By 1985, there were many regular meetings being held at higher levels, but these were not being monitored and evaluated as systematically as field channel meetings had been at the outset, so they were overlooked in the evaluation.

7. Asad Azfar, "Measuring Institutional Development: The AKRSP Approach," paper presented to workshop at the World Bank, Washington, D.C., January 31, 1997.

8. Process documentation was developed in a parallel way by the Orangi Pilot Project (Khan 1996, xxii).

9. Because the process documenters were part of the organizer cadre, they had a better understanding of the tasks and problems of organizing farmers, so their reports were more knowledgeable and realistic. Also, because they were part of the cadre, organizers did not regard them with suspicion or distrust, as happened to some extent when PD was undertaken separately from the work of farmer organizing in the Philippines. Feedback from PD to the rest of the cadre was quick and more readily accepted. Given that the cadre was committed to "embracing error," as discussed in Chapter 2, there was no resistance to critical observations in the PD reports, which were reviewed with each group of organizers before being sent to the Colombo office. This enabled process documenters to correct anything that had been omitted or misinterpreted, and it challenged the organizers as a group to engage in self-criticism and self-correction. Organizers did not wait for program managers to recommend remedial actions or new tactics. These could be adopted subsequently if certain efforts were still not succeeding.

10. In BRAC's oral rehydration therapy program, discussed later in the text, a detailed follow-up program was established to determine whether the knowledge imparted to village mothers, to save their children's lives when diarrhea occurred, was correct and remembered. The incentive system for trainers—giving them bonuses for every mother who passed the follow-up test—created a willingness to accept researchers' and evaluators' efforts to improve the effectiveness of the messages and the methods being used to train mothers. This enabled BRAC to avoid tensions or antagonisms between field staff and evaluators (Chowdhury and Cash 1996, 105–6).

11. The Orangi Pilot Project "from the very beginning, considered itself to be a research institution whose objective was to analyze the outstanding problems of

Orangi, and then through prolonged action research and extension education, discover viable solutions" (Khan 1996, xxi).

12. One farmer reported being able to increase his potato harvest enough to earn $1,200 more by investing just $18 in lupine seed. Farmers are doing experiments on randomized plots within their fields, assessing the effects of green manure, chemical fertilizer, animal manure, and combinations of all three. They also evaluate the productivity of different varieties, which are sensitive enough to differences in altitude, temperature, and sunlight that yields can vary as much as tenfold. Farmers can make substantial gains in output by systematically evaluating varietal and management differences. Once farmers understand the principle of randomization and significant differences, even if they could not previously do arithmetic, they become quite enthused about such research.

13. At first, it was believed that only women should be used, since mothers were the target audience for the training. Given local mores, men could not provide such training in rural Bangladesh. However, testing showed that women's acceptance and use of ORT was greater when village elders and men in the household understood and approved of the technique. So having a male team member educate men, though in less detail than the mothers, increased program impact (Chowdhury and Cash 1996, 51–2, 105–6).

14. Through a process of consultation, thirty-two measurable indicators were agreed on as criteria for desirable community development. Examples include the following: schoolchildren receive adequate food for nutritional requirements, measured in calories; pregnant women receive adequate and proper food to give birth to babies weighing not less than 3,000 grams; households possess a hygienic latrine; adequate clean drinking water is available year-round; all children get primary education; all primary schoolchildren are immunized; security of people and property (especially home gardens) is provided; fertilizers are used to increase yields; plant and animal diseases are prevented and controlled; families have no more than two children, and there is access to family planning services; people are involved in self-help activities; natural resources are preserved; family members are involved in religious practices at least once a month; there is no gambling or addiction to alcohol or other drugs (Piyaratn 1993). These were things that villagers themselves identified as important for a satisfying life in the village.

15. Any parent whose child was seriously underweight would be visited by the village health worker and by concerned members of the community, sometimes including extension workers from the health, agriculture, or social welfare departments. "The purpose of the visit is a combination of nutrition education, micro-level problem analysis, and social or political persuasion to induce behavioral changes" (Pelletier 1991, x). Follow-up visits would ensure that changes were being made to improve the child's status, and evidence of progress could be determined at successive village health days.

16. In the case of low-birth-weight babies, for example, once clusters of households were monitoring the weights of newborns, everyone took an interest in pregnant women and became solicitous about ensuring that they had sufficient nutritious

food. Public health nurses, who had previously approached their assigned duty of weighing every newborn rather casually, were now closely observed when a birth occurred and took great care to make accurate measurements.

17. The growth charts had a broad normal range; anything above one standard deviation below the international mean was colored green. The area between one and two standard deviations below the average was colored yellow as a warning. Below two standard deviations was the red zone, indicating danger.

18. In her study of successful government programs for development in the Brazilian state of Ceará, Tendler (1997, 15) reports that information about staff responsibilities and citizen rights contributed to markedly better performance by government personnel across several sectors. Pressures for staff to be accountable did not come from supervisors or formal monitoring bodies so much as from the better-informed public. With greater cooperation and expressions of appreciation from the public, personnel were more highly motivated to meet program objectives.

19. This was a limitation built into the World Bank–promoted training and visit (T&V) system of agricultural extension. The "contact farmer" was usually chosen by the extension agent (needing to meet targets in a timely way) rather than by the "follower farmers," as they are called in T&V terminology. The contact farmer was usually of higher socioeconomic status and usually owned more land, closer to roads. If messages got to him, they often did not get disseminated to and adopted by his neighbors. For critiques of the T&V system, see Antholt (1994), Chambers (1997, 71–2), and Uphoff (1986b, 121–2).

20. In Ghana, the Cornell International Institute for Food, Agriculture, and Development is collaborating with World Vision International/Ghana, the Ministry of Food and Agriculture, the Council for Scientific and Industrial Research, faculty at two universities, district assemblies, and (most importantly) community groups in what is called the Natural Resource Management and Sustainable Agriculture Partnership (NARMSAP).

    At the district level, the assembly has designated one of its zones (a collection of villages) to be the lead zone for farmer-centered research and extension. Each zone, in turn, has selected several villages to undertake experiments on its behalf. Within villages, volunteers are chosen to participate in the actual experiments, such as common paddocking, cashew planting, beekeeping, and inventory credit. Whole villages evaluate the experiences of individuals, and other villages within the zone participate in evaluation; ultimately, the whole district, through its assembly, decides where and how innovations can best be spread.

    This structure focuses initial efforts where there is the most enthusiasm and interest, working out and refining innovations rather than simply testing prepackaged technologies. It also makes for a more cooperative approach to technology development, avoiding the envy and jealousy that can otherwise impede innovation. There is friendly competition among individuals and villages, with the purpose of finding solutions to production and conservation problems that villagers have identified as urgent.

8 Utilization of External Assistance

Deriving benefit from information, the most nonmaterial of resources, requires various material means. Having reviewed how different resources can be managed to best effect in rural development programs, we now consider the question of outside funding and the use of resources external to a program. These may come from government agencies, nongovernmental organizations (NGOs), or foreign assistance agencies. Since such resources, especially those provided by donor agencies, appear to be declining in absolute terms and are certainly shrinking relative to need, it is important to consider how material support from abroad can best be utilized to improve capabilities and performance for broad-based rural development.[1]

Our endorsement of assisted self-reliance in Chapter 2 made it clear that we consider the receipt of external resources to be compatible with the goal of self-sustainability and the strategy of self-help, provided the aid relationship is appropriately conceived and maintained. How to do this can be learned from successful experiences with rural development that have gone beyond pilot stages and touched the lives of large numbers of people, which is what donor agencies say they want to accomplish.

There is much interest in and support for self-reliant approaches to development. Indeed, many donors are anxious to fund such efforts, often not understanding how paradoxical and problematic this can be. Public statements notwithstanding, donors sometimes shy away from organizations that insist on maintaining their own values and methods. By now, it should be clear that autonomy and self-sufficiency are not necessarily desirable in themselves, since they can amount to impotence or insignificance. Any community or program can find it advantageous to request and accept technical assistance, training opportunities, or financial support from outside sources, so long as these are compatible with its own goals. What must be avoided are external resources that divert programs from their goals or create long-term dependency on funds that may be unilaterally withdrawn or used as instruments of outside pressure. A strategy of assisted self-reliance is concerned with *how* aid is provided—on what terms, with what mutual expectations, on what schedule, with what matching resources?

It is tempting to argue that efforts toward the achievement of self-reliance are most satisfactory if the initiative comes from within the communities themselves. From previous analysis of a wide variety of experiences at the micro level, we have some evidence to support this claim.[2] But we also found a number of successful initiatives with substantial donor roles. Indeed, one that successfully championed and institutionalized self-reliance, the Orangi Pilot Project in Pakistan, was instigated entirely by an external donor—one now held in worldwide ill repute.[3] So qualitative factors—how outside resources are provided and managed—remain more important in our view than the source of funds, recognizing that the odds for success are greater to the extent that initiative and subsequent responsibility are local.

In this chapter, we review experience with external assistance in some of the most successful rural development ventures, looking particularly at modalities and principles that are most promising. There can be no guarantees of success. But at a time when there is so much disaffection with foreign aid, we are pleased to be able to document where and how outside assistance has been beneficial and even essential to successful ventures in rural development.

HOW NOT TO PROVIDE EXTERNAL ASSISTANCE

We begin with consideration of the Orangi Pilot Project (OPP). It is exemplary not only in its accomplishments for over 100,000 poor households but also for both benign and benighted outside aid. OPP was instigated by the Bank of Credit and Commerce International (BCCI), now known to have been engaged in financial skullduggery on a global scale. But in its home country, Pakistan, the bank offered substantial funds in 1980 to find ways to uplift living conditions in urban slums. Akhtar Hameed Khan accepted the challenge of finding organizational and technical means for improving sanitation and other services in a low-cost, self-managed way.

Orangi is a huge squatter settlement on the outskirts of Karachi, housing about one million residents of diverse ethnic origins in an area of 8,000 acres. OPP started with self-help sewerage, developing simple technologies that could be implemented by lane committees and that would provide sewerage at a cost of about $33 per household, mostly self-financed. During the life of the project, the ratio of local resources mobilized per rupee of external funding has been about *seventeen to one*. This is a remarkable demonstration of self-reliant development among the poor, showing that if genuine needs are being met in a cost-effective way, even the poor can contribute to their own development. It also shows what can be accomplished with the "pump priming" application of external resources.

OPP has moved on to establish education, health, credit, and other services for this large population, as described by Khan (1996, 1997). When Khan embarked in 1980 on this extrapolation of rural development techniques to urban areas, however, there was "skepticism, amusement, or outright hostility" among NGOs and bilateral and multilateral agencies working in urban areas in Pakistan (Khan 1996, xxiii). One outside agency, the United Nations Centre for Human Settlements (UNCHS), thought that it could improve on the approach that OPP was evolving and offered to provide expert services for sanitation, public health, program monitoring, and other areas. To oversee and coordinate these efforts, it furnished an experienced planner who would serve as joint director of OPP.

Most specialists in the field of rural development would have been hesitant to second-guess Khan, but apparently his reputation for insight, sagacity, and tenacity had not reached the urban planning profession, because the joint director began almost immediately finding fault with the OPP strategy.

> He found everything wrong with the Project. It had no targets and no "proper" physical, social or ethnic surveys. It had no master plan. It had no work programme. Its office was dilapidated and in the centre of a noisy and congested area of the settlement and as such was not conducive to serious work. And finally, its choice of sanitation technology . . . and implementation procedures were disastrous. He argued that the sanitation technology the OPP had opted for required sophisticated engineering and artisanal skills.
>
> This he felt could only be developed in association with local [government] bodies, elected councilors and professional contractors. Community organizations, simply backed by OPP professionals, technicians and social organizers could not deliver this technology. In addition, he felt that the social organizers recruited from Orangi communities were no more than "muscle men." (Arif Hasan in Khan 1996, xxiv)

After four months in Orangi, the joint director proposed that BCCI set up a project in the squatter settlement separate from the OPP, stating:

> Clearly there are two apparently irreconcilable approaches to project execution. One, open-ended, exploratory and evolutionary, with emphasis on sociological particularities, unconstrained by time and cost. The other, target-oriented, systematic, with a professional and technical focus, constrained by time and costs. (quoted in Khan 1996, xxiv–xxv)

In requesting BCCI funding, the technical adviser asserted that there should be no doubt that the UNCHS was uniquely equipped to provide specialized support for undertaking large-scale projects in low-income rural areas. Khan responded to this appraisal, suggesting that:

> The "target-oriented, integrated urban rehabilitation demonstration" approach may be suitable to an official agency like the Karachi Municipal Corporation or Karachi Development Authority, although previous efforts in [squatter settlements] along these lines have shown poor results. Such plans involve huge investments (not two million dollars, but hundreds of millions) besides the exercise of regulatory powers which are beyond the reach of an NGO. (Khan 1996, 151–2)

He cautioned, in conclusion:

> If the experts sent by UNCHS are completely obsessed with hackneyed, narrow and generally unsuccessful conventional techniques, unintelligently obtuse to pragmatic and innovative research and extension, blindly insensitive to local developments, and at the same time compulsively desirous of executive control, I am afraid the people of Orangi will derive little benefit from them, and the BCCI will get a miserable return from one million dollars. (153)

Nevertheless, Orangi was divided up as proposed by the outside adviser, and a new project under UN administrative control and technical guidance was set up. It was allocated $2 million for the first three years, and the OPP would continue to receive a small annual allocation in rupees. The new project, backed by a series of international experts, tried to establish the same programs as the OPP was operating. Yet after six years, it was able to develop sanitation facilities in only thirty-six lanes, while all its other programs went nowhere. The project was closed down in 1989, and responsibility for the whole area reverted to the OPP.

During the same period, at less than one-third the total cost, the OPP was able to catalyze sanitation services in over 4,000 lanes, covering more than 70,000 of the 94,000 houses in Orangi. This comparison makes the OPP *more than 100 times* more cost-effective in getting sewerage installed. In addition, its other activities to improve education, health, credit, and other opportunities took root and expanded beyond Orangi township.

Subsequently, several other agencies, including UNICEF and the World Bank, sought OPP assistance with their urban development projects. This collaboration is discussed in more detail later, but we note here that these relations were, if not always smooth, less rocky than the project's initial experience with external assistance. Subsequently, the OPP has received financial assistance from, besides UNICEF and the World Bank, the United Nations Development Programme (UNDP); the U.S. Agency for International Development (USAID); the Swiss Development Corporation; the Aga Khan, Rockefeller, and Winrock Foundations; and the government of Pakistan. It is significant that the OPP has been contracted by several of these agencies to give technical advice and assistance for other urban development programs. This gives substance to the idea that all international development transactions should be shifting from a concept of "foreign aid" to one of "development cooperation."

MORE BENEFICIAL RELATIONSHIPS

Some of the best examples of assisted self-reliance have been cases in which NGOs in Europe or North America—or, in the case of SANASA, an NGO from Australia—provided resources and support (see Table 8.1). The effectiveness of such aid is seen in the institutions that have been established, which enjoy the respect and support of rural people and the confidence of donors.

Readers may not be surprised to learn about cases in which NGOs in the North provided effective aid to incipient NGOs in the South. Less expected may be cases in which United Nations agencies played a similar supportive role, providing flexible funding and beneficial advice and assistance, considering that the UN is so often criticized these days for lacking such capabilities.

- The integrated pest management (IPM) program in Indonesia, which has now trained over 650,000 farmers in agroecosystem-based methods to control plant pests, was started, developed, and sustained with active technical and some financial assistance from the Food and Agriculture Organization (FAO). There was an active partnership between FAO personnel and Indonesian scientists and planners, with outsiders making the insiders more effective, and vice versa.[4]

- In Tanzania, staff from UNICEF and the World Health Organization (WHO), backed financially by the Italian government, forged a strong working partnership with Tanzanian counterparts to design, test, and then extend the Iringa model for improving child nutrition and survival. This effort attracted funding from the

Table 8.1   NGO External Assistance to NGOs in Developing Countries

Southern NGO	Program	External Assistance History
DESEC BOLIVIA	Technical and financial support of diversified rural development	Founder-members initially financed the program from their own resources; then early support ($1 million during the first five years) from European NGOs—Misereor (Germany), Vastenaktie (Netherlands), Fastenopfer (Switzerland), Entraide et Fraternité (Belgium)—enabled DESEC to get established; now diversified sources include the Food and Agriculture Organization and Belgian, Spanish, and Swiss aid
San Martin Jilotepeque GUATEMALA	Assist villagers to improve agricultural technology, health, and local capacities for technical innovation	Initial service and experimentation by medical missionary of Lutheran Church; then World Neighbors started technical assistance in health and agriculture with $25,000 grant; Oxfam (US) expanded program with $82,000 grant, supplemented by another $104,000; cost per household benefited was about $50 for many-fold increases in yields
Six-S SAHELIAN COUNTRIES	Grants and loans plus technical support and training to village groups for diversified agricultural and rural development activities	Initial encouragement from Swiss aid representative to find innovative ways to provide development assistance to rural villages; first grant of $12,000 from Misereor, followed by grants from other European NGOs and Swiss government; budget doubled every three years between 1978 and 1990; donors "lining up" now, program possibly expanding too fast
SANASA SRI LANKA	Savings and loan cooperatives to increase and mobilize local savings and make loans to members	Early modest funding from Community Aid Abroad (CAA), Oxfam affiliate in Australia; also Canadian Cooperative Association, World Council of Credit Unions, and HIVOS (Netherlands); external support covered salaries and some operating expenses during formative years; present external funding equals about 2 percent of value of loan volume; member deposits now over $40 million; local societies are fully self-financing
Population and Development Association THAILAND	Raise consciousness and acceptability concerning family planning to lower the birthrate; contribute also to community development	Started with a variety of small grants, including from the Ford Foundation and different donor agencies; self-financing village water supply program started with aid from AgroAction (Germany); assistance from Oxfam and other NGOs; set up a variety of for-profit activities that now finance 40 percent of education and technical assistance programs
CAMPFIRE Association ZIMBABWE	Get communities to take responsibility for protecting and preserving wildlife in return for share in benefits from it; almost all wildlife areas in the country are under local management	Staff member of Save the Children Federation (UK) provided initial support for meetings and planning, working with university and government partners; support from World Wildlife Fund for Nature and from Zimbabwe Trust, a national NGO; variety of donor funding now used for training, monitoring, research, capital investment, and income-generating projects; program generates own stream of funds from wildlife harvesting

World Bank, the International Fund for Agricultural Development
(IFAD), and SIDA, GTZ, and NORAD (Swedish, German, and
Norwegian aid agencies, respectively) to support programs along
similar lines elsewhere in Tanzania.

- The Small Farmer Development Program in Nepal was launched
  by the FAO with a grant of only $30,000 to the Agricultural Deve-
  lopment Bank in that country.[5] Within ten years, the program had
  gained enough experience and effectiveness that it was getting $40
  million in donor support and was assisting 40,000 rural households in some of the more remote areas of Nepal (Rahman 1984).

These examples show that large agencies can engage in innovative, constructive support of efforts at the grassroots that become large-scale programs. In each of these cases, there were some individuals within the UN
system who were more entrepreneurial and bigger risk-takers than is typical for international bodies. Such positive outcomes are possible, even if
they are not presently the rule.

One would expect international foundations, with the flexibility common to private agencies, to play a creative role in funding programs that
can make a difference.

- The Ford Foundation figured prominently in the early support of
  the Grameen Bank, the Bangladesh Rural Advancement Committee (BRAC), and the Philippines' National Irrigation Administration (NIA). In all three cases, financial assistance was given
  early in the process of program development; in the NIA case,
  foundation staff played an active role in helping to think through
  the requirements and processes for participatory development.
  Once these programs became established, they attracted substantial funding from the World Bank, USAID, IFAD, and other agencies, expanding tested practices and procedures to cover larger
  areas.

- The Aga Khan Foundation has played the lead role in setting up a
  series of rural support programs, the largest and most notable
  being the Aga Khan Rural Support Program (AKRSP) in northern
  Pakistan (World Bank 1987). This program underwrites rural
  development activities undertaken by 2,000 village organizations
  with more than half a million members, who make their own contributions of labor, money, and materials to improve irrigation,
  roads, health clinics, and other facilities.

- The Rockefeller Foundation supported Plan Puebla in Mexico in the latter 1960s, as one of the first interdisciplinary efforts to bring agricultural research to poor and marginal farmers. This initiative may have had more effect through the changes it brought about in the institutions that serve the rural sector than through the impact it had on 47,000 farm households in the state of Puebla. These efforts probably would have had more impact if private funding had not been terminated after six years, pushing the program into government hands, which were less supportive of innovative and self-critical approaches (Diaz Cisneros et al. 1997, 136).

Probably the most "mileage" from external funding comes when donor agencies can buy into a program that has already been developed with more limited resources. This provides a structure of organization, a pattern of operations, and a philosophy of service that can accomplish more than if donors try to build such capacities from the ground up themselves. The three examples we point to are ostensibly quite different, being an NGO, a cooperative, and a government program, but all invested in a learning process that produced both an effective doctrine of organization and a motivated cadre of personnel:

- BRAC started as a postwar relief operation and developed a philosophy and structure that enabled it to engage in a wide variety of grassroots development work, targeted to the poorest households (Lovell 1992; Abed and Chowdhury 1997). It now has an annual budget of $86 million, about 40 percent of which is self-financed; a staff of over 16,000; and a sophisticated capacity for research, monitoring, and evaluation, as discussed in the preceding chapter.

- The Anand dairy cooperatives began at the subdistrict level and, over time, refined their organization, technology, logistics, and incentives to the point where they could operate at the district, state, and national levels. In 1970, Operation Flood was launched as a World Bank–funded project to cover fifteen states. Today, the National Dairy Development Board, which is the institutional outgrowth of the Anand initiative, reaches and benefits over 9 million households in India (Doornbos and Nair 1990; Kurien 1997).

- The Malawi self-help water supply program was initiated by a government department through a pilot project in one village to test simple gravity-flow technology. As further small projects refined the technology and organizational mechanisms, donor funding was attracted from DANIDA and CIDA (Danish and Canadian aid agencies, respectively), Oxfam, UNICEF, Dutch church organizations, and particularly USAID. With external support from a variety of sources, potable water has been provided at very low cost to over a million rural residents (Hill and Mtwali 1989; Krishna and Robertson 1997).

In these three cases, donors were not trying to invent or design something new. Rather, they were enabling programs that had learned to be effective and efficient to expand (Korten 1980).

THE PROJECT APPROACH

Donor agencies are apparently wedded to designing, funding, and implementing projects, despite the accumulating evidence that this is not a good way to use scarce resources.[6] To the extent that a project can be planned and carried out in a learning process mode, it can avoid most if not all of the pitfalls of a "blueprint" style of operation (Korten 1980). We have been personally associated with some donor-funded projects that were able to work with communities in ways that built local capabilities and achieved technical objectives.

As noted earlier, one of the most successful projects in our view is the Orangi Pilot Project in Pakistan, which was most unusual in that it started with no plan, no targets, and no timetable. It adopted a learning process approach in the purest sense. We summarize in Table 8.2 how four project experiences featured in *Reasons for Hope* plus two others managed to avoid the difficulties and limitations that normally prevent donor-assisted projects from making the best use of available capital and human resources.

In each case, the project leadership treated the design as a starting point rather than as an injunction. Such instances, though few in number, show that project processes can be compatible with people-centered development. But each case required a degree of risk taking and perseverance that is not the norm in government agencies. The pathologies of normal project procedures constitute a subject in themselves (see Chambers 1993). Rather than focus on critiques of the project approach, we have tried in this book to map out constructive concepts and methods that are likely to produce more beneficial and lasting results.

Table 8.2   Donor Assistance for Successful Rural Development Projects

Project	Donors	External Assistance History
Rajasthan Watershed Conservation Project INDIA	World Bank	Donor funds of $25 million were made available for watershed conservation and development work, topping up $45 million from the government of India; a new government department was created to implement the project; using state-of-the-art principles, the project was able to proceed rapidly by working with user groups; it increased the rate of implementation ten-fold, satisfying both government and donor and giving the project leadership room to maneuver
Agroforestry Outreach Project HAITI	USAID	The project design was based on social science research, and the first project manager was an anthropologist; the donor gave ample and flexible support for ten years, although the NGO implementing the project sometimes had to proceed independently; a new donor mission director throttled the project, despite its success in involving 20 percent of rural households in planting 60 million trees, with a 60 percent survival rate
Gal Oya Water Management Project SRI LANKA	USAID	Donor added a farmer organization component in the final stages of project design; got a government research institute and a U.S. university to implement the participation component; some success was more in spite of rather than because of donor personnel; water productivity was increased fourfold; subsequent World Bank projects in the irrigation sector failed to build on what this project had learned and achieved
Iringa Child Survival and Development Project TANZANIA	UNICEF/WHO, Italian aid	Donors established a strong working partnership with a national research institute, did field analyses and diagnoses; started with a pilot effort in part of a district, then expanded systematically based on what was learned; strong government support and commitment to expanding successful innovations to the rest of the country; made rapid measurable advances
Nepal-Australian Forestry Project NEPAL	Australian aid (AIDAB)	Project started technocratically in 1966 and made little progress; learned of an experiment with community management supported by the district forest officer (DFO); Australian National University worked on behalf of the donor with the DFO and the community to refine this approach, which required considerable local contributions; the project spread, and national policy changes were implemented supporting community management
Moneragala Integrated Rural Development Project (MONDEP) SRI LANKA	Norwegian aid (NORAD)	Donor adopted the process approach over the blueprint approach; made flexibility, learning, and participation the three core principles of planning and implementation; worked according to "rolling plans" (Bond 1997); commitment of donor and government to a twenty-year time frame allowed the process approach to take place

THE DONOR CONSORTIUM APPROACH

As donors gain more experience working with rural development initiatives, they are becoming more sensitive to the need for flexibility and complementarity in efforts. Rather than insisting on the submission of detailed project designs for approval, a number of donors, when they have confidence in a certain approach to rural development and a certain leadership and mode of operation, have become willing to fund programs on a "wholesale" rather than a "retail" basis through the formation of a donor consortium.

After 1980, Six-S, which serves village organizations in the Sahelian countries, was able to construct a consortium arrangement with several large German and Dutch NGOs to support local self-help investments. Three-year pledges of funds gave the program some stability and continuity. The donors in this case were willing to make commitments on the basis of the quality of previous work, backing Six-S's participatory process for making fund allocations. At an annual meeting, donor representatives sit together with Six-S staff and representatives from the grassroots to review progress and needs, leaving specific allocation decisions to lower-level consultations (Lecomte and Krishna 1997, 83).

By the end of the 1980s, BRAC found that its methodology was working well enough that much more rapid expansion of its program was justifiable. The Dutch agency NOVIB agreed to consult with other donors to put together a consortium that could fund a new, more comprehensive development thrust called the Rural Credit Program. Nine agencies pledged $50 million to see this implemented. They were willing to do this because BRAC was covering almost half of its total budget from its own revenue-generating activities. BRAC has a self-imposed rule that no more than one-third of its external funds can come from any one donor, to avoid too much dependence on any single source of support (Abed and Chowdhury 1997, 55).

In Sri Lanka, the SANASA savings cooperative movement had some unhappy experiences with donor intrusion, discussed below. But some donors have been willing to engage with SANASA on a partnership basis, holding an annual meeting to share experiences and discuss future plans. With both national and international organizations involved, the meeting is more than foreign donors sitting around a table with SANASA leadership. The central premise of the discussions is partnership, which implies mutual respect and objectives, on which basis financial support is offered and accepted. Although the absolute amount of assistance is substantial for Sri Lanka ($660,000 in 1992), this is not more than 2 percent of the volume of loans. External support contributes to the substantial SANASA training program and to central organization operations; the primary societies are all self-financing. As Kiriwandeniya says, these societies "could operate even if central organizations were cut back, although probably not as effectively" (1997, 72). The principle of assisted self-reliance is well illustrated by this financing strategy.[7]

The Center for Economic and Social Development (DESEC), which operates a program with community organizations in Bolivia similar to that of Six-S in the Sahel, does not have any formal consortium arrangement, but it works with a network of international agencies and domestic institutions to maintain a stable and expanding base of funding through multiyear commitments (Demeure and Guardia 1997, 93). This is a "program" rather than a "project" approach, leaving it to the NGO to assure technical quality and operational effectiveness in the activities supported with donor funds.[8]

From the recipient side, programs in less-developed countries have often been reluctant to become engaged with a donor consortium, for fear that this would compromise their independence. Some thought that they would be better off dealing separately with a large number of donors, able to play them off against one another, possibly fearing that donors would get together and dictate terms. But this is a shortsighted view. The concept of partnership, which needs to be fostered with and among rural communities, is one that applies equally well with donors and with other supporting institutions. Accordingly, consortium approaches can benefit both the programs receiving funds and the donor agencies providing them.

MANAGING RELATIONS WITH DONORS

Rural development programs have had some unhappy experiences with donor agencies that have operated in unilateral, even imperious ways. The SANASA savings cooperative movement has had to put up with donor interventions that undercut its internal discipline and democracy. In the 1980s, the prime minister of Sri Lanka was promoting a scheme to get a million housing units built for low-income households. The repayment rate for loans for these houses, given out on a political basis, was only about 60 percent, however. USAID was willing to provide money to expand the program, but not without better loan recovery. Knowing that SANASA's collection of loans was practically 100 percent, USAID suggested that its funds for housing loans be channeled through SANASA's primary societies. SANASA was pressured into agreeing to this, although it had previously maintained a nonpolitical posture.

The lure of cheap loans doubled SANASA membership in three years' time, but it also made the cooperatives the target of threats from a violent insurrectionary movement. More important, the overall repayment rate dropped, although defaults did not reach more than 10 percent. When USAID pulled out of the housing scheme after three years, the government, in the heat of an election campaign, said that it would write off housing loans—without consulting SANASA. Overall repayment rates, including those loans financed with SANASA's own resources, dropped to 80 percent, a sharp departure from the discipline that SANASA had instilled and insisted on. Fortunately, the government did not press SANASA to make good the housing credits that were not repaid, and members did not stop repaying their other loans. The movement survived this involvement with external funds, wiser about the dangers of politicization.

Unfortunately, SANASA's effectiveness as a mobilizer and manager of money attracted the attention of the World Bank in the 1990s. The bank was helping to finance a poverty reduction program and saw SANASA as a good conduit for getting funds to the poor. The problem was that the World Bank was not willing to pay SANASA's overhead, which supports an ambitious program of member education that helps sustain their commitment to cooperative ideals and practices.[9] To get around a fairly modest overhead charge, the bank sought to work directly with district-level cooperative unions, which created tensions and challenged the working of the organization as a whole (Hulme, Montgomery, and Bhattacharya 1996, 242).

One would think that any donor that endorses the importance of local organizational capacity, which the World Bank does, would be willing to contribute to a human resource development effort as solid as that which SANASA has mounted. But this is an example of what we have seen on many occasions: commendable statements articulated by donors at the policy level often do not get translated into practice by operational staff.[10]

The Orangi Pilot Project started up surrounded by considerable donor skepticism. But the merits of its approach are now well documented, and many donors are anxious to learn and benefit from this experience, seeking the OPP's involvement in their projects. There are still some major differences over issues of planning and implementation, but with the confidence derived from its good performance, the OPP has been reluctant to back down when faced with conventional practices and attitudes from donors, even well-meaning ones.[11]

An increasing number of donor agencies are trying to move in the directions described here. The CAMPFIRE Association in Zimbabwe, which began operating in 1989, enjoyed flexible donor support that enabled it to proceed in an adaptive manner. Especially appreciated was that the donors did not attempt "to carve the territory up into project fiefdoms, as has happened in some other countries" (Metcalfe 1997, 287). There is a willingness to provide funds on a programmatic basis and less preoccupation with discrete projects. Any implication that activities are owned by the funding agency is antithetical to the kind of participatory rural development we have been examining in this book. Ownership of rural development initiatives needs to rest firmly in the hands of rural people. To the extent that donor agencies think and act in possessive rather than facilitative ways, they defeat their own purposes, assuming that they seriously want to see their resources result in sustainable development.

External assistance can never be entirely trouble free or risk free. In principle, rural development programs should attempt to become increasingly self-reliant financially over time. Yet most such programs do not produce revenues for the organizations that sponsor them, and it is no easy matter to raise operating funds from low-income families who are the main beneficiaries of rural development programs. Some of the most successful programs in terms of self-financing—BRAC in Bangladesh and the Population and Development Association in Thailand—are now able to generate as much as 40 percent of their multimillion-dollar budgets from their own efforts, but this means that they still receive a majority of their annual operating costs from external sources.

TOO MUCH FUNDING?

In a time when external resources for the support of development in the Third World are becoming more limited, it may seem strange to even raise this question: can a program ever have too much money? But the answer is yes. Two of the programs reported in *Reasons for Hope* found that at certain times there was too much funding available for the good of their long-term effectiveness. By the early 1990s, Six-S had demonstrated such an attractive ability to assist poor and remote communities in the Sahelian region of West Africa that donors were practically lining up to offer funds. As a result, in the view of the Six-S directors, the membership and program grew at a faster rate than was sustainable without sacrificing the discipline that had been insisted on and instilled earlier. Today there are concerns that the rapid infusion of external funds has caused overall quality to decline. A similar concern has been expressed about the rapid expansion of BRAC's rural credit program (Montgomery, Bhattacharya, and Hulme 1996, 174–6).

Some disappointments and trade-offs of quality for quantity must be expected, because the high standards that are possible in a pilot project are seldom retainable with expansion and are certainly very difficult to sustain with rapid expansion. In the early years of the Rajasthan watershed conservation program, the improvement of 80,000 hectares a year was ten times the previous rate achieved by government agencies, and this was done with an improvement in quality as well as extent because of the more participatory mode of operation. But the government's new infusion of funding has pressed the program to expand even faster, without regard to the organizational and technical foundations that made the earlier high-quality spread of activities possible (Krishna, Uphoff, and Esman 1997, 297). Thus it is possible that many of the gains made in the first years of the project may be undermined by too rapid expansion under pressure from the government and donor sources.

There is an unfortunate equation in most governmental, and even some nongovernmental, circles that assumes that *money spent equals development done* (Korten and Uphoff 1982). We should by now be wary of any suggestion that development is something that can be "done," especially by anyone from outside the country or even outside the rural sector. Development is something that must be created and sustained by the people themselves, recognizing that certain kinds of external assistance can spark and nurture this process of development, particularly if aid comes in a catalytic manner.

A rigid policy of rejecting all external assistance in the name of self-reliance can be unnecessary and self-defeating. All the successful experiences reported in *Reasons for Hope* took advantage of at least some outside assistance to provide resources that would otherwise have been unavailable. They accepted such assistance, however, on a selective basis, choosing only those forms that were compatible with their own principles and policies and that did not compromise their independence (see, for example, Kiriwandeniya 1997, 69–72).

Although having money is a necessary condition for many if not all such changes, it has never been a sufficient one. Money cannot buy development any more than it can buy happiness. Frequently the most useful assistance from external sources is in the form of ideas, information, inspiration, and encouragement, which often require only modest funding. The development and spread of new and better ideas, the forging and nurturing of stronger social relationships, the creation of organizational capacities, and the mobilization of internal resources so that communities are only optimally dependent on exchanges with the rest of the world are all essential elements in a developmental process. All these require certain material support, but the money needs to be understood and used as being facilitative. This is the bottom line for the use of external resources. We have seen many instances in which donors played roles in rural development that were creative, catalytic, and critical. As external financial resources for development become scarcer, everyone will need to pay more attention to indigenous and nonmaterial resources, the aim being to utilize both material and nonmaterial resources better, from both internal and external sources.

NOTES

1. A variety of resources can be considered under the heading of external assistance: training, technical assistance, advisory services, food aid, grants-in-kind. Here we deal primarily with financial assistance, which gives receiving programs some flexibility in how the funding will be used. Some references are made to other forms of assistance, but the focus is on funding. We should note a connection between information and external assistance that is not always benign. Donor requirements for information and reporting often tend to draw the recipient toward a more top-down, data-seeking, content- (rather than process-) oriented posture. This has been seen in many programs that, despite their other merits, have become less autonomous and member-controlled as a result of donor influences.

2. In our evaluation of 150 cases of local organization in developing countries around the world, we found that overall performance scores averaged 153 when local residents had taken the initiative to start the organization ($N = 14$), 135 when local leaders had taken the initiative ($N = 26$), 50 when there was shared initiative between government and communities ($N = 24$), and only 16 when government agencies had started the local organization ($N = 53$). When the initiative came from government or NGO personnel acting in a catalyst role, however, the score was 114 ($N = 33$), indicating that how a program was initiated made a difference (Esman and Uphoff 1984, 163–6).

3. The Bank of Credit and Commerce International (BCCI) approached Akhtar Hameed Khan in 1980, after his retirement at age sixty-five from the Pakistan Academy for Rural Development, to apply what he had learned in over three decades of rural development work to improve the situation in periurban squatter settlements. The initiative for the Orangi Pilot Project, discussed later in text, thus came entirely from the donor side, although in inviting Khan to take responsibility for design as well as implementation, it was seeking some of the most creative and experienced leadership to be found.

4. In this very successful endeavor, the creativity and exertions of Peter Kenmore, from his base in Manila as the FAO's IPM adviser for Southeast Asia, were critical. It should also be noted that advisers with the Planning Ministry from the Harvard Institute for International Development played similar key roles with Indonesian colleagues to get and sustain political and bureaucratic support for IPM measures, which produced huge foreign exchange savings while increasing agricultural production.

5. This is one of the cases we had hoped to include in *Reasons for Hope*, but the person who could write the best account of it, S. K. Upadhyay, general manager of the Agricultural Development Bank of Nepal, had recently been appointed to the National Planning Commission and could not accept the writing assignment. The program grew out of some innovative workshops that the FAO organized and conducted literally at the field level, with small farmers participating alongside government and FAO personnel. See FAO (1978–79).

6. See Lecomte (1986) and Uphoff (1990). The standard concept of a project is a set of activities with defined starting and termination dates, time-phased targets for expenditures and performance, and a specification of all contributions to be made to project implementation by the donor agency, the host government, and the organization(s) responsible for the project. The conventional project plan is commonly treated as a "blueprint" for activities to be implemented.

7. Another NGO in Sri Lanka, Sarvodaya Shramadana, has had less happy experiences when working with a donor consortium. According to Perera (1997), instead of being a partner, donors have made it more of a subcontractor, with tight controls and expatriate interference giving its staff an inferiority complex. Although some donors have probably acted too intrusively and in a high-handed manner, there have been grounds for concern over Sarvodaya's effectiveness and use of funds. It has articulated the principles of self-reliance very eloquently, but it has also been willing to depend heavily on outside funds and has become somewhat removed from its village roots.

8. Consortium arrangements depend on having some continuity among the donor personnel working with them, who have built up knowledge about and confidence in the partner organization. One limitation that rural development programs can do nothing about, but which donor agencies could remedy, is the frequent turnover of their personnel. This creates incentives for agencies to continually embark on new ventures rather than persist in building up capacities.

9. Over 200,000 members participate in cooperative education courses each year at the village level, and over 100,000 are trained at divisional and district levels. SANASA has built and maintains a national training center that conducts forty one-week residential courses a year. The World Council of Credit Unions and other NGOs have supported the development of this training capacity, but SANASA needs to generate operating funds from its ongoing operations.

10. The World Bank's role in undercutting SANASA is reported in Hodson (1997).

11. Hasan Arif has listed some of the differences in approach by the World Bank that were eventually resolved according to OPP thinking:

> The World Bank wanted to begin more than one pilot project. It had hoped that work could begin in three Sindhi towns. However, the OPP felt that it could only handle one project, and that if that project was properly developed, it could serve as a training and demonstration area for other towns. . . . [The World Bank further felt] that government staff should be employed for motivating people, organizing

them and giving them technical advice. The OPP, on the other hand, was adamant that this function could not be performed by government functionaries but only by community members supported by NGOs . . . the World Bank saw the project office as a government institution under the Hyderabad Municipal Corporation . . . the OPP saw it as a community office run temporarily by the OPP.

The World Bank felt that a big seminar should be organized at the commencement of the project in which all the actors, including the community, should participate. The OPP disagreed. It felt that this would jeopardize the project as the community would see a lot of money being spent and a lot of foreigners participating in the seminar. They would immediately say that this money could have been used for development purposes instead. In addition, they would feel that the style of the project was not one that was conducive to the development of self-help and self-finance. The same differences between the two parties surfaced with regard to the nature of the project office. The OPP wanted an austere, non-air-conditioned office in the settlement. The World Bank envisaged a more elaborate affair. (quoted in Khan 1996, xxxii–xxxiv)

9 Dealing with Government and Politics

Any undertaking that seeks to change economic and social relationships will have some impact on political relations and will itself be affected by politics, whether formal or informal. We have deferred discussion of these factors not because they are unimportant. Indeed, they are ubiquitous. But they are also something to be dealt with discretely. Successful rural development programs have worked to keep partisan politics at arm's length, handling political relationships usually in a low-key way, seeking to avoid being drawn into political controversies and conflicts, which arise whenever interests and values are being pursued and redefined.

Managing these dynamics in ways that harness political energies and opportunities for forward movement, rather than dissipating them in struggles or confusion, has been necessary in rural development efforts that move from small-scale efforts to larger programs. The degree to which rural development programs operate under government auspices or with some governmental sanction or cooperation can vary. When official agencies are absent, incapable, or oppressive, rural development is more likely to be undertaken independently of government. Also, given the current popularity of nongovernmental organizations (NGOs) with donors, such initiatives are now more common. But even then, some accommodation with the powers that be is usually necessary. In this chapter, we consider experience with and strategies for working with government and dealing with political dynamics.

Politics is inherent in all collective human undertakings, but those that involve large numbers of participants and seek to produce significant societal changes are particularly attractive to political actors. Mobilizing and empowering low-status individuals and groups that were previously unorganized and subordinated will change existing political equations of power, whether they are balanced or hierarchical. No longer must rural people passively endure poverty and helplessness or wait to get assistance from patrons, governments, or employers. Through rural development programs of many kinds, it has been possible for rural people to acquire some greater control of their destinies. But such efforts are themselves a form of politics, so the challenges of political reasoning and action are always present.

The macropolitics of development initiatives that were considered in *Reasons for Hope* was not designed to overturn the prevailing social order or to supplant the current political regime. Instead, these initiatives sought space within the existing political order to build their own organizations, engage in self-help, and take advantage of opportunities available under the operative rules of the economic system. Although their goals are not revolutionary nor their tactics violent, such initiatives can alter old systems of subordination and insecurity and open avenues for the next generation that were, until now, very restricted.

Such programs may be considered by certain interests, however, to threaten sufficient change in the distribution of local power and status to precipitate clashes over policies and social practices. Yet powerful interests, even governments, can be outmaneuvered, or sometimes simply outwaited, through strategies that take advantage of inherent or shifting sources of power.

- The school programs initiated by the Bangladesh Rural Advancement Committee (BRAC) and the Grameen Bank at first met with much antagonism from conservative rural Islamic clergy, and some of the schools that villagers constructed and operated under NGO auspices were burned down. These organizations have persisted in their ambition to educate girls and young women, and with skillful management of local relationships, rural schools have continued to expand (Montgomery, Bhattacharya, and Hulme 1996, 163–5).

- Rich persons controlling the trade in oilseeds in India have opposed, sometimes with violence, the efforts of the National Dairy Development Board to establish cooperatives for oilseed-producing small farmers, similar to the Anand dairy co-ops. These rural elites have not been able to keep such co-ops from getting started; 5,300 societies now have almost a million members. But current laws are inadequate to protect and support cooperative development, so traders and moneylenders continue to challenge people's organizations.

- The killings of Guatemalan Indian leaders caused World Neighbors to withdraw from its rural development program around San Martin Jilotepeque. There was nothing that a small international NGO could do in the 1970s to curb the devastation.[1] Recently a national peace and reconciliation accord has been reached, acknowledging the injustices against the indigenous population. In the intervening period, villagers made further advances in agricultural productivity.

- The corrupt and brutal Duvalier regime in Haiti had to be bypassed, working through NGOs, when the Agroforestry Outreach Project was started in the early 1980s. Eventually that regime was ousted, although the military regime that installed itself after expelling an elected government was little better. Now that civilian rule has been restored, the situation in Haiti is somewhat more hospitable to NGOs and local action, so reforestation work could be resumed with more freedom than before.

These examples represent some of the more extreme situations in which rural development efforts have had to cope with adverse political forces and governments. More often, the contexts are less oppressive but nevertheless complex, presenting a variety of interests and sectors to be reckoned with. Just as good situations can deteriorate, bad ones can improve. Sustainable successes require maintaining a strategic long-term view and commitment, grounded on solid support from rural populations, and balanced by short-term tactical moves that build up goodwill and blunt attacks so that the meshing of improved technology and social organization can take hold.

WORKING WITH GOVERNMENTS

Successful rural development can stem from either governmental or non-governmental initiatives. Even with the latter, there are usually some modes and degrees of collaboration with political authorities. An assessment of the relationships that the thirty development efforts reviewed here have had with their respective governments is reasonably representative of how programs relate to the political authorities in their countries (see Table 9.1). There was highly visible support for innovative programs of rural development coming from a prime minister and from presidents in three cases reported in *Reasons for Hope*—in India, Indonesia, and Tanzania. Getting such high-level backing involved considerable planning and maneuvering by program leaders, but in each case, giving support served the political interests of the national leader, who could see this for himself. What had to be communicated to him were the economic, social, health, or other advantages that could accrue to large numbers of people

Table 9.1   Relationships between Rural Development Programs and Governments

Government Programs

Rajasthan Watershed Program INDIA	Government created a special department to carry out new effort for watershed conservation and development
Integrated Pest Management INDONESIA	Government decree banned the import of certain pesticides, cut subsidies, and supported training
Posyandus and Women's Associations INDONESIA	Government-supported health posts were able to work with communities better through the cooperation of women's organizations
Kenya Tea Development Authority KENYA	Government parastatal undertook to establish high-quality tea production among smallholding producers
Self-Help Water Program MALAWI	Government department initiated programs for low-cost, gravity-flow community water supply systems
Program for Integrated Rural Development MEXICO	Government with World Bank assistance created new system for promoting integrated rural development
Nepal-Australia Forestry Project NEPAL	Donor working with government department revamped policy toward management of country's forest resources
Small Farmer Development Program NEPAL	Government bank undertook innovative program with groups of smallholding farmers in disadvantaged areas
National Irrigation Administration PHILIPPINES	Government agency needing to be financially autonomous began working closely with water user associations
Gal Oya Water Management Project SRI LANKA	Government department with donor funding and initiative began experiment with participatory irrigation management
Moneragala Integrated Rural Development SRI LANKA	Government project operating in participatory and experimental mode with long-term donor support
Iringa Child Survival and Nutrition TANZANIA	Government department with UNICEF and WHO assistance devised comprehensive, community-based program
Khorat Integrated Rural Development THAILAND	Provincial governor co-opted government departments and experimented with them to establish new approach

Cooperative Relationship

BRAC BANGLADESH	NGO initially had an independent stance; now works closely with government programs in various sectors
Grameen Bank BANGLADESH	Initially encountered resistance from government banks; now accepted as an independent bank with its own approach

(cont.)

if technology and social organization were appropriately combined and extended on a national scale.[2] Both the Iringa child nutrition program and the Malawi self-help water program benefited for a time from close ties with their countries' ruling parties during those parties' heyday. But both

DESEC BOLIVIA	Similar to BRAC; now has strategy of "triangular" relationships involving NGOs, donors, and government agencies
North Potasi Program BOLIVIA	Program operates independently of government, but some ministers and top officials are supportive
Anand Dairy Cooperatives INDIA	Cooperative model was expanded through government support to much of the country
Plan Puebla MEXICO	University-initiated program taken over by government, with diminished flexibility and innovativeness
Baglung Bridge Program NEPAL	Local government initiative accepted and modestly aided by government; also assisted by UNICEF
Aga Khan Rural Support Program PAKISTAN	NGO operating in an area where government is very weak; services are much appreciated by communities; government has adopted the approach on a national scale, opening it to politics
Orangi Pilot Project PAKISTAN	NGO able to work with only a few Karachi Municipal Council members at first; now cautious cooperation
Population and Develop- ment Association THAILAND	NGO undertook a task that government could not manage itself; now there is a close cooperative relationship
CAMPFIRE Association ZIMBABWE	NGO undertook a task that government could not carry out itself; there has been close cooperation and support from start

Distant/Opposed Relationship

Six-S BURKINA FASO AND SAHEL	Some initial opposition; governments generally so weak that village organizations operate quite independently
San Martin Jilotepeque GUATEMALA	Government so repressive toward local population that the program had to be closed down; people continued it
Agroforestry Outreach Project HAITI	Government so corrupt that project had to bypass it by working with and through NGOs
Self-Employed Women's Association INDIA	Government disinclined to assist poor and low-caste women, but forced at times to come to their assistance; founder now appointed to National Planning Commission
SANASA Savings and Loan Cooperatives SRI LANKA	Government did not respect co-op autonomy; interference temporarily set back organization; now staying "courteously 'distant' from state" (Hulme, Montgomery, and Bhattacharya 1996, 244)
Organization of Rural Associations for Progress ZIMBABWE	NGO was banned by the government for a while as "tribalist" but now maintains an uneasy relationship; founder recently became a deputy minister in the cabinet

then lost popularity with the public when it became disaffected with partisan excesses and these single-party regimes fell.

We discuss in this chapter various strategies for dealing with governments and with the political forces they represent or that challenge them. A consistent theme is that successful rural development programs base their dealings on an impressive and reasonably united membership base. In the realm of politics, this is respected even more than money, although some of the political difficulties a program may encounter involve holding that base together and keeping it from being divided by political competition. Some governments are suspicious of and resistant to any autonomous rural mass organizations, regarding them as potential breeding grounds for opposition and even subversion. In such situations, programs must either accept sponsorship or regulation by the government or go out of business.[3]

It is axiomatic that programs must maintain benign relations with those power centers that can affect their operation and survival. Politics surely play a part in this, but influence with political actors derives at least as much from demonstrating good results as it does from the campaigning or maneuvering skills of top leadership. Although efficient and honest management does not guarantee success, failing to meet expectations in this regard can doom a program. Especially in socioeconomic settings where efficiency, equity, and honesty are not widespread, demonstrating these qualities not only gives a program great advantages with the publics it intends to serve but also gains the grudging if not enthusiastic support of politicians and bureaucrats who might not be persuaded to cooperate merely on the grounds of equity and helping the disadvantaged. For example, a lot of reservations and resistance were weakened when the Anand dairy cooperatives in India could point out that, thanks to their organization, technology, and infrastructure, small producers were getting 70 percent of the consumer rupee spent for milk and milk products. Thus good development performance contributes to successful political positioning.

One area affecting relations with government that is often overlooked is the legal context (or lack thereof) for cooperative and other people's organizations. Having a favorable framework of laws within which to operate and a legal status that provides rights as well as obligations is important for expanding a program and working on a large scale. Often the laws under which rural development programs must work are decades old and outmoded, dating sometimes from the colonial era and not suitable for the contemporary tasks at hand. Some provisions of law are restrictive or onerous. People's organizations can be burdened with regulations, inspections, and reporting requirements that harass or stymie their operation. But almost as limiting is a situation of legal limbo, where officers are personally and individually liable for any and all actions, and this becomes a deterrent to collective action. A certain amount of "social" authority may be created by consensus among members and by status with persons outside the organization, as was accomplished in the Gal Oya case (Uphoff 1992a). But political and legal authority are needed for opening bank accounts, signing contracts, and conducting business operations. We can only highlight this concern here, but legal enfranchisement and requirements must always be considered in connection with efforts to scale up programs, if not necessarily to start them.

INTERNAL POLITICS

The image that some may have of rural societies as harmonious, cooperative communities of the altruistic poor is a product of the idealized world of urban intellectuals more than a description of reality. Rural societies are usually differentiated along a number of lines of cleavage. They can be divided based on kinship associations or networks; along class lines, usually larger landowners against smallholders, tenants, and the landless; according to gender—men versus women; often according to age—elders, middle age, and youth; by ethnic origin or other characteristics of race, religion, or language; or by specific circumstances, such as head-enders against tail-enders in irrigation schemes.

These differences may be contained by accommodative arrangements, which are commonly disadvantageous to the poor, one example being patron-client networks in which landlords ensure the basic needs of their tenants and laborers in highly inequitable exchanges of labor, services, and deference. Divisions may be regulated by ties of affection or by social control, such as the deference of children toward parents, or of wives to their husbands. They may be regulated by religious or legal sanctions, such as prohibitions against the taking of life, or the accepted obligations of borrowers to lenders. All such relationships are vulnerable to tensions and even to conflicts that may be caused by economic distress, personality clashes, technological changes, or the circulation of fresh ideas that generate grievances or frustrated aspirations. Established authorities often have difficulty managing such conflicts according to traditional norms or patterns of regulation. NGOs that cannot invoke the sanctions of authority must rely on goodwill to minimize conflicts.

Contemporary rural development programs tend to be democratic and even egalitarian in their outlook. In their concern with alleviating poverty through participatory self-reliance, they champion the causes of the disadvantaged—women, smallholders, the landless, youth, debtors—who collectively make up the majority of the rural poor. It is they who have the most to gain from measures that raise economic productivity, improve quality of life, elevate dignity and self-esteem, and empower them to act in behalf of their collective interests. Some of these changes may not be considered seriously threatening by their more privileged and prosperous neighbors, in which case the latter acquiesce in the changes. Some shifts, however, may be construed as damaging to their economic interests, social status, or values, in which case change will be resisted by a variety of tactics that do not exclude violence. When BRAC was promoting oral rehydration to save the lives of children with diarrhea, there was no opposition from local power holders. But when BRAC promoted the social and economic independence of women, this initiative was greeted in some places by campaigns of vilification, intimidation, and violence by religious dogmatists.

Those responsible for rural development initiatives need to be aware of potential conflicts of interest within the organizations they create. They can set up mechanisms to minimize conflicts, conciliating and managing them when they occur. The wisest course is to bring divergent views and interests into the open, where they can be dealt with under the rubric of a united organization and where sorting out differences is framed by overarching goals on which there is agreement. In *Reasons for Hope*, there is not much discussion of internal conflicts or of the problems involved in managing them, which is surprising, because we know from previous work that many rural development programs have confronted troublesome internal conflicts of interests. The contributors to that volume were unanimous, however, in prescribing methods to avert one common and very destructive type of conflict that can ruin participatory associations—the conflict between officeholders and rank-and-file members. These methods include regularly scheduled meetings; periodic elections; rotation of officeholders; and especially transparency in financial transactions, along with periodic external audits, to ensure the accountability of officers to members. Meticulous honesty and openness in managing funds are critical for maintaining the confidence and trust of members and for removing the temptation for some officeholders to exploit the organization for personal benefit. We find financial irregularities to be the most common, and clearly legitimate, cause of internal divisions.

Some programs attempt to ensure internal solidarity by requiring potential members to develop and demonstrate a sense of commitment, discipline, and esprit de corps before they are accepted as full participants, for example, before becoming eligible for financial assistance. The Aga Khan Rural Support Program in northern Pakistan has a rigorous set of criteria that village organizations must meet in terms of savings and self-help before they are accepted into the program. Village groups seeking to join the Six-S program in the Sahel must complete at least one local improvement project on their own before they can request program funding for additional activities. In Bangladesh, the Grameen Bank requires prospective members to go through training on the rules and expectations of its savings and loan program, and BRAC has a prescribed six-month course of education and compulsory savings, albeit in tiny amounts, for village organizations before they are entitled to participate in the credit program. Rather than having premembership requirements, SANASA in Sri Lanka has a large-scale educational program for members. Few programs make such extensive efforts to educate members about organizational rules and goals while reinforcing the values that underlie their mission, but this is an excellent example for others to learn from.[4]

One way to minimize internal divisions is to start with relative homogeneity of membership. Programs such as BRAC, the Grameen Bank, and Six-S have designed their membership base to be purposefully homogeneous, restricted in terms of income levels, asset holdings, or age. Programs such as the Self-Employed Women's Association (SEWA) in India, created to serve the interests of poor and marginalized women, find homogeneity by gender essential (Rose 1992). It should be appreciated, however, that homogeneous membership does not eliminate conflicts; it only minimizes certain sources thereof. Even an organization composed only of poor women can have internal divisions. Occupational or caste differences remain, and the drives and complexities of personality are ever present, making it necessary for program leaders to be vigilant about division, reconciling and preempting conflicts as part of their duties.

Programs that have a geographic basis, such as irrigation or watershed programs or even integrated pest management, need to take a more inclusive approach to membership. They must find ways to ensure representation and articulation of divergent interests as part of the program planning and development process. The Rajasthan watershed program and the participatory irrigation management programs in the Philippines and Sri Lanka had to include all landowners and water users. Wealthier ones were encouraged to participate and to benefit from the technical innovations sponsored by the program, which nevertheless sought to assist particularly the large majority of smallholders.

Generally, programs that require sustained cooperation among members and contributions of money or labor function better on the basis of self-selection of members, screened by characteristics such as occupation or asset ownership, as well as commitment to the program's goals. When eligibility for financial assistance or government subventions is involved, inclusive membership may protect the program from the opposition of those who would otherwise have been excluded and resentful and who could undercut the program from outside if not inside. In such cases, a strategy is needed to ensure support for objectives and means of operation. Education programs such as SANASA's or the National Dairy Development Board's can help, but attention needs to be paid to ensuring the production of sufficient as well as equitably distributed net benefits.[5]

As indicated earlier, dealing with external political influences is made easier by having an internally cohesive membership base. Maintaining this base requires continual effort by program leadership at all levels. Although internal democracy will periodically stir the pot of dissension and difference, it can bring forth criticism and self-criticism, as well as ideas that strengthen the organization. Truly active internal democracy is hard to achieve and sustain, as development programs are no more able to evade "the iron law of oligarchy" than are other people's organizations.[6] Most successful programs have strong leadership, as discussed in Chapter 3, but this can be compatible with democratic procedures and values. Especially because leaders are not immortal, there is a need to continually search for and draw forth leadership talent from within the ranks. If the ethos of the organization is one of solidarity, of creating benefits that will be equitably shared, those who are chosen to fill leadership roles will be persons who can deal with conflicts as well as problems and who are unifying in their approach. Solidarity coupled with shared decision making also helps expand the base of leadership, often to the extent that leader-follower relations are replaced by rotating leadership, as in Six-S.

PARTISAN AND ELECTORAL POLITICS

Any large and successful program that has the support of many members will be an attractive target for politicians, who see in mass organizations a chance to secure votes for their parties, raise funds for their treasuries, and possibly provide patronage jobs for loyal followers. Overtures from politicians at the national or local level are reported in two-thirds of the cases in *Reasons for Hope*. Program leaders are unanimous in their recognition that partisan political entanglements can seriously jeopardize their organizations by generating and exacerbating internal cleavages based on political loyalties. By identifying their programs with particular political contenders, they are likely to make enemies of these persons' political opponents. This makes avoiding partisan politics important, yet at the same time, programs usually need to be working cooperatively, or at least not at cross-purposes, with the government.

In our experience, rural people are increasingly sophisticated about such matters. Many, even most, may have been attracted (some would say seduced) by the appeals of different political parties in the past. But the failure of formally democratic institutions and elections to represent adequately the interests and needs of the poor majority under prevailing socioeconomic conditions and within existing political processes has become abundantly clear. Accountability has been short-circuited by the power of money and incumbency, so that the majority is subordinated rather than represented. The restoration of democracy in many countries will depend not so much on constitutional or legal reforms as on the advancement of mass-based rural organizations that wield enough electoral power—not in a narrow or partisan way—to enforce accountability on elected officials.

Sri Lanka has been one of the most partisan countries, with control of the government changing partisan hands through elections periodically in the five decades since independence. When participatory irrigation management was introduced in the Gal Oya irrigation scheme, the divisive effects of partisan allegiances were considered one of the most likely obstacles to farmer cooperation. But farmer-representatives quickly established a norm of nonpartisanship within the water user associations. Anyone chosen as a representative was expected to resign any party offices. (This norm has also been established by SANASA.) If the chairman of a group belonged to one party, the group would choose a member from a different party as secretary. This showed that party interests would not dominate group decisions.

In 1981, when the Gal Oya program was getting started, Uphoff discussed this norm with a group of farmer-representatives, who said that politics was all right in the home but had no place within their organizations. They knew that because of divisions along partisan lines in the past, they had squabbled and not cooperated. Equitable and efficient water distribution had been made impossible by the intrusion of partisan influences and considerations. Farmers explained their thinking by using a powerful metaphor (in Sri Lanka, each party has its own special color, such as green or blue, for its campaign posters, flags, flyers, and so forth): "Water has no color, and if you put color into water, that spoils (pollutes) it." This concept, that irrigation water management must be kept free from partisan politics, is something that farmers in Gal Oya have made a principle of organization and have maintained steadfastly over the past fifteen years.[7]

In a country where there is political competition between or among parties, it is difficult for any large program, especially a popular one, to remain aloof. The Grameen Bank, with its national and international reputation for assisting over 2 million of the rural poor, has made it a policy to remain independent politically, at the same time urging member-borrowers to register to vote and to support the condidates they consider most suitable. Member groups interview candidates at the local level and make their own decisions on whom to support. When some complained that most of the persons they spoke with were not very sympathetic or agreeable, the national leadership suggested that they choose "the lesser devil," a Bengali version of "the lesser evil."

In 1992, managing director Muhammad Yunus was surprised to learn that about 400 Grameen Bank members had been elected to local government councils, and two had been elected as council chairmen. (This was brought to his attention by unhappy politicians who now saw Grameen as a competitor for electoral allegiance.) When Yunus inquired how this had happened without any initiative from the central office, he was told that members had decided not to accept the "lesser devil" theory. "We are not devils," they said, so hundreds had run for local offices themselves. Given the public esteem for Grameen, many candidates with connections to the bank were able to succeed without party backing. Where this will lead remains to be seen. The Grameen Bank does not want to discourage its members from electoral activity, as this would further diminish their influence. As long as the organization remains free of all party alliances and its members compete for office as individuals, the influence of the rural poor can be increased (Counts 1996, 258–60).

It is hard to divorce rural development programs from electoral politics. A number of the leaders of the user committees involved with the Rajasthan watershed program in India were elected to local *panchayats* in 1995 in recognition of the constructive roles they had been playing in their communities (Krishna 1997, 271). This also happened with the Small Farmer Development Program in Nepal. Similarly, the popularly chosen managers of lane committees working with the Orangi Pilot Project have usually been elected to local offices whenever they have run (Khan 1997, 33). One member of the Gal Oya farmer organizations in Sri Lanka has been elected to parliament.[8]

Elections are invariably times of emotional arousal and many kinds of conflict. The World Neighbors program in Guatemala faced a situation in which the majority Indian population was discriminated against, even brutalized, by dominant economic, social, and political forces. Two years after the project was started, an Indian was elected mayor of San Martin, the first of his ethnic background. Although this enhanced the status and security of Indians, it also heightened conflict with the privileged minority population (Krishna and Bunch 1997, 149). Any time one enters into the electoral arena, one must be prepared for all kinds of surprises, backlash, recrimination, and even violence. As discussed with regard to internal politics, whether a program can withstand the buffeting of political forces, internal or external, depends in large part on how much solidarity and unity have been forged among the poor rural majority.

Many of these influences are beyond the control of the program. The SANASA savings and loan cooperatives in Sri Lanka have had an explicit and sophisticated nonpartisan stance from the outset, though that has not always protected them against political interference from the highest levels. Currently they face the detrimental influences of success. With membership over 700,000 and a positive reputation in rural communities, an increasing number of local branches are being infiltrated by aspiring politicians, who seek to build a broader support base through leadership roles within SANASA. Although SANASA has a policy that its elected leaders at various levels are not supposed to be politically aligned, in a mass organization like this, especially one that is based on democratic governance starting in its primary societies, excluding anyone is difficult, because higher levels would be imposing their views. SANASA tries through its educational programs to reinforce a commitment to nonpartisan functioning, but the larger and more successful it becomes, the more difficulties it faces in maintaining such a stance. That SANASA has built up its own financial base from member savings gives it more scope for independence than if it relied on government or donor support.[9]

As we observed earlier, politicians are invariably concerned about the rise of mass rural organizations. These can undercut the prevailing power structure or the bases of elite politics, bridging the cleavages of class or ethnicity, which politicians rely on for mobilizing votes in the service of particularistic interests of the rural elite. The breakdown of clientelistic relations and the emergence of popular leadership raise new issues over which the local politician may have little or no control.[10]

Politicians have sometimes attempted to control emergent rural organizations through coercion or outright violence, as we saw in the cases from Guatemala and Bangladesh. Alternatively, they can try to co-opt or buy off the leadership of local organizations. Knowing that the more visible an organization is, the more attractive it will be to politicians, many successful rural programs have commenced work quietly and unobtrusively, with a minimum of publicity. The organization's profile has been raised only at a later stage, when internal processes and group attachments are strong enough to withstand external threats and when group solidarity is adequate to contain individual ambitions.

ADVOCACY AND POLITICAL ALLIANCES

If rural development programs can avoid the snares of partisan political involvement and play their electoral cards in a nonpartisan manner, it is advantageous to find ways to have some influence on the way that authority is exercised, even if they do not determine who will be exercising it. Political initiatives can come from rural organizations that attempt to impress their interests and values on public policy and the behavior of government officials. When rural development organizations develop multi-tiered federated structures, they achieve, in addition to economies of scale, opportunities for advocacy. They can make the needs of their organization and its members known to policy-making officials and politicians, lobby for favorable policies and allocations, and resist measures that they deem harmful. Exerting political influence can and should remain, however, resolutely nonpartisan.

When relationships are somewhat or very adversarial, as with SEWA in India, advocacy can be a confrontational matter (Rose 1992). We are pleased to note that with a recent change in government at the national level, the founder of SEWA was appointed the first woman member of the Indian National Planning Commission. Her advocacy has won respect and a degree of influence beyond what the NGO she established can accomplish. Similarly, Sithembiso Nyoni, the founder and executive director of the Organization of Rural Associations for Progress in Zimbabwe, after several periods of repressive measures against the people's movement she heads, has been appointed a deputy minister in the cabinet. So programs that present good ideas that are well articulated and backed by a credible base of popular support can gain entry into national councils of decision making.

In some of the cases we studied, we have seen how co-optation can work in the other direction, with influence being exercised in such a way that government decision makers are drawn into helping programs assess problems and plan innovations. Getting officials to "buy in" makes the source and the extent of prople's influence less visible but not less effective. The CAMPFIRE association in Zimbabwe achieved far-reaching changes in that country's wildlife management system by drawing in government personnel who worked with it from its inception. Experiments started under local government auspices with CAMPFIRE backing were supported by the Department of National Parks and Wildlife Management, which then promoted CAMPFIRE innovations within government circles.

The Gal Oya program in Sri Lanka led to changes in the attitudes and behavior of irrigation department staff, as well as to a cabinet policy endorsing participatory irrigation management within eight years (Uphoff 1992a, 261). After four years in the field, there were already 12,500 farmers participating in the organizations managing the Left Bank of that scheme. Ten years later, there were twenty times that many, about 250,000 farmers, participating in organizations that co-manage all the major irrigation schemes under the jurisdiction of the irrigation department. Just as many are participating in the farmer organizations that are taking a larger role in managing irrigation schemes under the Mahaweli Development

Authority. A core of Sri Lankan professionals and expatriates who had been involved in planning and implementing the Gal Oya work from the start persevered with the original objective. A number of them were recruited to the staff of the International Irrigation Management Institute (IIMI), coincidentally based in Sri Lanka after it was created in 1984. The prestige and expertise of IIMI reinforced what the handful of nationals were trying to institutionalize—participatory management—with some policy analysis support from USAID. This transformation of the irrigation sector was achieved through a much more complex process than the term *advocacy* implies (de Silva et al. 1992).

Advocacy may be directed not only at national policy-making levels but also at regional and local officials to apprise them of the needs of rural people, to demand more responsive behavior, and to negotiate more satisfactory relationships.[11] Activating and empowering the rural poor to deal with officials, especially at local levels, can have the consequence of improving the effectiveness and efficiency of government services. It can promote positive-sum relationships as government staff become better acquainted with the needs, preferences, and capabilities of the publics they are committed to serving. The experience of the Program for Integrated Rural Development (PIDER) in Mexico shows that regional and local politicians may initially perceive participatory rural development activities as transferring power from themselves to ignorant, unlettered, incompetent peasants. These politicos eventually recognized that the organization and activation of rural publics could be mutually beneficial, and the program gained their acceptance.[12]

Effective advocacy can be legitimated by collective self-help and efforts for self-reliance. Some advocates of participatory development emphasize empowerment, in terms of making effective demands for goods and services from government. This overlooks the fact that the rural poor will be more respected and attended to when they are contributing to their own advancement by their own efforts. Demand-making is usually zero-sum in its orientation and effect, whereas self-help efforts are more positive-sum, expanding the resource base from which needs can be met.

Advocacy that expects subventions and handouts from governments invites exploitation by politicians and reinforces a relationship of dependency from both directions. Also, advocacy alone is unlikely to maintain the interest and participation of the rural poor, who have learned to expect very little from the state. The core of participatory rural development in our view is self-reliance. Technical and economic assistance from outside sources can be productive, but it is even more so if it is building on a base of self-help.[13] Lobbying on behalf of rural interests is more credible when the organization speaking up has demonstrated successful performance that has won the loyalty of many members. When the Anand cooperatives lobby the government of India for more favorable legislation or administrative support, their claims are fortified by a record of achievement for hundreds of thousands of members and for millions of urban consumers. Had they sought support for the same provisions before they recorded these successes, the government would have paid less heed. The success of the Kenya Tea Development Authority (KTDA) in maintaining political support from the highest levels of government to operate a first-class operation benefiting its smallholder members was similarly based on the excellent efficiency, quality, and reputation that KTDA operations had achieved (Leonard 1991, 125–44).

Of course, all programs need to start somewhere. When the Orangi Pilot Project (OPP) began in a squatter settlement on the outskirts of Karachi, there was an entrenched system centered in the Karachi Municipal Council that had profited politically from the marginalization of Orangi residents. Middlemen were able to extract money from residents on behalf of politicians and bureaucrats who doled out minimal urban services for very high prices. The self-reliant approach of OPP would undercut this exploitative structure. Most municipal councilors wanted nothing to do with this initiative, but a few were sympathetic. The project began by organizing committees to install self-help sewerage in those lanes where the councilors were most sympathetic. This rewarded the few political friends the project had, thanks to the popularity of the new services and the new sense of enfranchisement that Orangi residents felt. Although total opposition from all officials will stymie a rural development program, it can start with the cooperation of a few individuals in relevant positions of authority and build from there. Strong support, commonly referred to as "political will," is not necessary from the outset. This can be built over time, so long as some minimum support is available at the start. With good performance, others who initially opposed the venture have reason to come around.[14]

Coalition building is a process. Some of the early friends of a program may prove to be disappointments, but by the same token, some initial antagonists can become allies. Program leadership, appreciating the need for support in high places, should undertake to inform and educate high-ranking politicians and administrators, as was undertaken by the Rajasthan watershed program. Legislators and even cabinet ministers and party leaders were invited to visit the project area and observe activities in the field. The enthusiasm of user committees for the changes being made was communicated directly to persons whose support could sustain the funding and authorization for the program, particularly ensuring appropriate flexibility. Even so, such intermediation by the program management was, in the words of the program's director, a makeshift solution. "Sustainable solutions can result only from linking village-level [user committees directly] with higher-level political structures" (Krishna 1997, 271). This is what we see as the objective of coalition building—not alliances managed by program leadership, but connections between political and administrative authorities, on the one hand, and rural communities speaking through their chosen representatives, on the other. This is the best way to deal with politics and government.

POLITICS: A CONTINUING PROCESS

All participatory rural development programs require interaction among various stakeholders, each with distinctive interests, values, agendas, and preferences. Within every organization in which the rural poor participate, contribute their resources, and share the burdens of membership, differences will arise that must be reconciled so that joint efforts can proceed. The same may be said of organizations in which base-level units and higher echelons in federated structures periodically have differences and tensions.

The more centralized an operation is, the more attention, effort, and envy will be focused on the center. The central leadership needs to be attentive to these dynamics and tensions, but it should not try to control them by centralized management, as this cure will exacerbate the disease. Along with decentralization, there must be democratic processes that express confidence in the judgment and maturity of members, who are expected to make decisions that serve the long-term interests of the whole enterprise. Favoritism or factionalism that is evident at the center will set the tone for the rest of the organization, so central leadership is responsible for providing examples. It needs to actively present to members the principles and rationale for a cohesive, goal-directed organization, supported by good technical performance, that gives reasons as well as incentives for maintaining solidarity in the face of whatever political or economic challenges might draw members off in different directions. Training programs such as those of BRAC and SANASA can serve such a purpose, provided they have strong normative as well as technical content.

Politics in its various manifestations involves the mobilization of power resources to achieve or protect certain values or interests. These may relate to one another in positive-sum or zero-sum ways, with the danger that the latter will lead to negative-sum dynamics and outcomes. Whenever value is being created or things of value are being distributed, there will be conflicts unless people take satisfaction in one another's advancement, and even then, some criteria of equity need to be satisfied. Program leaders need to anticipate conflicts and address them as they arise. Some of the antagonists (preferably outside the program rather than within) will be strong and even aggressive. If they have government backing or are part of the government, this will put severe strains on the program. Yet we have seen a number of cases in which rural development programs contributed to progress in environments as unpromising as Haiti and Guatemala in the 1970s and 1980s.

Programs need to have both tactical maneuverability and strategic perseverance in the political realm. The nature of rural development is such that culture and values are being changed along with technologies and institutional arrangements. Bureaucratic reorientation within the agencies of government, including the banking system and political parties, needs to accompany the growth in the capacity of people's own organizations that reach upward from the grassroots. This process is one that strengthens what is increasingly referred to as civil society. The process changes the higher-level institutions at the same time as it builds local capabilities. The founder of the Anand dairy cooperatives in India has expressed a vision of where such organizational development should lead. He says that local institutions

> provide means whereby the poor can act together to obtain for themselves the benefits of modern science and technology and a fair share of the country's economic growth. In the process, they obtain the means to build for themselves, in every village, a society that is confident and at peace with itself, secure in the vision of a better future for its children. This also represents real growth in the nation's social and political capital, as a plurality of local institutions is created and strengthened that can underpin democracy at the grassroots. (Kurien 1997, 106)

Out of civil politics should emerge a learning process from which all participants benefit, a dialectic in which they may revise their strategies and even their goals. In this sense, politics, both internal and external, is a continuing feature of rural development programs, especially as they embody a participatory ethos that encourages and enables people at the grassroots to express and implement their needs and preferences.

Needs and preferences evolve. For this reason, the criteria for "success" should be viewed in a dynamic sense. In the concluding chapter, we look at how successful programs do not simply meet the initial needs and preferences expressed by founders and members but embark on a process of organizational development and change, diversifying their activities to meet new or additional needs as initial ones are met and as capabilities expand. This is, we think, the most important feature of successful rural development.

NOTES

1. In 1997, mass graves were discovered in San Martin, proving that the area served by the San Martin cooperative had become a "killing field" for the Guatemalan military, which sought to suppress the Indian population that constituted the cooperative's membership base.

2. Shortly after the Gal Oya irrigation management program began, the minister of lands, one of the most powerful members of the cabinet, met with farmer-representatives in an impromptu meeting set up at his initiative to "check out" the program. He was persuaded from this encounter that they would remain nonpartisan and that their effectiveness would reflect well on his government. The district minister for the ruling party had already reached this conclusion from his knowledge of the program (Gamini Dissanayake, personal communication, August 1985).

3. We should note that political climates have been changing in most developing countries since the collapse of communism as an international movement and a credible political alternative. The rise of international concern and support for human rights has also altered the climate of opinion. In previous decades, there were numerous confrontations between authoritarian governments—of either the Left or the Right—and people's movements. This limited the opportunities for the kinds of rural development initiatives considered here. We are not sure what effect political changes at the international level during the 1990s will have, but we can hope that the end of the cold war and stronger human rights norms will make for fewer oppressive situations in the future.

4. See Chapter 6 and note 9 in Chapter 8.

5. The National Dairy Development Board now seeks to reinforce positive qualities and discourage negative ones among cooperative leaders by working with officers and members of co-op boards of directors as soon as they are elected. Leadership training focuses initially on their developing a mission statement, a long-term plan, and a strategy for efficient production, including establishing monitoring procedures. Tom Carter reports: "What we have seen is virtually a transformation of attitudes and, with time, the apparent replacement of negative with positive values. It is too early as yet to claim success, but the lesson appears to be that when leaders play a role in defining the future of an institution and have a personal and political stake in achieving positive goals, their values become much more supportive of institutional interests" (personal communication).

6. Swiss sociologist Robert Michels (1959), based on his study of trade unions and socialist parties in Europe at the turn of the century, predicted that the emergence of oligarchical rule was almost unavoidable in organizations. But see discussions in Fisher (1994) and Uphoff (1996, 27–31) on how this "iron law" may not be so inevitable.

7. Gal Oya farmers' reasoning on how to control partisan politics is quoted in Uphoff (1992a, 100–1). "Those days [when politicians could get support by

offering special favors] are gone," said one farmer. "Politicians should do things not just for individuals or groups but for the community as a whole. If a politician has helped the community, he need not ask for our vote. He will get it." Farmers said that they "would have to remove any politicians who try to interfere" in their organizations. They said that they had been misled by politicians in the past but would be misled no longer, and that farmers across Sri Lanka now realized how they had been deceived. When Uphoff revisited Gal Oya in March 1996, farmer-representatives proudly told him, as evidence of their continuing nonpartisanship, that they had staged demonstrations against both the previous government and the recently elected one.

8. To his credit, the minister for the district where the Gal Oya project was centered had been willing not to interfere with the farmer organizations for partisan purposes. He had his chief civil servant meet with farmer-representatives instead of meeting with them himself, so it would not appear that he was seeking political advantage through the organizations (Uphoff 1992a, 109). This posture paid off politically, since the success of the farmer organizations and his being a benign patron made him more popular among farmers. He was reelected in 1988 and became the country's minister of irrigation. He survived the electoral landslide that ousted his party from power in 1994, making him one of the top leaders of the opposition.

9. Organizational size can be an asset for keeping adverse political influences in check. The farmer organizations in the Polonnaruwa district of Sri Lanka, established along the lines of those in Gal Oya, faced a challenge in 1988 when a member of parliament (MP), who was also a deputy minister in the government, instructed the engineer operating the reservoir to make a special issue of water for farmers along a certain canal, who were his supporters. The engineer consulted the farmer organizations before doing this, because it had become normal practice to seek agreement on any change in plans for water issues. The organizations asked that the original schedule be followed, since this was a water-short season, and the farmers to be benefited by political intervention had already gotten their assigned share of water.

The MP was furious when his instruction was not carried out. He got a transfer order issued against the engineer (a penalty that politicians commonly use against civil servants who incur their displeasure—moving them abruptly to another location). But when farmer-representatives learned about this, they were equally furious. They sent a delegation to meet the state secretary for irrigation. Once he was informed of the circumstances, he countermanded the transfer order, wanting to support the system of participatory irrigation management. The secretary told Uphoff that he was pleased but surprised to see such solidarity among farmers, who normally would not dare to stand up to a politician in this way. In the past, they would have been intimidated by the politician's henchmen (A. A. Wijetunga, personal communication, July 1990). With 10,000 farmer-members in the organization and several times that many voters backing the negotiated system of water allocation, the MP had to back down. He was defeated in the next election for parliament.

10. The Savings Development Movement in Zimbabwe grew to a quarter of a million members without external assistance and with only deft guidance from a

small secretariat in the capital city. It was evidently seen as a threat by the national government, which closed this potential mass movement down in the late 1980s. Its decentralized structure permitted local savings groups to continue without central support. Had it maintained its previous momentum, it would certainly have been included among our profiled cases in this book. See Chimedza (1985).

11. One of the lessons drawn from the Moneragala integrated rural development program experience in Sri Lanka was that "national political support cannot be assumed to be unchanging and does not automatically mean support from local political leadership. Both need attention from programme management" (Bond 1997, 107).

12. Under PIDER, local committees helped plan and construct rural roads, increasing the road network within the project area from 25,000 to 100,000 kilometers within just six years. This was possible because the program shifted from capital-intensive to labor-intensive construction methods, which local communities could manage with limited outside assistance. The reorientation came partly because the government agency responsible for rural roads was not given enough funding to pursue a heavy equipment–intensive approach and had to look to local communities to mobilize the labor needed to meet construction targets (Cernea 1979).

13. In the Gal Oya case, a donor decision that contributed paradoxically to success was the fact that the project budget for rehabilitating the irrigation system included no funds for restoring the tertiary-level field channels. Project designers expected this to be done by the farmers as a form of participation, as their contribution to the project, without ever consulting them. But because rehabilitating primary and secondary levels would produce few benefits unless the field channels were also desilted and reconditioned, engineers had to be solicitous of farmers' suggestions and their willingness to assist in project implementation. The engineers' more cooperative and less contemptuous attitude helped establish more positive relations with the farmers. When the latter proved to have some excellent ideas for rehabilitating the system (see, for example, Uphoff 1992a, 50–1), they gained the engineers' respect. Thus the self-help requirement, which Cornell and Sri Lankan advisers for the farmer organizations initially objected to because it was being imposed, turned out to enhance farmers' influence and even their power within the system.

14. The Karachi Municipal Council (KMC) was notorious for official corruption. Contractors regularly profiteered with the connivance of council staff, resulting in substandard work. Fortunately, once the project began to demonstrate good results, the mayor became supportive. (Sanitation facilities were provided for 80 percent of the settlement at no cost to the government.) Although KMC personnel continued to resist local people's participation in monitoring government programs and revealing irregularities, over time, the communities were able to pressure the KMC and its contractors into meeting higher technical and ethical standards. Now "a good working relationship between KMC engineers, contractors, and the community [has] evolved after a very turbulent beginning. As a result the OPP now has supporters in the KMC set-up" (Khan 1996, xxxv).

10 Success and Sustainability

We hesitated before putting the words *success* and *sustainability* together—words highly favored these days by governments and donor agencies—because they are often used in overblown ways and are easily overstated. But both have much in common, representing fortuitous confluences of human, material, and mental factors. They depend on relationships that are multiply and mutually productive, relationships that reinforce one another in positive-sum ways. In fact, these are both very fragile constructions, at risk of being undone from various directions. Changes in government policy, in external economic conditions (world prices, for example), or in ethnic or regional cooperation can undermine these carefully assembled structures of collaboration, as can changes in leadership within a program or in upper political or bureaucratic ranks.

We were somewhat hesitant to use the word *success* in the title of this book, knowing that it creates often exaggerated expectations that can never be fully met or sustained. Anticipations of perfection, which the idea of success conjures up, are bound to be disappointed. Nothing is perfect, and even programs that defy the law of averages and are excellent for a while may regress over time. Yet, because we think that there are some principles of organization and operation that give programs a chance to be much better than average, we have ventured onto this tricky terrain. Even a glass three-quarters full, which is better than the usual glass half full, is one-quarter empty and can be discounted and deprecated because there is still room for improvement.

Success and sustainability warrant analysis in part because they are so much sought by decision makers and investors in rural development. They deserve attention even more because rural people desire and require them. We have tried throughout this book to draw out from varied experiences—those better than average and some very much better—the most promising approaches to meeting the needs and hopes of rural people. These should be what decision makers and investors, as well as advisers and academics, aspire to meet.

Whenever success is spoken of, one should ask, by what criteria? The objectives of rural development should be those things that rural people seek. The three that stand out are productivity, well-being, and empowerment. The first means that rural people are able to utilize those factors of production under their control (particularly labor) and others to which they have access (especially land, but also capital) to produce combinations of goods and services that are demanded and reasonably remunerated by others through market transactions. Being productive according to market criteria gives one purchasing power and thus the ability to command others' resources, goods, and services. It reduces dependence on charity and the need to "do without." Although one should not consider success only in economic terms, there are many reasons, from rural people's perspective, why they value improvements in this domain.

Well-being refers to a wide range of attributes that enhance a feeling of self-worth and fulfillment. Good health and the vitality that comes from good nutrition and freedom from disease are part of this. The knowledge of opportunities, of culture, of religious and other concepts that comes from literacy, at a minimum, and further degrees of education is vital to a sense of self-worth. Other aspects of one's existence—a respectable occupation, a decent living place, the amenities such as water, electricity, and clothing that permit one's family to live with dignity and reasonable comfort—are also part of this concept of well-being. The income that comes from productivity is a major contributor to well-being, but many of its elements are public goods or culturally determined characteristics outside the operations of the market.

The third factor we emphasize is empowerment, a degree of control over the circumstances and destiny of individuals, their families, and their communities. This security is enhanced by increased productivity, and both add to a sense of well-being, which is itself an affirmation of personal worth and dignity that should not be subsumed under purely economic or physical headings. Empowerment includes the ability to resist encroachment on the economic or cultural interests that are valued by the individual and the community and to promote those interests by means that others are willing to respect. The rural development programs that we consider most successful have been able to contribute in different ways and to differing degrees to all three aspects of people's fulfillment as human beings—to their productivity, their well-being, and their empowerment.

In this book we are concerned with the planning and implementation of programs that benefit individuals, families, and communities in these ways. Thus we focus on processes that make the widespread achievement of these outcomes more feasible. Four criteria in particular represent reasonable goals for rural development programs, as well as standards for evaluation. We consider them in light of experience that makes both the ends and the means of rural development more concrete. The four criteria are:

- *Resource mobilization*, with the aim of self-reliance and self-sufficiency;

- *Scaling up and expansion*, so that larger numbers of persons can benefit from technical and organizational innovations;

- *Diversification*, so that organizational capabilities are applied to solving other problems in rural areas; and

- *Continual innovation*, utilizing learning process and problem-solving strategies, with maturing institutional relationships, both internally and externally, that enable rural people to have more control over their situations and futures.

RESOURCE MOBILIZATION

The concept of assisted self-reliance has guided most of the successful initiatives in rural development. There was an understanding that external resources could be useful and often were necessary for breaking through material and psychological constraints that kept rural people less productive, secure, and enabled than they could be. Often the initiative came wholly from outside of rural communities—from government agencies, nongovernmental organizations (NGOs), or donors. Sometimes it came from persons outside those communities who identified with them and served as catalysts and intermediaries. Not as often as one would like—because of the constraints mentioned above—the initiative came from within communities and was adopted and aided from outside. But no matter what the origin of an idea for change, the critical factor was its making sense to rural people and being taken over as their own.

The next crucial step was for them to be willing to contribute substantial resources from their own meager endowments to make the new venture succeed. The contributions could be cash, but also labor, materials, land, right-of-way, local knowledge, management skills, and assumption of responsibility. Both success and sustainability require this engagement and commitment so that the initiative does not remain dependent on outside largesse. No matter how well intended, the changes do not constitute development until financial and other resource responsibilities are shared and eventually taken over by rural people.

A dramatic example of this is the Orangi Pilot Project in Pakistan, where each rupee of outside financial support has been matched by seventeen rupees of local resource mobilization. The residents of this sprawling and neglected squatter settlement outside Karachi literally "bought into" the initiatives that Akhtar Hameed Khan and his associates introduced, after appropriate (quite informal) consultations with the people whose lives would be affected and whose efforts were needed to make this project a success. Total investment in Operation Flood to spread the Anand dairy cooperative model to twelve other states of India has been about $400 million. Now each year, cooperative dairy producers earn twice as much as this from their milk sales, a vastly favorable benefit-cost ratio.

Three of the largest NGO programs in the Third World, the Bangladesh Rural Advancement Committee (BRAC), the Population and Development Association in Thailand, and the Organization of Rural Associations for Progress in Zimbabwe, have purposefully set about to create a financial base to support their operations. This meant, among other things, entering into commercial, for-profit enterprises and providing credit on commercial terms (but more cheaply than village moneylenders). The result is that these NGOs now mobilize almost half of their annual multimillion-dollar budgets from their own activities. They can set and maintain their own agendas that are responsive to expressed rural needs, rather than having to chase after donor-offered projects.[1]

The SANASA savings and loan cooperative societies in Sri Lanka have benefited from rather modest amounts of external support from overseas cooperatives and NGOs. Their strategy for resource mobilization was to make all the primary societies at the grassroots self-sufficient, so that they could function no matter what transpired at higher levels. It was up to the higher levels of the cooperative to provide services and opportunities that would be attractive to the member groups at the base. In particular, external support was sought to fund training facilities and programs, which are hard to finance from member contributions in a poor country. Even so, the total amount of external assistance amounts to no more than 3 percent of the volume of loans outstanding. Although one can say that the cooperative is not fully self-sufficient, its degree of dependence is small enough that it could dispense with external aid if this did not serve the organization's and its members' interests. Partly because it mobilizes a lot of volunteered time to manage savings and loan operations, SANASA's administrative costs are only 3.5 percent of transactions, a very sustainable level.

Organizations need not be completely self-supporting to be sustainable and essentially self-reliant. There is controversy over the Grameen Bank's operations in this regard, since its loans are still subsidized by donor agency contributions, that is, the rate of interest paid by loan recipients is not enough to cover operating costs. It can be argued that the Grameen Bank should have placed more emphasis on savings. The SANASA experience in Sri Lanka has shown that with modest outside assistance, a process of rural savings can be institutionalized that generates large flows of funds from the rural sector. But SANASA does not try to provide as full a range of development services as the Grameen Bank does. The two organizations make different kinds of contributions to rural development.

There have been critiques of the Grameen Bank, comparing it with the massive rural loan operations of the Bank Rakyat Indonesia (BRI). This, indeed, is one of the most impressive rural credit programs to be found, having started its rural branch unit operations about the same time as the Grameen Bank. Since then, it has expanded its network of depositors to over 11 million, with over $2 billion in savings, many times more than that accumulated by Grameen Bank member-borrowers.[2] It is able to finance these operations without any current subsidization, but it differs from the Grameen Bank in that it does not aim at or assist the very poorest potential borrowers. Grameen undertakes to provide various livelihood- and quality-of-life enhancing opportunities to its more than 2 million member-borrowers, so this program should be evaluated not only as a bank but also as a development agency. The benefits produced in terms of health, education, housing, and income generation need to be weighed against the cost of external resources furnished to the Grameen Bank. Considered as a poverty alleviation program in which small-scale loans are the entry point and core activity, but with other activities included, the Grameen program becomes more cost-effective.[3]

In the case of watershed conservation and development in the Indian state of Rajasthan, there is a requirement that 10 percent of the cost of activities be borne by villagers, the intended beneficiaries. As only a small share of the direct project cost is locally financed, this could be seen as evidence that the program is not sustainable. But there is a complicating factor: for decades, the government of India has provided program benefits to villagers free of charge. For the beneficiaries to have to pay all or part of the cost of land improvements is a new idea, and in the minds of most, it is still unnecessary. Many think that they can always lobby politicians to get free goods and services, if past experience is any guide. Introducing a scheme of self-financing, even partial financing, has been difficult, although the program is trying to move the local contribution up to 25 to 40 percent of the cost of land improvement practices.[4] Similar difficulties in getting local contributions had to be overcome by the National Irrigation Administration (NIA) in the Philippines, where politicians had discouraged self-help requirements.

Programs need not always start out demanding full-cost contributions by rural participants. This may be exceedingly difficult, either because participants are not fully convinced about the promised benefits or because they may be unable to provide so much funding at the outset.

Asking for resource contributions in the form of labor or local materials, things that local residents can usually generate more easily than cash, is one way around this difficulty. Another way is to share costs on a sliding scale, with participants in pilot programs paying a lower share of costs, and those who subscribe to the program at a later stage, when benefits have been more amply demonstrated, required to contribute a higher proportion of costs. Also, smaller payments may be expected from poorer households, following the principle of ability to pay.

In addition to making the program financially self-regenerating, local resource mobilization serves other important purposes. A sense of commitment is more likely to be instilled among local residents when they pledge their own resources to a program. This thinking may be missing when program benefits are perceived as coming free of charge. Sadly, there is evidence that residents are less likely to value and maintain physical assets if they made no investment in creating these facilities (Narayan 1995).

Just as important, by contributing a share of resources, local residents are more likely to acquire an effective voice in program management. When agency staff need to rely on local contributions for their programs to proceed, they are more disposed to listen to the ideas and suggestions of rural people, as seen in the NIA in the Philippines and Gal Oya in Sri Lanka. By refusing to make contributions unless their opinions are respected, people can acquire a veto over project decisions they disapprove of. Contributing a share, even a small share, of project resources thus assures local people of a voice in the management and oversight of program expenditures.

The Iringa child survival and development program in Tanzania set a goal of mobilizing two-thirds of the resources from local sources, figuring that one-third of the cost being paid by the government could be justified, since improving public health, and particularly that of the next generation, is something that governments invest in around the world. Efforts by communities and local administrations to absorb costs and keep budget requirements low should also be considered resource mobilization, as this reduces the amount of resources needed to operate a program. This has been a premise of the self-help water supply program in Malawi to make its continuation and expansion more sustainable.

Such contributions, being hard to measure and aggregate, make resource mobilization and self-sufficiency more difficult to assess, however. Rather than being preoccupied with percentages of resources from outside or from local sources, it is important to focus on how much commitment of resources, of all kinds, communities are making to the maintenance and spread of a program. When this is at least steady, and preferably increasing, this provides good basic evidence of both success and sustain-ability. One can never know whether a program is sustainable decades into the future. But present contributions are a measure of how much the ben-efits of a program are valued, and they are an indicator of willingness to make further contributions, possibly even sacrifices, to maintain this capacity to meet people's needs.

SCALING UP AND EXPANSION

One of the most important tests of success is whether a program is expanding, indicating that more and more persons judge its goods and services to be desirable. If the expansion is occurring because government or donor sources are promoting it, this is less persuasive than if there is spontaneous joining of the program or if local governments take over responsibility. A good sign that the integrated pest management (IPM) program in Indonesia was making effective contributions to rural people was when district governments began putting up their own funds to expand the training beyond what the central government, with Food and Agriculture Organization (FAO) support, could provide (Oka 1997, 189–90).

Working in a learning process mode, as suggested in Chapter 2, requires that the initial efforts be limited in scale, starting small with pilot projects or learning laboratories, to gain and refine knowledge of what will work under particular conditions. Learning to be effective and then efficient should lead to a phase of learning to expand, where the program is demand driven, meeting needs that are recognized and real.

We are concerned with two kinds of expansion. The first concerns the size of the area and the population served, commonly referred to as scaling up. The second involves taking on new kinds of tasks, moving into new functional areas of activity. This is quite different, and we consider this below in terms of diversification.[5] Both kinds of expansion can be under-taken concomitantly, but this adds to the complexity and risks of man-agement. We think that they are separate tasks, conceptually even if not operationally.

BRAC has gone from working in a few communities almost twenty-five years ago to working in 35,000 of the 60,000 villages in Bangladesh. Much of this expansion occurred after 1990, when BRAC's program involved about 4,000 villages. This growth was achieved as the share of internally generated resources was markedly increased. For this expan-sion, the groundwork had been carefully tested and laid through a series of projects and programs (Abed and Chowdhury 1997, 47–51). BRAC's oral rehydration therapy program to reach and train most of the rural mothers in the country through a systematic campaign in the 1980s sharpened the organization's operations research, evaluation, and management capabilities (Chowdhury and Cash 1996, 39–84; see also Lovell and Abed 1993).

The NIA in the Philippines deliberately started with just two communities in 1976 as pilot projects, with Ford Foundation support. Then a series of program expansions, regarded as experimental scaling up, took place—first in smaller communal (community-run) systems and then in larger national (government-run) systems. This increased the NIA's capability to support the new approach of participatory irrigation management. With a carefully thought through strategy, 60 percent of the irrigated area of the national systems (over 350,000 hectares) is now under participatory management, and about 480,000 hectares of the smaller communal systems constructed or improved with farmer participation have been fully turned over to irrigation associations for operation and maintenance (Korten and Siy 1988; Bagadion 1997).

It takes self-discipline to avoid being rushed into too rapid expansion. The self-help water supply program in Malawi recognized the importance of having and maintaining an effective cadre of staff within its department who were skilled and experienced in working with communities if the quality of construction and maintenance in the pilot projects was to be preserved. Accordingly, the government controlled the pace of program growth, not accepting as much donor assistance as was offered once the self-help water supply methodology had proved to be cost-effective and was attractive to donor agencies as well as to communities (Hill and Mtwali 1989, 60).

Deliberateness and restraint should not be taken as an absolute rule. For the farmer organizations in Gal Oya, Sri Lanka, there was a tentative plan to start at the field channel level with small, informal groups, which would be the foundation for federating farmers at successively higher levels. Circumstances and popular acceptance overtook the plan, however. Farmer-representatives wanted to begin meeting to have communication and coordination at the branch and main canal levels before distributary canal organizations had been established, and the government agreed to farmer requests to have some farmer-representatives become members of the District Agriculture Committee, which made policy for the whole area. This meant that the third and fourth levels of organization took form before the second level was in place. Such unplanned scaling up was accepted by program managers because it meant that farmers and officials were taking responsibility for the organizations as their own vehicles for problem solving.

The pace of expansion has to be assessed on a location-specific basis. As a rule, rural people, who are to bear the costs and get the benefits of new initiatives, are the most appropriate persons to make decisions about expansion and the turnover of responsibilities to local decision makers. But program managers need to exercise some judgment of their own, in consultation with local representatives. When working in a learning process mode, it is important that there be enough spatial concentration of effort and attention so that interaction and evaluation are taking place from which to learn.[6]

Scaling up always involves certain risks of dilution and diminution of effort. Probably the most broadly scaled-up program is Operation Flood in India, which took the organizational model of the Anand dairy cooperatives and extended it to twelve other major states, by now bringing 9.5 million producers within a massive cooperative structure supported by the National Dairy Development Board (NDDB). Dr. Kurien, who was the driving force behind Anand's development, acknowledges that the basic pattern of organization and operation, which was very successful in Kheda district in the state of Gujarat, was compromised by this scaling up:

> The stages of growth had to be telescoped and attenuated. District unions would be formed first by state governments. . . . State-level federations were created to administer policy and to assist the district unions. Since the large investments in existing state-run dairies could not be simply wished away, the state federations had to absorb within them the existing bureaucratic apparatus of state dairy boards. (Kurien 1997, 110)

This was quite a different organizational creation than had been evolved in Gujarat over the prior two decades, with less "weight" at the bottom of the structure. Membership was massive, but participation of members within the newer cooperatives was considerably less. Given that substantial benefits could be created for members in this top-down way, that the organizations were legally within farmers' hands, and that the leadership supported democratic control of the co-ops' bureaucracy, such a trade-off in participation—less quality for more quantity—may be justified.

Although the experience has not been entirely a happy one, much can be learned from this scaling-up effort (Doornboos and Nair 1990). The catalytic "spearhead teams" deployed by the NDDB might have produced more local initiative and empowerment if the process had not been driven so much by targets and numbers. Even so, structures now exist in tens of thousands of communities across India that can be used as vehicles for small and marginal farmers, even landless households, to reach collective decisions about improving their economic and social positions.

Whether the human resource and institutional development that these cooperatives represent will be used to deal with problems beyond increasing returns from milk production remains to be seen. For us, a criterion of success, beyond expansion, is whether the capacity for collective action that has been fostered is used by rural people to improve their lives in other ways.

DIVERSIFICATION

We look on diversification as a critical measure of success and as a key factor contributing to sustainability. This is often overlooked by donor agencies and governments when planning and evaluating rural development efforts. They identify a particular need and try to meet it in the most reliable, cost-effective way. The added expense and complexity, and possible delays, can discourage them from investing in local organizational capacity. Certain rural development tasks, such as the dispensing of rural credit as done by BRI, do not require the social infrastructure that improving irrigation management does. But a broader and longer view of what rural development is all about gives credence to the value of making such investments in social capital because of the additional benefits obtainable—what economists call positive externalities. Of the eighteen cases in *Reasons for Hope*, two-thirds demonstrated the ability to move beyond their initial problem focus to find other ways in which the mobilization of local resources and talents could improve people's lives (Table 10.1).[7]

There has been some controversy in the literature about whether single-function rural organizations are more likely to be successful than multifunction ones.[8] However, two large-scale studies have found multifunction organizations to be more successful overall, even when controlling for number of functions.[9] Certainly correlation does not prove causation. It is probably more correct to argue that successful organizations are, or become, multifunctional than to assert that multifunction organizations are, or will become, necessarily successful. As a rule, more successful organizations and programs tend to take on and perform more functions as they gain capability and confidence, having started in a very focused manner. Referring again to the Anand cooperative experience in India:

> Dairy cooperatives have catalyzed road building, and occasionally they have themselves taken up the construction of village-approach roads. Some of the dairy cooperatives have set up rural health services for their members, and some are using their incomes to provide social and economic services. None of these activities are part of the original charter; they have been

Table 10.1 Diversification of Rural Development Activities

Program	Initial Activity	Subsequent Activities
Grameen Bank BANGLADESH	Making small-scale loans	Members encouraged/assisted to make improvements in housing through loans; health insurance; nursery schools; adult education; fisheries, agriculture, horticulture; textiles and handicrafts; also tackled social issues (such as dowry, child marriage)
Orangi Pilot Project PAKISTAN	Self-help sewerage	Health (insurance for $4/household); credit at commercial rates plus markup, lowered default rate; women's work centers (for income generation, now self-supporting); low-cost housing; kitchen gardens; family planning (44 percent accepters, compared with 10 percent national average); urban social forestry; rural water supply; pilot project to spread self-help measures to rural areas
BRAC BANGLADESH	Postwar relief	Education (28,000 alternative schools with 1.1 million children enrolled); health and family planning; oral rehydration therapy (12 million mothers trained); employment generation (sericulture, poultry, textiles, tubewells for agriculture); legal aid; income generation for vulnerable groups (food for work); commercial operations (to earn revenue, such as printing); savings and credit operations
SANASA SRI LANKA	Cooperative savings and loans	Preschools; environmental protection; cultural events (festivals, children's dramas); consumer shops, loan operations, and barter exchanges among regions to lower prices; sustainable agriculture initiatives; paddy mills for processing rice harvest; purchasing agricultural inputs
Six-S BURKINA FASO	Construction of wells and dams to combat drought	Promotion of horticulture, poultry, schools, theaters, stores, woodlots, village health programs, rural pharmacies, adult literacy, grain mills, cereal banks, soil conservation, vegetable gardens
DESEC BOLIVIA	Improvement in potato production	Handicraft production; agroforestry; consumer cooperatives; health and housing; peasant education; appropriate technology; marketing

(cont.)

taken up incrementally as farmer-members gain the confidence to act for themselves through the institutions that work for them. (Kurien 1997, 107–8)

It is possible for programs to expand their functions too widely or too fast. For this reason, it is important that any decisions about scope and pace of program development be made by, or at least with, the people who will get the benefits and bear all or much of the costs of expansion. The mobilization of needed resources is more likely and sustainable when a program's growth is demand driven rather than supply oriented.

Program	Initial Activity	Subsequent Activities
Anand Dairy Cooperatives INDIA	Collection and sale of milk	Cattle fodder; veterinary services; artificial insemination; milk processing and milk product marketing; improving road infrastructure; health services; model for oilseed production and marketing; fruit and vegetable cooperatives; cooperative forestry
Plan Puebla MEXICO	Improvement of maize production	Maize-bean system improvement; trench silos; expanded irrigation; women's groups; fruit production; rural infrastructure; animal production; credit union for loans; family microenterprises
San Martin Jilotepeque GUATEMALA	Increase in farm yields	Soil conservation; fruit trees; composting; animal health; new crops; crop rotation; credit cooperative; land purchase scheme for landless; reconstruction of housing after earthquake; health and nutrition programs for women; potable water; latrines; family planning and nutrition; literacy programs
Gal Oya Farmer Organizations SRI LANKA	Improvement in irrigation	Savings and credit programs; crop protection (IPM); income-generation activities for women and youth; collective marketing of paddy, rice milling, civil defense; successor organizations in Polonnaruwa: dispute resolution to avoid court costs; negotiated cancellation of land mortgages
Population and Development Association THAILAND	Promotion of family planning	Rural water storage and supply; animal health and production; renewable energy (biogas); marketing; handicraft production; employment generation (relocation of urban enterprises to rural areas); tourist shops and restaurants (to increase revenue)
Iringa Child Nutrition Program TANZANIA	Reducing child malnutrition and mortality	Local initiatives for increased agricultural production; better caring practices and access to basic services; environmental improvements

Single-function organizations may have some advantages in efficiency terms. But we do not see organizational capacity as something simply instrumental to achieving certain specific objectives, such as small farmer credit, dairy production, reforestation, or family planning. Rather, the capability of rural people to plan, manage, and evaluate programs is something fungible and thus valuable in its own right. Following the logic of Hirschman (1967), organizational capacity should not be viewed as an "externality," something extraneous or supplemental, but as central to the enterprise of development.[10] Poverty does not have only a single dimension. As people develop the capacity and the confidence to deal with one or some of the various problems they live with, they will see others that are amenable to solution. A development agency can go along with this impetus or stultify it. How it responds to this choice reflects whether it sees development as a task or as a process of strengthening human capacities.

CONTINUAL INNOVATION AND MATURING
INSTITUTIONAL RELATIONSHIPS

For the long run, the most important criterion for success and sustainability is that the program and associated organizations remain continually in a learning mode, identifying problems and weaknesses, experimenting, evaluating, and modifying. The three phases of the learning process—learning to be effective, learning to be efficient, and learning to expand—all presume that learning is ongoing. Even after expansion, there needs to be further evolution of program, structure, incentives, and philosophy. This requires a self-critical posture and self-image that convey to all an ongoing search for relevance and excellence.

We began reviewing many of the cases considered here a decade ago, when we became interested in finding alternatives to the "project" mode of development assistance and cooperation. A working group of faculty and students under the auspices of the Rural Development Committee at Cornell University called this effort, ironically, "the non-project project." Some of the main ideas coming from an analysis of Anand, BRAC, Plan Puebla, the Mexican Program for Integrated Rural Development (PIDER), the Malawi self-help water program, and other initiatives that went well beyond the pilot stage were reported by Uphoff (1990). The overarching concept was that the "project cycle" should be replaced by the "development cycle," divided into four stages using a biological metaphor.

The first stage is conception and gestation, when a problem is identified and a potential solution is conceived. Whether the enterprise being gestated is called a project, program, experiment, or social movement is not important. There needs to be some period for considering alternatives, designing activities, and bringing together the necessary resources to launch an initial effort. This stage is quite variable, as the time between the start of an idea and the start of a program can range from months to many years (see Tables 1.1 and 1.2). The Anand dairy experiment in first Kheda district and then Gujarat state lasted twenty years before Operation Flood was launched as a national program. The length of time the Anand-model cooperatives spent adjusting and improving both their technology and their organization, and the fit between these, is part of the explanation for their success.

The Khorat Integrated Rural Development Program was "a gleam in the eye" of Suwai Pramanee in the late 1970s when he was assigned to Khorat province as deputy governor. He spent a year persuading the provincial department heads for agriculture, education, health, and community development of the need for a more integrated and participatory approach. Once they were on board, it took a year for them to persuade their subordinates at the district level. With the concurrence of these officials, another year was spent enlisting the understanding and enthusiasm of the subdistrict staff of these four departments. They became the core team that then worked at the village and cluster levels to bring households into the process of self-evaluation and self-improvement described in Chapter 7. Although this program was initiated from above, there was a critical period of gestation when the idea was implanted at local levels, where it could become widely owned. Once the participatory methodology had been demonstrated and refined, the national government, with United Nations Development Programme (UNDP) assistance, adopted the basic minimum needs approach for national application.

The second stage starts with the birth of the enterprise in some programmatic form. There may be a formal inauguration, some legal enactment, even groundbreaking. The idea conceived some months or years before is now in the hands of others than its progenitors and planners. The enterprise acquires a life of its own. The further control exercised by those who conceived it will be quite variable. It could even be adopted by others, severing the connection with progenitors and planners at birth or sometime thereafter. If there is a continuing connection, the relationship will evolve and change. The more successful nurturers support the enterprise with experimentation and evaluation to help it grow and mature; trying to exercise too much or too tight control is likely to lead to resistance and cessation of growth.

Some of the first steps of the newborn enterprise are likely to be awkward, often halting, with some stumbles and falls. The enterprise needs to pick itself up and keep trying to walk on its own. Gaining motor control and strengthening cognitive capabilities are both part of the early childhood experience. This biological metaphor is not an exact analogy, but we see some parallels. This early period is a time when skills are being developed, integrated, and consolidated. There is often a temptation to try to run before walking has been mastered. There can be rapid growth, often coming in spurts, which makes consolidation even more necessary. And at times, there can be little visible change. This period of organizational childhood takes perhaps five to ten years, which corresponds to the human scale.

The third phase is one of maturing, which contains the pitfalls of youthfulness. There are often identity crises, when the relationship with the founders can be difficult. This is the time to learn to run, to expand, to diversify (although some diversification may have started earlier, as part of the initial learning period). Some enterprises may have a smooth maturing period; for others, it can be turbulent. Just as there can be childhood mortality, there is no guarantee that all enterprises will survive through their adolescence. Some risk taking may be part of the maturing process, and this will not always be successful.

For enterprises, the entry into the fourth period can be as gradual as for people. As more responsibilities are taken on and handled routinely with confidence and effectiveness, the enterprise is performing in an adult manner. One never knows the life expectancy of an adult, but having reached this stage in life, the odds of survival are more favorable than before. One of the reasons we were attracted to this metaphor is that it implies that adulthood is not final or static. There needs to be continual learning and adjustment to succeed in the world, because it is always changing, sometimes for the better, but often for the worse. These figures of speech also raise questions about senescence and eventual mortality.

This metaphor suggests why a "blueprint" model for project planning and management is inappropriate for rural development activities and why we stress continual learning as one of the criteria for success. This metaphor also directs attention to the fact that an enterprise's relations with others will be changing and maturing, particularly with those institutions or actors that helped it come to life. This speaks to the issue of withdrawal, which is often suggested as a criterion of "success." If an outside agency—governmental, NGO, donor—that nurtured a program can leave the scene without the program falling down, this is regarded as a mark of success. But this reflects too much the mechanistic "project" thinking that has shaped and often deformed thinking and practice in development circles.

The CAMPFIRE Association in Zimbabwe puts the issue thoughtfully: "The agencies that helped implement CAMPFIRE can realistically plan to reduce their involvement within the next decade and allow these community-based institutions, coordinated through the CAMPFIRE Association, to carry the program forward" (Metcalfe 1997, 288). Local people are now actively involved, Metcalfe says, debating the issues themselves and developing their own capabilities to tackle problems. The university, NGO, and government actors who helped bring CAMPFIRE into being will continue their personal if not institutional involvement with the movement. The relationships they have with rural communities will be different from when they first approached villages in Nyaminyami and Guruve districts. Although they tried to relate to the villagers as peers, proposing rather than imposing, there was no clear bond of mutual interest and understanding at the outset. Over time, the relationships, with some tensions and disappointments on both sides, matured and evolved. What strengthened the effort most were the emerging relationships among communities and between districts that made interactions more multilateral rather than just bilateral. CAMPFIRE and the Rajasthan watershed program, the "youngest" cases reported in *Reasons for Hope*, are probably best regarded as still in their adolescence, but they are approaching adulthood quickly, partly because they deliberately observed and tried to learn from the experiences of other rural development enterprises around the world that had preceded them.

As noted already, there can be premature withdrawal of outside support and involvement. The university supporters of Plan Puebla had no choice but to play a less active role in that enterprise once outside foundation support was withdrawn, and operational responsibilities for the experimentation and extension work were passed over to the government. In the view of the plan's initiators, five years of relative autonomy—provided by foundation funding and International Center for Maize and Wheat Improvement (CIMMYT) administrative support—was not enough to carry the innovation and testing of new options through to solid programmatic strength:

> In the early days of Plan Puebla, the evaluation component was understood to have two main objectives: identify problems limiting progress and take an active role in finding appropriate solutions; and document quantifiable changes brought about by plan activities. . . . With time, however, almost all the effort of the evaluation unit was directed to the measurement of progress. It is likely that many adjustments in Plan Puebla strategies would have been made and would have been better focused had greater attention been given . . . to diagnosing conditions limiting progress and to prompting corrective action, rather than simply trying to document and report performance. The loss of a diagnostic capability with some administrative authority behind it constrained Plan Puebla from remaining as engaged with learning and adapting as it was in the beginning—and as is required for effective and sustainable rural development. (Diaz Cisneros et al. 1997, 136)

Considering withdrawal as a mark of success can undermine what is attainable from investing in social infrastructure. Social organization is not like physical infrastructure that, once it is built, will stand without any further work. Such a view ignores the fact that even roads, dams, and buildings require some continuing expenditure on maintenance to remain functional. The Gal Oya farmer organizations in Sri Lanka were introduced during just four years of fieldwork after a year of preparatory (gestational) activity. When U.S. Agency for International Development (USAID) funding stopped at the end of 1985, there was a precipitate withdrawal, even removing motorcycles and bicycles from the few remaining organizers.[11] Although the situation was far from ideal, and not what was envisioned when the program was planned, the farmer organizations survived and gained ground because members and leaders had anticipated the assumption of responsibility and considered the organizations theirs.

Although the organizations did not work on as broad a range of issues as the program's initiators had hoped for, or with as much systematization as would have enhanced effectiveness, the organizations continued to diversify their activities and to innovate, identifying and tackling problems that farmers saw impeding their progress. If this had not occurred, the organizations probably would have become purely perfunctory or dissolved by now, like so many other participatory development initiatives in Sri Lanka and elsewhere. Enough improvement in irrigation was evident that such organizations were promoted throughout the country.

An important point is that organizational capacities should not be seen as finished products that can be walked away from once they are in place and operating. The relationship that organizations have with the government, NGO, or donor agency that sponsored them should naturally change, mature, and evolve. If the progress achieved has been underpinned by relations of mutual respect and appreciation—in short, friendship—it is a changing and maturing relationship in which friends do not just leave and forget friends. They may not see each other as frequently once the period of intense interaction is over, but they can pick up the strands of social connectedness and maintain positive supportive connections.

Another way in which diversification and continual innovation combine is in the spin-off organizations discussed in Chapter 5. To the extent that additional functions are taken on to address new problems not part of the original mission, it makes sense to devolve responsibility to autonomous institutions that take over implementation in association with the sponsoring program. Numerous examples of this were given in Table 5.1. The Center for Economic and Social Development (DESEC) in Bolivia has experimented with a variety of such spin-off arrangements, where new enterprises become self-supporting and fully locally managed. DESEC's experience suggests that the supporting agency may need to stay involved longer than initially expected, which is to say that the termination of support should not become a goal in itself (Demeure and Guardia 1997, 96).

To the extent that there are mutual interests and complementary tasks involved, at least a system of loose connections and some cooperation should be maintained. Following the theme of this section, the relationship is one that matures and evolves over time. This is the philosophy of BRAC, which takes satisfaction in the number of NGOs, many of them more specialized, that have been started by former staff who wanted to initiate new problem-solving activities with communities (F. H. Abed, personal communication). The Orangi Pilot Project has had similar spin-offs, with an OPP Society Council providing an umbrella arrangement (Khan 1997, 35).

We need to keep in mind that "success" is itself a fragile thing. It results, as suggested at the beginning of this chapter, from a complex weaving together of human capabilities, aspirations, expectations, and commitments, bolstered by material resources and institutional structures. There can be reversals and setbacks. The Agroforestry Outreach Project achieved some remarkable mobilization and concertedness of rural efforts to reforest barren hillsides of Haiti. But this could be undone by a USAID mission director who abruptly shifted donor policy at a time when the government was still too dysfunctional to take over responsibility for such conservation measures.

Plan Puebla had an auspicious start and contributed to much learning within and outside of Mexico. But it also fell short of its potential when donor support was withdrawn, and the government took over with less commitment to a learning process and to participatory approaches. Certainly external factors can challenge and even undo what has been accomplished. It is hard to imagine any programs, with associated organizational capacity, that are so strong that nothing can diminish their effectiveness. Success and sustainability are not once-and-for-all things but rather matters of degree and probability. The analysis in this book has been oriented to improving the odds of having rural development initiatives succeed and last.[12]

RENEWING THE PRIORITY FOR RURAL DEVELOPMENT

There is currently much celebration of the private sector as offering more efficient and cost-effective solutions to the challenge of achieving developmental change. NGO and government operators in their production and marketing activities are advised to learn from the successes of competitive private enterprise. They need to be attuned to market dynamics, as Abed and Chowdhury (1997, 56) contend, although the limitations of free-market approaches must always be kept in mind (Soros 1997). The same kinds of mental and personal qualities are required for success in rural development as in the commercial marketplace: analytical skills, good interpersonal relationships, energy and persistence, willingness to take risks balanced by appropriate prudence, and the ability to inspire and retain others' confidence.

The critical question, however, is what is to be maximized? Private profit? Or socially defined and distributed benefits, especially for the disadvantaged? In the realm of business, we know that the lessons of creative

entrepreneurs such as Henry Ford and Sam Walton concerning the organization of production and distribution can be learned and adapted by
others. This has been demonstrated by the rural development entrepreneurs whose experiences are reported in *Reasons for Hope*. They applied
these lessons, however, not for private profit but for opportunities to
increase the productivity, well-being, and empowerment of millions of
rural people around the world. For them and their associates, these were
adequate incentives.

Fortunately, the state of the art, the knowledge underlying successful
ventures in rural development, has expanded and matured in the past two
decades. Evidence for this is provided in the experiences reported in
Reasons for Hope, with additional evidence presented and analyzed in this
volume. We are well beyond the stage where those initiating and managing
rural development efforts must be purely experimental. Although knowledge must be sustained by personal commitment and determination, it is
available to underpin effective performance. This means that NGOs, governments, donors, universities, and others that would sponsor rural development initiatives are far better equipped in this regard and thus more
likely to succeed than were their predecessors a generation ago.

During the last two decades, rural development has been an increasingly neglected priority in economic development circles. Aggregate economic growth based on neo-orthodox prescriptions of private industrial
and service investment and globalized market processes has become the
reigning solution for problems of economic development. But with few
exceptions, these policies, even when they have promoted rapid growth,
have failed to improve the living conditions of the hundreds of millions
who are mired in the struggle for survival at, near, or below subsistence
levels in rural areas of Asia, Africa, and Latin America. The effectiveness
of economic development programs must surely be judged, at least in
part, by their success in alleviating widespread poverty. So development
strategies are due for revision. We think that a great deal can be accomplished, at relatively low cost, as demonstrated in *Reasons for Hope*, to
raise the productivity, increase the well-being, and enhance the security
and dignity of rural people through the principles and practices of assisted
self-reliance.

Because the need for rural transformation remains imperative, because
current policies are unresponsive to the need, and because solid foundations of experience and knowledge have been built up, we expect that the
new millennium will see renewed attention to the remediable predicaments
of the rural poor. Enough successful work has been done and documented
to provide reliable guidance for achieving rural development, not just for
the few but for the majority. The emergent generation of entrepreneurs

who launch these fresh initiatives will be indebted to the pioneers whose efforts generated the body of knowledge that has been explored and summarized in this book. The question before us is whether the necessary support can be mobilized from a variety of actors—public, private, community-based, nongovernmental, university, grassroots activist—to put such knowledge to practical use.

NOTES

1. In the case of BRAC, a deliberate strategy of investment and earmarked donor assistance raised this percentage from 15 to 40 percent in just five years' time.

2. Considering its scale of operation, the BRI experience could have been included in *Reasons for Hope*. But the BRI has no local organizational base, since the bank deals with all borrowers as individuals, thereby having less broad social impact than the other cases in that book. The BRI is being thoroughly documented in a forthcoming book by Marguerite Robinson of the Harvard Institute for International Development. See Robinson (1992, 1995).

3. The Grameen Bank cannot be 100 percent successful in limiting its loans to the poorest, but it targets efforts in that direction, and the BRI does not. Between 85 and 95 percent of Grameen borrowers are below the poverty line. About one-third of BRI depositors have per capita monthly incomes below $15; the majority are thus better off than those getting Grameen loans. Hossain (1988) has calculated that the effective interest rate paid by Grameen borrowers is about twice as high as officially set if one considers the obligatory savings and the emergency fund and group fund payments. However, these uses of resources provide benefits rather than simply being costs. Hossain's critical verdict is from a single-function perspective. BRAC's rural credit program also has some shortcomings, as discussed by Montgomery, Bhattacharya, and Hulme (1996, 155–62), but it has had substantial impact.

4. Villagers are contributing land to many of these ventures, a very real cost when land is privately owned, although if the improvement measures raise production, this cost is easily recouped. When common land is contributed, there are opportunity costs, although these are not assigned much economic value, because it is usually wasteland. If productivity is increased (fodder production has been boosted as much as ten times through project innovations), what is counted as a cost in the first instance becomes a handsome benefit in the second.

5. In his assessment of ten rural development programs, four of which we have included in our analysis (AKRSP, BRAC, Iringa, and Plan Puebla), Uvin (1995) suggests four kinds of scaling up: quantitative, functional, political, and organizational. His first two categories are the ones we consider here. His third concerns an evolution in objectives from service delivery toward engagement with more structural causes of underdevelopment. Since not all the cases we consider started in a service delivery mode rather than addressing structural issues, this

third category does not apply to all cases. His fourth category, increasing organizational strength at the grassroots, is what most of our analysis is concerned
with, so it is not considered separately.

6. Shortly after the Gal Oya project started in Sri Lanka, USAID supported a project with similar objectives in Indonesia to introduce participatory irrigation
management there. Activities were started up at ten sites across the length and
breadth of the country, to gain experience in a wide variety of environments and
to avoid any appearance of favoring one region over another. The first aim is consistent with a learning process, but this aim was thwarted by scattering the few
professionals with experience and commitment to the project's goal across the
whole country. No critical mass was attained. More learning and eventual impact
would have resulted if there had been more initial concentration of effort.

7. Similarly, there was some diversification of activities beyond initial focuses in
two-thirds of the dozen cases listed in Table 1.2. The cases in which activity did
not evolve much beyond the original conception were programs defined in such
specific sectoral terms that communities did not extrapolate organizational
capacities to other arenas. Also, some of these programs were in countries such
as Kenya and Indonesia, whose governments were quite control-oriented and did
not encourage much local initiative.

8. Tendler (1976, 7) argued in favor of single-function organizations: "They [local
organizations should] organize around a concrete goal, which can be achieved in
a limited time period and would not necessarily require the organization thereafter. . . . Though the organization may continue and expand into other activities, once the concrete goal is achieved, the farmers perceive themselves as
organizing to achieve this one goal, and not to create an organization."

9. A multiple regression analysis found a positive correlation (.26) between number
of functions and overall performance, which was assessed independently of
number of functions. This was one of the four (out of twelve) independent variables that were statistically significant. The average performance score for organizations with only one function was 35; with two, 44; with three, 87; with four
or five, 146; and with six or more, 189 (Esman and Uphoff 1984, 180, 140). When
we reanalyzed data from the forty rural development cases documented previously by Development Alternatives Inc. (Gow et al. 1979), we found a significant
correlation of .52.

10. Almost all the principles that Peters and Waterman (1982) propose for effective
organization apply to planning and management rural development enterprises.
But one—"stick to your knitting," concentrate on what you are good at, and do
not get involved in other lines of activity—need not. As seen from Table 10.1, the
most successful development efforts have diversified widely to meet needs that
are identified sequentially and as capacities are developed that can be extrapolated to new domains.

11. A government-appointed project manager was supposed to work with and assist
the farmer organizations. But this official, who had good political connections,
had previously been a crop insurance representative in the area. As such, he
did not have the farmers' confidence, because that program was notoriously

unresponsive to farmers' claims unless they were backed by political or economic clout. This official and the farmer organizations, assisted by several remaining organizers, worked out a sufficient degree of cooperation to keep the new capabilities intact.

12. In the Gal Oya program, an informal motto was "We proceed with the knowledge that there are no permanent successes, and with the confidence that there are no permanent defeats." The latter part gave expression to the aphorism, "If at first you don't succeed, try, try again." But the first part was more original in that it counseled against overconfidence and encouraged continual self-critical assessment of where the program could get off track.

References

Abed, F. H., and A. M. R. Chowdhury. 1997. The Bangladesh Rural Advancement Committee: How BRAC learned to meet rural people's needs through local action. In *Reasons for hope: Instructive experiences in rural development*, edited by Anirudh Krishna, Norman Uphoff, and Milton J. Esman, 41–56. West Hartford, Conn.: Kumarian Press.

Aluwihare, P. B., and Masao Kikuchi. 1991. *Irrigation investment trends in Sri Lanka: New construction and beyond.* Colombo: International Irrigation Management Institute.

Antholt, Charles H. 1994. *Getting ready for the twenty-first century: Technical change and institutional modernization in agriculture.* Washington, D.C.: World Bank.

Aqua, Ronald. 1982. Local institutions and rural development in Japan. In *Rural development and local organization in Asia.* Vol. 2, *East Asia*, edited by N. Uphoff, 328–93. New Delhi: Macmillan.

Bagadion, Benjamin U. 1997. The National Irrigation Administration's participatory irrigation management program in the Philippines. In *Reasons for hope: Instructive experiences in rural development*, edited by Anirudh Krishna, Norman Uphoff, and Milton J. Esman, 153–65. West Hartford, Conn.: Kumarian Press.

Blunt, Peter, and D. Michael Warren, eds. 1996. *Indigenous organizations and development.* London: Intermediate Technology Publications.

Bond, Richard. 1997. Operationalising process: The experience of the first decade of the Moneragala IRDP in Sri Lanka. IDPM discussion paper series. Manchester, U.K.: Institute for Development Policy and Management, University of Manchester.

Bornstein, David. 1996. *The price of a dream: The story of the Grameen Bank and the idea that is helping the poor to change their lives.* New York: Simon and Schuster.

Bunch, Roland. 1982. *Two ears of corn: A guide to people-centered agricultural development.* Oklahoma City: World Neighbors.

Cernea, Michael. 1979. *Measuring project impact: Monitoring and evaluation in the PIDER rural development project—Mexico.* Staff Working Paper no. 332. Washington, D.C.: World Bank.

———. 1983. *A social methodology for community participation in local investments: The experience of Mexico's PIDER program.* Staff Working Paper no. 598. Washington, D.C.: World Bank.

Chambers, Robert. 1985. *Managing rural development: Ideas and experience from East Africa.* West Hartford, Conn.: Kumarian Press.

———. 1993. *Challenging the professions: Frontiers for rural development.* London: Intermediate Technology Publications.

———. 1997. *Whose reality counts? Putting the first last.* London: Intermediate Technology Publications.

Charlick, Robert. 1984. *Animation Rurale revisited: Participatory techniques in improving agriculture and social services in five francophone nations.* Ithaca, N.Y.: Rural Development Committee, Cornell University.

Chimedza, Ruvimbo. 1985. Savings clubs: The mobilization of rural finances in Zimbabwe. In *Rural development and women: Lessons from the field*. Vol. 1, edited by S. Muntemba, 161–74. Geneva: World Employment Programme, International Labour Organization.

Chowdhury, A. M. R., and Richard A. Cash. 1996. *A simple solution: Teaching millions to treat diarrhoea at home*. Dhaka: University Press.

Cohen, John M., and Norman Uphoff. 1980. Participation's place in rural development: Seeking clarity through specificity. *World Development* 8(3): 213–35.

Counts, Alex. 1996. *Give us credit*. New York: Times Books.

Coward, E. Walter. 1979. Principles of social organization in an indigenous irrigation system. *Human Organization* 38(1): 28–36.

de los Reyes, Romana. 1984. Process documentation: Social science research in a learning process approach to program development. *Philippine Sociological Review* 32(1–4): 105–20.

de Silva, N. G. R., Douglas J. Merrey, and R. Saktivadivel. 1992. A participatory approach to building policy consensus: The relevance of the irrigation management policy support activity in Sri Lanka to other countries. *IIMI Review* 6(1).

Demeure, Juan, and Edgar Guardia. 1997. DESEC: Thirty years of community organization in Bolivia. In *Reasons for hope: Instructive experiences in rural development*, edited by Anirudh Krishna, Norman Uphoff, and Milton J. Esman, 91–101. West Hartford, Conn.: Kumarian Press.

Diaz Cisneros, Heliodoro, Leobardo Jiménez Sánchez, Reggie J. Laird, and Antonio Turrent Fernández. 1997. Plan Puebla: An agricultural development program for low-income farmers in Mexico. In *Reasons for hope: Instructive experiences in rural development*, edited by Anirudh Krishna, Norman Uphoff, and Milton J. Esman, 120–36. West Hartford, Conn.: Kumarian Press.

Doornbos, Martin, and K. C. Nair, eds. 1990. *Resources, institutions and strategies: Operation Flood and Indian dairying*. New Delhi: Sage Publications.

Edwards, Michael, and David Hulme, eds. 1992. *Making a difference: NGOs and development in a changing world*. London: Earthscan.

Eliot, T. S. 1934. *The rock*. London: Faber and Faber.

Esman, Milton J. 1983. *Paraprofessionals in rural development: Issues in field-level staffing for agricultural projects*. Staff Working Paper no. 573. Washington, D.C.: World Bank.

———. 1991. *Management dimensions of development: Perspectives and strategies*. West Hartford, Conn.: Kumarian Press.

Esman, Milton J., and Norman Uphoff. 1984. *Local organizations: Intermediaries in rural development*. Ithaca, N.Y.: Cornell University Press.

FAO. 1978–79. *Field action for small farmers, small fishermen and peasants*. Vol. 1, *The field workshop: A methodology for planning, training and evaluation of programmes for small farmers/fishermen and landless agricultural labourers*. Vol. 2, *Small farmer development manual*. Bangkok: Food and Agriculture Organization.

Fisher, Julie. 1994. Is the iron law of oligarchy rusting away in the Third World? *World Development* 22(2): 129–43.

Ghai, Dharam, and Anisur Rahman. 1979. *Rural poverty and the Small Farmers' Development Programme in Nepal*. Geneva: Rural Employment Policies Branch, International Labour Organization.

Gow, David, et al. 1979. *Local organizations and rural development: A comparative reappraisal.* 2 vols. Washington, D.C.: Development Alternatives, Inc.

Guha, Ramachandra. 1989. *The unquiet woods: Ecological change and peasant resistance in the Himalayas.* Berkeley: University of California Press.

Hadden, Susan G. 1980. Controlled decentralization and policy implementation: The case of rural electrification in Rajasthan. In *Politics and policy making in the Third World*, edited by Merilee Grindle, 170–91. Princeton, N.J.: Princeton University Press.

Haverkort, B., W. Hiemstra, C. Reijntjes, and S. Essers. 1991. Strengthening farmers' capacity for technology development: Participatory technology development. In *Sustainable agriculture: An introduction.* Leusden, Netherlands: Information Centre for Low External-Input and Sustainable Agriculture (ILEIA).

Hill, Catherine B., and Katundu M. Mtwali. 1989. Malawi: Lessons from the gravity-fed piped water scheme. In *Successful development in Africa: Case studies of projects, programs and policies*, edited by R. Bheenick et al., 57–78. EDF Development Policy Case Studies no. 1. Washington, D.C.: World Bank.

Hirschman, Albert O. 1963. *Journeys toward progress: Studies in economic policy making in Latin America.* New York: Twentieth Century Fund.

———. 1967. *Development projects observed.* Washington, D.C.: Brookings Institution. (Republished in 1995.)

———. 1984. *Getting ahead collectively: Grassroots experiences in Latin America.* New York: Pergamon Press.

Hodson, Roland. 1997. Elephant loose in the jungle: The World Bank and NGOs in Sri Lanka. In *NGOs, states and donors: Too close for comfort?* edited by David Hulme and Michael Edwards, 168–87. New York: St. Martin's Press.

Holdcroft, Lane. 1978. *The rise and fall of community development in developing countries: A critical analysis and annotated bibliography.* MSU Rural Development Paper no. 2. East Lansing: Department of Agricultural Economics, Michigan State University.

Hossain, Mahabub. 1988. *Credit for alleviation of rural poverty: The Grameen Bank in Bangladesh.* Research Report no. 65. Washington, D.C.: International Food Policy Research Institute.

Hulme, David, and Michael Edwards, eds. 1997. *NGOs, states and donors: Too close for comfort?* New York: St. Martin's Press.

Hulme, David, Richard Montgomery, and Debapriya Bhattacharya. 1996. Mutual finance and the poor: A study of the Federation of Thrift and Credit Co-operatives (SANASA) in Sri Lanka. In *Finance against poverty*, edited by David Hulme and Paul Mosley, 2:177–245. London: Routledge.

Hulme, David, and Paul Mosley, eds. 1996. *Finance against poverty.* 2 vols. London: Routledge.

Ilchman, Warren, and Norman Uphoff. 1969. *The political economy of change.* Berkeley: University of California Press. (Republished by Transaction Books, 1997.)

Jain, S. C. 1994. Managing for success: Lessons from Asian development programs. *World Development* 22(9): 1363–77.

Jiggins, Janice. 1989. *Farmer participatory research and technology development.* Occasional Papers in Rural Extension no. 5. Guelph, Canada: Department of Rural Extension Studies, University of Guelph.

Jonsson, Urban, Björn Ljungqvist, and Olivia Yambi. 1993. Mobilization for nutrition in Tanzania. In *Reaching health for all*, edited by Jon Rohde, Meera Chatterjee, and David Morley, 185–211. Oxford: Oxford University Press.

Khan, Akhtar Hameed. 1996. *The Orangi Pilot Project: Reminiscences and reflections.* Karachi: Oxford University Press.

———. 1997. The Orangi Pilot Project: Uplifting a periurban settlement near Karachi, Pakistan. In *Reasons for hope: Instructive experiences in rural development,* edited by Anirudh Krishna, Norman Uphoff, and Milton J. Esman, 25–40. West Hartford, Conn.: Kumarian Press.

Kiriwandeniya, P. A. 1992. The growth of the SANASA movement in Sri Lanka. In *Making a difference: NGOs and development in a changing world,* edited by Michael Edwards and David Hulme, 111–7. London: Earthscan.

———. 1997. SANASA: The savings and credit cooperative movement in Sri Lanka. In *Reasons for hope: Instructive experiences in rural development,* edited by Anirudh Krishna, Norman Uphoff, and Milton J. Esman, 57–74. West Hartford, Conn.: Kumarian Press.

Korten, David C. 1980. Community organization and rural development: A learning process approach. *Public Administration Review* 40(5): 480–511.

Korten, David C., and Norman Uphoff. 1982. *Bureaucratic reorientation for participatory rural development.* NASPAA Working Paper no. 1. Washington, D.C.: National Association of Schools of Public Affairs and Administration.

Korten, Frances F. 1982. *Building national capacity to develop water users' associations: Experience from the Philippines.* Staff Working Paper no. 528. Washington, D.C.: World Bank.

———. 1988. The working group as a catalyst for organizational change. In *Transforming a bureaucracy: The experience of the Philippines National Irrigation Administration,* edited by Frances F. Korten and Robert Siy, 61–89. West Hartford, Conn.: Kumarian Press.

Korten, Frances F. and Robert Siy, eds. 1988. *Transforming a bureaucracy: The experience of the Philippines National Irrigation Administration.* West Hartford, Conn.: Kumarian Press.

Krishna, Anirudh. 1997. Participatory watershed development and soil conservation in Rajasthan, India. In *Reasons for hope: Instructive experiences in rural development,* edited by Anirudh Krishna, Norman Uphoff, and Milton J. Esman, 255–72. West Hartford, Conn.: Kumarian Press.

Krishna, Anirudh, with Roland Bunch. 1997. Farmer-to-farmer experimentation and extension: Integrated rural development for smallholders in Guatemala. In *Reasons for hope: Instructive experiences in rural development,* edited by Anirudh Krishna, Norman Uphoff, and Milton J. Esman, 137–52. West Hartford, Conn.: Kumarian Press.

Krishna, Anirudh, with Urban Jonsson and Wilbald Lorri. 1997. The Iringa nutrition project: Child survival and development in Tanzania. In *Reasons for hope: Instructive experiences in rural development,* edited by Anirudh Krishna, Norman Uphoff, and Milton J. Esman, 216–27. West Hartford, Conn.: Kumarian Press.

Krishna, Anirudh, with Lindesay H. Robertson. 1997. The self-help rural water supply program in Malawi. In *Reasons for hope: Instructive experiences in rural development,* edited by Anirudh Krishna, Norman Uphoff, and Milton J. Esman, 228–38. West Hartford, Conn.: Kumarian Press.

Krishna, Anirudh, Norman Uphoff, and Milton J. Esman, eds. 1997. *Reasons for hope: Instructive experiences in rural development: Instructive experiences in rural development.* West Hartford, Conn.: Kumarian Press.

Kurien, V. 1997. The AMUL dairy cooperatives: Putting the means of development into the hands of small producers in India. In *Reasons for hope: Instructive experiences in rural development*, edited by Anirudh Krishna, Norman Uphoff, and Milton J. Esman, 105–19. West Hartford, Conn.: Kumarian Press.

Lamb, Geoff, and Linda Mueller. 1982. *Control, accountability and incentives for a successful development institution: The Kenya Tea Development Authority.* Staff Working Paper no. 550. Washington, D.C.: World Bank.

Lassen, Cheryl J. 1980. *Reaching the assetless poor: Projects and strategies for their self-reliant development.* Ithaca, N.Y.: Rural Development Committee, Cornell University.

Lecomte, Bernard J. 1986. *Project aid: Limitations and alternatives.* Paris: Development Centre, Organization for Economic Cooperation and Development.

Lecomte, Bernard J., and Anirudh Krishna. 1997. Six-S: Building upon traditional social organizations in francophone West Africa. In *Reasons for hope: Instructive experiences in rural development*, edited by Anirudh Krishna, Norman Uphoff, and Milton J. Esman, 75–90. West Hartford, Conn.: Kumarian Press.

Leibenstein, Harvey. 1976. *Beyond economic man: A new foundation for microeconomics.* Cambridge, Mass.: Harvard University Press.

Leonard, David K. 1991. *African successes: Four public managers of Kenyan rural development.* Berkeley: University of California Press.

Lovell, Catherine. 1992. *Breaking the cycle of poverty: The BRAC strategy.* West Hartford, Conn.: Kumarian Press.

Lovell, Catherine, and F. H. Abed. 1993. Scaling-up in health: Two decades of learning in Bangladesh. In *Reaching health for all*, edited by Jon Rohde, Meera Chatterjee, and David Morley, 212–32. Oxford: Oxford University Press.

March, Kathryn, and Rachel Taqqu. 1986. *Women's informal associations in developing countries: Catalysts for change?* Boulder, Colo.: Westview Press.

Mechai Viravaidya. 1997. The Population and Community Development Association in Thailand. In *Reasons for hope: Instructive experiences in rural development*, edited by Anirudh Krishna, Norman Uphoff, and Milton J. Esman, 203–15. West Hartford, Conn.: Kumarian Press.

Metcalfe, Simon. 1997. The CAMPFIRE program: Community-based wildlife resource management in Zimbabwe. In *Reasons for hope: Instructive experiences in rural development*, edited by Anirudh Krishna, Norman Uphoff, and Milton J. Esman, 273–88. West Hartford, Conn.: Kumarian Press.

Michels, Robert. 1959. *Political parties.* New York: Dover. (First published in 1915.)

Milliken, Max F., and David Hapgood. 1967. *No easy harvest: The dilemma of agriculture in underdeveloped countries.* Boston: Little, Brown.

Montgomery, Richard, D. Bhattacharya, and David Hulme. 1996. Credit for the poor in Bangladesh: The BRAC Rural Development Programme and the government Thana Resource Development and Employment Programme. In *Finance against poverty*, edited by David Hulme and Paul Mosley, 94–176. London: Routledge.

Murray, Gerald F. 1997. A Haitian peasant tree chronicle: Adaptive evolution and institutional intrusion. In *Reasons for hope: Instructive experiences in rural development*, edited by Anirudh Krishna, Norman Uphoff, and Milton J. Esman, 241–54. West Hartford, Conn.: Kumarian Press.

Narayan, Deepa. 1995. *The contribution of people's participation: Evidence from 121 rural water supply projects.* Environmentally Sustainable Development Occasional Paper Series no. 1. Washington, D.C.: World Bank.

Oka, Ida Nyoman. 1997. Integrated crop pest management with farmer participation in Indonesia. In *Reasons for hope: Instructive experiences in rural development*, edited by Anirudh Krishna, Norman Uphoff, and Milton J. Esman, 184–99. West Hartford, Conn.: Kumarian Press.

Olson, Mancur. 1965. *The logic of collective action: Public goods and the theory of groups.* Cambridge: Harvard University Press.

Paul, Samuel. 1982. *Managing development programs: The lessons of success.* Boulder, Colo.: Westview Press.

Pelletier, David. 1991. *The uses and limitations of information in the Iringa nutrition program, Tanzania.* CFNPP Working Paper no. 5. Ithaca, N.Y.: Cornell Food and Nutrition Policy Program, Cornell University.

Perera, Jehan. 1997. In unequal dialogue with donors: The experience of the Sarvodaya Shramadana movement. In *NGOs, states and donors: Too close for comfort?* edited by David Hulme and Michael Edwards, 156–67. New York: St. Martin's Press.

Peters, Tom J., and Robert Waterman. 1982. *In search of excellence: Lessons from America's best-run companies.* New York: Warner Books.

Piyaratn, Prapont. 1993. Basic minimum needs: Concepts and practices. In *Integrating food and nutrition into development: Thailand's experiences and future visions,* edited by P. Winichagoon et al., 63–70. Bangkok: Institute of Nutrition, Mahidol University, and UNICEF/EAPRO.

Porter, Doug, Bryant Allen, and Gaye Thompson. 1991. *Development in practice: Paved with good intentions.* London: Routledge.

Pradhan, Prachanda. 1980. *Local institutions and people's participation in rural public works in Nepal.* Ithaca, N.Y.: Rural Development Committee, Cornell University.

Putnam, Robert D., with Robert Leonardi and Raffaella Y. Nanetti. 1993. *Making democracy work: Civic traditions in modern Italy.* Princeton, N.J.: Princeton University Press.

Rahman, Md. Anisur. 1984. The Small Farmer Development Programme of Nepal. In *Grassroots participation and self-reliance: Experiences in South and South East Asia,* edited by M. A. Rahman, 121–51. New Delhi: Oxford University Press.

Raper, Arthur. 1970. *Rural development in action: The comprehensive experiment at Comilla.* Ithaca, N.Y.: Cornell University Press.

Repetto, Robert. 1986. *Skimming the water: Rent-seeking and the performance of public irrigation systems.* Research Report no. 4. Washington, D.C.: World Resources Institute.

Robertson, L. H. 1981. The development of self-help gravity-piped water projects in Malawi. In *Rural water supply in developing countries,* 9–11. Ottawa: International Development Research Centre.

Robinson, Marguerite. 1992. Rural financial intermediation: Lessons from Indonesia. Part 1, The Bank Rakyat Indonesia—rural banking, 1970–91. Development Discussion Paper no. 434. Cambridge: Harvard Institute for International Development.

———. 1995. Indonesia: The role of savings in developing sustainable commercial financing of small and micro enterprises. In *New perspectives on financing small business in developing countries,* edited by E. A. Brugger and S. Rajapatirana, 147–72. San Francisco: Institute of Contemporary Studies Press.

Roe, Emery, and Louise Fortmann. 1982. *Season and strategy: The changing organization of the rural water sector in Botswana.* Ithaca, N.Y.: Rural Development Committee, Cornell University.

Rohde, Jon. 1993. Indonesia's Posyandu accomplishments and future challenges. In *Reaching health for all,* edited by Jon Rohde, Meera Chatterjee, and David Morley, 135–57. Oxford: Oxford University Press.

Rohde, Jon, Meera Chatterjee, and David Morley, eds. 1993. *Reaching health for all.* Oxford: Oxford University Press.

Rondinelli, Dennis. 1983. *Development projects as policy experiments: An adaptive approach to development administration.* New York: Methuen.

Rose, Kalima. 1992. *Where women are leaders: The SEWA movement in India.* London: Zed Books.

Ruddell, Edward, Julio Beingolea, and Humberto Beingolea. 1997. Empowering local farmers to conduct experiments. In *Farmers' research in practice: Lessons from the field*, edited by L. van Veldhuizen et al., 199–208. London: Intermediate Technology Publications.

Sebstad, Jennifer. 1982. Struggle and development among self-employed women: A report on the Self-Employed Women's Association, Ahmedabad, India. Washington, D.C.: Office of Urban Development, USAID.

Small, Leslie E., Marietta S. Adriano, and Edward D. Martin. 1986. *Regional study on irrigation service fees: Final report.* Kandy, Sri Lanka: International Irrigation Management Institute.

Smyth, Rebecca. 1995. Trip report regarding future collaboration between Cornell University and the Indonesian IPM movement. October 11. Ithaca, N.Y.: Cornell International Institute for Food, Agriculture, and Development.

Soros, George. 1997. The capitalist threat. *Atlantic Monthly* 279(2): 45–58.

Tendler, Judith. 1976. *Inter-country evaluation of small farmer organizations in Ecuador and Honduras: Final report.* Washington, D.C.: U.S. Agency for International Development.

———. 1997. *Good government in the tropics.* Baltimore, Md.: Johns Hopkins University Press.

Thomas, John W. 1975. The choice of technology for irrigation tubewells in East Pakistan: Analysis of a development policy decision. In *The choice of technology in developing countries: Some cautionary tales*, edited by C. Peter Timmer, 31–68. Cambridge: Center for International Affairs, Harvard University.

Thorbecke, Erik. 1990. Institutions, X-efficiency, transaction costs, and socioeconomic development. In *Studies in economic rationality: X-efficiency examined and extolled*, edited by Klaus Weiermair and Mark Perlman, 295–313. Ann Arbor: University of Michigan Press.

UNICEF. 1993. *We will never go back: Social mobilization in the child survival programme in the United Republic of Tanzania.* New York: UNICEF.

Uphoff, Norman. 1986a. *Improving international irrigation management with farmer participation: Getting the process right.* Boulder, Colo.: Westview Press.

———. 1986b. *Local institutional development: An analytical sourcebook with cases.* West Hartford, Conn.: Kumarian Press.

———. 1988. Participatory evaluation of farmer organizations' capacity for development tasks. *Agricultural Administration and Extension* 30(1): 63–74.

———. 1990. Paraprojects as a new mode of international development cooperation. *World Development* 18(10): 1401–11.

———. 1991. A field methodology for participatory self-evaluation. *Community Development Journal* 26(4): 271–85.

———. 1992a. *Learning from Gal Oya: Possibilities for participatory development and post-Newtonian social science.* Ithaca, N.Y.: Cornell University Press. 2d ed., London: Intermediate Technology Publications, 1996.

————. 1992b. Monitoring and evaluating popular participation in World Bank–assisted projects. In *Participatory development and the World Bank: Potential directions for change*, edited by B. Bhatnagar and Aubrey C. Williams, 135–53. Discussion Paper no. 183. Washington, D.C.: World Bank.

————. 1996. Why NGOs are not a third sector: A sectoral analysis with some thoughts on accountability, sustainability, and evaluation. In *Beyond the magic bullet: NGO performance in the post–cold war world*, edited by Michael Edwards and David Hulme, 23–39. West Hartford, Conn.: Kumarian Press.

Uphoff, Norman, and Milton J. Esman. 1974. *Local organization for rural development: Analysis of Asian experience*. Ithaca, N.Y.: Rural Development Committee, Cornell University.

Uphoff, Norman, M. L. Wickramasinghe, and C. M. Wijayaratna. 1990. "Optimum" participation in irrigation management: Issues and evidence from Sri Lanka. *Human Organization* 49(1): 26–40.

Uvin, Peter. 1995. Fighting hunger at the grassroots: Paths to scaling up. *World Development* 23(6): 927–39.

VanSant, Jerry, David Gow, and Thomas Armor. 1982. Managing Staff to Promote Participation. *Rural Development Participation Review*, Special Supplement 3(3): A1–A3.

Veneracion, C., ed. 1989. *A decade of process documentation research: Reflections and synthesis*. Quezon City: Institute of Philippine Culture, Ateneo de Manila.

Volante, Jesus R. 1984. A manual for participant observers in process documentation research. *Philippine Sociological Review* 32(1–4): 121–33.

White, T. Anderson, and C. Ford Runge. 1994. Common property and collective action: Lessons from cooperative watershed management in Haiti. *Economic Development and Cultural Change* 43(1): 1–41.

Whyte, William F., and Damon Boynton, eds. 1983. *Higher yielding human systems for agriculture*. Ithaca, N.Y.: Cornell University Press.

Wijayaratna, C. M., and Norman Uphoff. 1997. Farmer organization in Gal Oya: Improving irrigation management in Sri Lanka. In *Reasons for hope: Instructive experiences in rural development*, edited by Anirudh Krishna, Norman Uphoff, and Milton J. Esman, 166–83. West Hartford, Conn.: Kumarian Press.

Williamson, John. 1994. The emerging development policy consensus. Working Paper Series no. 5. Madison: Global Studies Research Program, University of Wisconsin.

World Bank. 1987. *Aga Khan Rural Support Program in Pakistan: An interim evaluation*. Washington, D.C.: Operations Evaluation Department, World Bank.

Yunus, Muhammad. 1997. The Grameen Bank story: Rural credit in Bangladesh. In *Reasons for hope: Instructive experiences in rural development*, edited by Anirudh Krishna, Norman Uphoff, and Milton J. Esman, 9–24. West Hartford, Conn.: Kumarian Press.

Index

Subjects

Cases

Authors

About the Authors

Norman Uphoff has been a professor of government at Cornell University since 1970. In 1990 he was appointed director of the Cornell International Institute for Food, Agriculture, and Development (CIIFAD), an interdisciplinary program dedicated to sustainable agricultural and rural development. Before that he chaired the Rural Development Committee at Cornell and directed its Rural Development Participation Project under a cooperative agreement with USAID from 1977 to 1982. During 1978–79 he spent a sabbatical year in Sri Lanka at the Agrarian Research and Training Institute and then worked with ARTI colleagues on the Gal Oya irrigation water management project from 1980 to 1985, making follow-up visits through 1989. He also helped introduce participatory irrigation management in Nepal between 1986 and 1989.

Milton J. Esman is John S. Knight Professor Emeritus of International Studies and former director of the Center for International Studies at Cornell. A veteran participant, observer, and analyst of development policies and programs, he has been particularly interested in the institutional and administrative dimensions of development. His publications include *Management Dimensions of Development* (Kumarian Press, 1991) and, in collaboration with Norman Uphoff, *Local Organizations: Intermediaries in Rural Development* (Cornell University Press, 1984). He served as senior adviser in public administration to the prime minister's office of the government of Malaysia, 1966–68, and taught at the Graduate School of Public and International Affairs at the University of Pittsburgh before coming to Cornell.

Anirudh Krishna is a member of the Indian Administrative Service, Rajasthan cadre, currently serving as director of tourism and culture. He was responsible for setting up and directing the Department of Watershed Development in Rajasthan in 1991, which is protecting 400,000 hectares of degraded or deteriorating land and which twice received the Indian government's National Merit Certificate for best watershed development, involving user committees as well as interdisciplinary teams of technicians and officials. He has master's degrees in economics from the Delhi School of Economics and in international development from Cornell, where he was a Humphrey Fellow during 1993–94.

Books of related interest
from Kumarian Press

Reasons for Hope:
Instructive Experiences in
Rural Development
Anirudh Krishna, Norman
Uphoff, and Milton J. Esman,
editors

Eighteen of the world's most exemplary rural development success stories are told in the words of the originators and managers working closely in the projects. Presents a true picture of hope and shows what can be done.

US $19.95 Paper   1-56549-063-0
US $40.00 Cloth   1-56549-064-9

Players and Issues in
International Aid
Paula Hoy

This one-stop source of introductory information provides a basic overview of the issues surrounding development assistance. It offers multiple perspectives of the complexities of international development assistance and aid.

US $21.95 Paper   1-56549-073-8
US $45.00 Cloth   1-56549-072-X

Achieving Broad-Based
Sustainable Development:
Governance, Environment,
and Growth With Equity
James H. Weaver, Michael T.
Rock, Kenneth Kusterer

This comprehensive and multidisciplinary work provides an excellent overview of economic development and the results of growth. The authors provide a model that looks through economic as well as social, political, and environmental lenses.

US $26.95 Paper   1-56549-058-4
US $38.00 Cloth   1-56549-059-2

Beyond the Magic Bullet:
NGO Performance and
Accountability in the Post-
Cold War World
Michael Edwards, David Hulme

In this volume, experts review the issues of NGO performance and accountability in international development assistance and provide guidance with respect to the process of assessment. Case studies from Central America, Asia, South America, East Africa and North Africa.

US $18.95 Paper   1-56549-051-7
US $38.00 Cloth   1-56549-052-5

Governance, Administration
and Development:
Making the State Work
Mark Turner, David Hulme

Provides a comprehensive introduction to public policy and management in developing countries and transitional economies. The book assesses both traditional and new models of public administration with particular emphasis on the challenge to the centrality of the state in development and current debates about the conditions of effective governance.

US $24.95 Paper 1-56549-070-3
US $48.00 Cloth 1-56549-071-1

Management Dimensions of Development:
Perspectives and Strategies
Milton J. Esman

The author critiques the thinking of the founding development administration practitioners and emerging generations and demonstrates how to go beyond early development approaches. Esman builds a case for multiorganizational strategies sensitive to all players within a society—government, private enterprise, and voluntary organizations.

US $16.95 Paper 0-931816-64-5
US $30.00 Cloth 0-931816-65-3

Promises Not Kept:
The Betrayal of Social Change
in the Third World,
Fourth Edition
John Isbister

This book develops the argument that social change in the Third World has been blocked by a series of broken promises, made explicitly or implicitly by the industrialized countries and also by Third World leaders themselves.

The fourth edition takes into account the success stories in the Third World, particularly in East Asia, asking why those experiences have not been more widespread.

US $18.95 Paper 1-56549-045-2

Kumarian Press, Inc.
14 Oakwood Avenue
West Hartford, CT 06119-2127
USA

Inquiries: 860-233-5895
Fax: 860-233-6072
Order toll free: 800-289-2664

e-mail: kpbooks@aol.com
internet: www.kpbooks.com

 Kumarian Press is dedicated to publishing and
distributing books and other media that will
have a positive social and economic impact
on the lives of peoples living in "Third World"
conditions no matter where they live.

As well as books about International Development,
Kumarian Press also publishes books
on the Environment, Peace and Conflict Resolution,
Nongovernmental Organizations, Government,
International Health, Gender, and Development.

To receive a complimentary catalog or to request writer's
guidelines, call or write:

Kumarian Press, Inc.
14 Oakwood Avenue
West Hartford, CT 06119-2127 USA

Inquiries: 860-233-5895
Fax: 860-233-6072
Order toll free: 800-289-2664

e-mail: kpbooks@aol.com
internet: www.kpbooks.com